VOICE IN THE AMERICAN WEST

ANDY WILKINSON

Series Editor

PHOTOGRAPHS BY BUTCH HANCOCK

FOREWORD BY DAN FLORES

TEXAS TECH UNIVERSITY PRESS

IF I WAS A HIGHWAY

ESSAYS

Michael Ventura

This book is typeset in Monotype Dante.

The paper used in this book meets the minimum
requirements of ANSI / NISO Z39.48-1992
(R1997). ♾

Designed by Barbara Werden

*Title spread: Highway and clouds,
New Mexico, 1968*

Library of Congress Cataloging-in-Publication Data
Ventura, Michael.

    If I was a highway : essays / Michael Ventura ;
foreword by Dan Flores ; photographs by Butch
Hancock.

      p. cm. — (Voice in the American West)
    Summary: "Forty-five essays—many of which
first appeared in the Austin Chronicle—that convey the author's impressions of America, particularly Texas and the Southwest. Also includes photographs by Butch Hancock"—Provided by
publisher.

    Includes index

    ISBN 978-0-89672-706-9 (hardcover : alk.
paper)

    1. Southwest, New—Social life and customs—
Anecdotes. 2. Texas—Social life and customs—
Anecdotes. I. Austin chronicle. II. Title.

    F386.6.V46 2011

    979—dc22   2010042827

Printed in the United States of America
11 12 13 14 15 16 17 18 19 / 9 8 7 6 5 4 3 2 1

Texas Tech University Press | Box 41037
Lubbock, Texas 79409-1037 USA
800.832.4042 | ttup@ttu.edu
www.ttupress.org

for Irene
in thankful, loving memory

We have to become lost before we can find ourselves. That sort of map you make up as you go along.

STIRLING SILLIPHANT

Route 66

CONTENTS

CONTENTS

OUR SERIES is built upon the evocative power of the first-person voice, not so much in the sense of a summoning or a calling to mind, though both apply, but particularly in the sense that *to evoke* means to create anew. It is a point not to belabor, for there is no better illustration of the difference in these senses than in the essays that follow.

But before I leave you to them and them to you, I am compelled to add that the first-person voice is also an invoca-tion, a putting into action. In the pages that follow, Michael Ventura's evocative voice serves as the incantation for two other personal voices, for we are further graced here with both a foreword by Dan Flores, one of America's finest narrative historians, and the photography of Butch Hancock, a troubadour whose voice sings in images as well as in words and notes. Each voice is itself a highway, each run-ning sometimes in parallel and sometimes at criss-cross, but each always leading us into the same horizon.

ANDY WILKINSON
Lubbock, Texas—2011

SOUTHWEST OF EVERYTHING

A Foreword

I HAVE JUST released Michael Ventura from a Time Machine.

What that means, to be more helpful, is that a few minutes ago I dug out of a box in my closet a DVD that preserves a videotape I shot in the spring of 1994. This requires some context. That spring, almost two decades ago now, I had already left Lubbock—the West Texas town Michael Ventura has never been able to abandon—for greener (and rather brisker) pastures in Missoula, Montana. But I had not been able to give up the magical property I owned in Yellow House Canyon or the house I had finished there. So here I was, on a sabbatical from my university duties and back in Lubbock, of all places. In Texas that spring I met a girl who owned a health-food store in town, who among other talents threw fantastic parties. And my canyon place was something of a legendary flame-out party ground in any case. So as had happened so many times before (and after), the throng assembled that night and the April full moon drifting up over the mesa convinced us that we inhabited a rare and enviable world. And we did.

In the videotape I have of that party, twenty-five or thirty unforgettable faces—smiling, laughing, raising their glasses to the music and the camera—appear out of memory. And sure enough, as I'd thought I recalled, there was Michael. I am fairly certain he had arrived with our mutual friend, Deborah Milosevich. I also believe we had never met before. Although I was only a few years younger and we were in the same cultural solar system, Michael and I orbited differently. I had certainly read him; he probably hadn't read me. How much we got to converse I cannot say (not much, I don't think), but I am gratified that the video confirms my vivid memory image. There were other writers there that night, but Michael—his dark fedora never removed, his eyes narrowed behind black Buddy Holly glasses, dragging off a cigarette and taking in the scene—was a writer at *work*. Later, reading some of his columns in *The Austin Chronicle*, I realized, well, the guy never *isn't* working. As the Native American painter T. C. Cannon observed sagely of himself, "My restless heart, my passionate soul, provide windows from which I look out on the world ceaselessly." Glancing at Michael Ventura at a party—better yet, reading his essays and books—is to confront an artistic mind at full engagement. Watching. Thinking. Taking notes. On all the time.

What I am about to say next may require a suspension of disbelief from some, but for nearly forty years Michael Ventura has been a card-carrying member and chronicler of the Lubbock counterculture. And yes, I do mean *that* Lubbock, the town famous for its crucifix skyline and where political diversity means adopting positions to the right of rightwingers, *has* a counterculture. Of course it does, and by way of a gonzo style he seems to have just stumbled into, since the early 1970s Michael Ventura has seen from the inside what he calls here "an isolated, hedonistic, country-western-folk-music-Zen-rock-&-roll honky-tonk/monastery." Many of the Lubbock counterculture's inspirational heroes—musicians, artists, and ad hoc philosophers like Spider Johnson, Don Dykes, Paul Milosevich, Terry Allen, Deborah Milosevich, Joe Ely, Butch Hancock, Jimmie Dale Gilmore, a collective group Ventura refers to as "among the smartest, most original, generous, multitalented people I've known"—have themselves become High Plains expatriates. But they never stay away for long, and neither has Ventura, who finally abandoned Los Angeles and moved back to Lubbock full-time a few years ago. Not

bad for a Brooklyn boy. Texas wants you anyway.

This book, as Michael tells us, is a collection of some of the columns he has long written for the Austin alternative press—not really essays in the high literature sense, but as he admits, more like "letters." Readers from a certain generation will recognize them as Kerouac-like musings about the world as it is encountered. Those from another generation will think of this kind of writing as blogging. He himself from a generation between those two, the generation of Sex, Drugs, and Rock & Roll, Ventura doesn't usually write about sex, and almost never about drugs, but he does write "about God" (as he has put it elsewhere, "America is the Bible running wild in the wilderness"). As both a novelist and a writer of nonfiction, he most definitely writes about rock & roll. And film. Long a film critic, he has authored books about both John Cassavetes and Marilyn Monroe.

Here what he writes most about, however, is the road, and it is music and that forward trajectory across America that give this book its title, *If I Was a Highway*. "In the music of the Southwest," he offers in one of these essays, "one image is constant: the road. . . . Somebody is always arriving, always leaving, and there's always something immeasurable just past the outskirts of town." So off we go in Ventura's vintage '69 lime-green Chevy

Malibu, from Lubbock to Arizona, to Los Angeles, Seattle, Minnesota (to see the town that produced Bob Dylan), Maine, New York, even my home country of Louisiana, where the lime-green Malibu (which survives everywhere else) is very nearly kilt off. And finally back to Lubbock again, although en route we have met the wild mélange of characters the road throws at you, learned from Carolyn Cassady that what husband Neal and Jack Kerouac wanted most was to settle down, and from Carlos Castaneda (Ventura's one of the few people I've ever heard of who *met* Carlos Castaneda) that a consequence of being a famous mystic is that

people impersonate you at parties. And from George Maharis, who costarred in the 1960s television program *Route 66*, a series about a couple of guys who drove their Corvette around America, that he was picked for the part because he was a dead ringer for Kerouac.

This, then, is classic Michael Ventura: smart, observant, generous, honest, throwing himself at the world and seeing what happens. And always watching, thinking, and taking notes.

If I were a highway, I think I'd want Michael Ventura to write about me.

DAN FLORES
Santa Fe, New Mexico

I've lived in Lubbock, Texas, for a while now, but on April 19, 1995, I dwelt in West Hollywood, just north of Santa Monica Boulevard—which, as it happens, was the last stretch of old Route 66 before it reached the Pacific. My apartment was on the top floor of an art deco building designed to seem a bit fantastical, as though never meant for normal people. In 1932 a film studio built it to house starlets. Years had not changed the mood of the building or the neighborhood. Steve Erickson, author of exceptional novels, lived one floor below. Below him lived an actress who would play a role on *Buffy the Vampire Slayer*. Everybody in that neighborhood was—or was trying to be—an actor, screenwriter, director, producer, or model. On the street strangers often seemed oddly familiar; you wondered where you'd met them, then realized you viewed them recently on TV or in a movie. The neighborhood teemed with the faces of bit players, supporting roles, and commercials. In restaurants it wasn't unusual to see a current celebrity. Shops displayed glossy photos of famous, would-be

famous, and no longer famous patrons. It was a neighborhood that said, "I am not mainstream America, but I play mainstream America on TV"—which is very American, making West Hollywood, in its quirky way, as much U.S.A. as anywhere.

That April morning seemed no different from any other as I walked to the corner to buy newspapers, intending to read over brunch at Hugo's, one of the area's more "Hollywood" eateries. As I entered the restaurant I saw Erickson and Lori Precious at a table. They waved me over. They seemed tense. Steve asked what I thought of it all. I didn't know what he was talking about. "Oklahoma City," he said.

I hadn't turned on a radio or TV, hadn't yet heard of the explosion at the Federal Building in Oklahoma City. Steve told me what details he'd learned. "They're saying it was Arabs"—*they* being the media.

I said, "Arabs? Arab fanatics conspiring unobserved in Oklahoma City? I doubt it. Anyway, Arabs would be playing for their people back home, where—"

Steve finished my sentence: "Where

Oklahoma City is not exactly a household name. Who, then?"

"They hit the federal building? Probably antifederalist militia."

Before the Oklahoma City bombing, homegrown antifederalist militias hadn't made much news, so my well-informed friends hadn't heard of them. Driving around the country, as I do whenever the chance and coin present themselves, I'd run across a couple of militiamen, listened to their views—appalled but interested—in a garage in Arizona while waiting for an oil change.

Later in my apartment the phone rang. Steve's voice was stern: "I *don't* want to hear you crow about this for the rest of my life, but they've just arrested a guy identified as antifederalist militia."

Human beings being what we are, I enjoyed being right—even about something so gruesome. But I deserved no credit. It doesn't take much cleverness to strike up a conversation in a garage or anywhere else. I'd met two militiamen, jotted some notes about them afterward, then forgot them until the bombing.

THE POINT of this story is that trusted names in American media immediately said "Arabs" with neither proof nor the scantiest knowledge of circumstances in Oklahoma City.

America is written about and reported upon largely by people in our major coastal cities who rarely go anywhere else in America until *after* something happens. Not that the coastal cities are less American than the heartland; but they're a different America, for there are many Americas on this wide continent, all equally American but, even in this time of homogenization, very different from each other, with different ways, geographies, cultures, problems, and very different pasts and futures.

This book is a selection of essays about some of those Americas, though "essay" may be too highfalutin a word. I've always thought of them as letters—the words of a traveler writing to a friend in the wee hours of the morning. They're arranged such that each piece reflects the piece it follows and the piece it precedes, making this book a kind of switchback journey in image and thought up and down the roads of the West, with occasional detours into the South, Midwest, New England, New York, and Los Angeles. Detours in time, too—scenes of the past, intimations of the future. An interior journey as well, a personal journey, for I am a "journalist" in the original sense of the word: one who records, journal-like, the sights, thoughts, and feelings of passing days. Musicians, sorcerers, and wanna-bes appear on these pages, as well as laborers, priests, kids in trouble, and kids finding their way—also friends, strangers, farmers, UFOs, garage mechanics, conquistadors, gunfighters, and storms. These pieces record the country in motion as seen from the road, an America often in trouble but still unfinished, still recreating itself, always to be discovered anew.

WITH THREE EXCEPTIONS, these essays appeared as installments of my biweekly column in *The Austin Chronicle*, "Letters at 3AM." For the most part they appear as they were originally published. Marjorie Baumgarten has been my editor at the paper for sixteen years; her patience, generosity, and consummate professionalism can't be overpraised. She and the *Chronicle*'s intrepid crew of fact-checking proofreaders often save me from myself.

Thanks also to my great friends Deborah Milosevich and Butch Hancock, my friend the ace car mechanic Ron Rothstein, and to Andy Wilkinson. Andy helped shape this manuscript and his suggestions have been invaluable. And the people of Texas Tech University Press could not have been more supportive.

An Appendix notes the dates of original publication. A few essays have been updated where necessary.

Some quotes and a couple of incidents are repeated in several contexts in different essays—think of them as refrains in a prose ballad of the American road.

MICHAEL VENTURA
Lubbock, Texas—2011

IF I WAS A HIGHWAY

IT WAS A PLACE to drive to through a storm—through a storm, and after a dream. That isn't poetry. That's how it was. I'd dreamed the dream in Oakland, and it told me to move on. The storm hit in El Paso, the worst in years, the whole world iced and white from Flagstaff to Nashville—Irene and Crash and I in a VW Bug, with gas not yet thirty cents a gallon and not enough money between us for a motel, and the de-icer not working, and every twenty miles or so we'd edge up to a snowdrift and carefully pour our bottle of *sake* across the windshield. The *sake* melted the ice and we'd go on to that place I'd never heard of before they told me where they were headed: Lubbock, Texas.

"The house they call 14th Street," Irene named it, on the corner of Avenue W. By the time we got to Lubbock, the snowdrifts were high, the ice was thick on every road, the sky was white and clear. Nixon was president and we were still in Vietnam, and that dark fact hung over America like a daylight moon, a pale hole incongruous in a powder-blue sky—and people like us searched the country for

each other, and for the fulfillment of a promise no one had ever made but that we intended to keep.

Neither the door on the 14th Street side, nor the door on the Avenue W side, ever was locked. One day for some reason we tried to find the key and no one could, not Butch nor Jimmie Dale nor Joe, nor Sharon nor Janette nor Lora nor Elyse, nor Vicki and the two Lindas, nor Debby, nor the Debby we called "Little Debby" (as opposed to the Debby who wasn't little), nor Lora nor Jic, nor Terry nor Jerry, nor Charlene nor Tommy nor Connie nor Traci nor Joaquin, nor Ron, nor Mickey, nor George, nor any of the many who lived there, slept over, or passed through. Nor Irene, nor me, the only Yankees. There were wind chimes on the porch. In the spring there were enormous bright sunflowers. But there were never any keys.

There was Sharon making beans and cornbread and talking about clowns. There was Butch Hancock singing the song that had come to him in a dream only a month ago: *If you were a bluebird, you'd be a sad one—I'd give you a true word,*

*but you've already had one . . . If I was a
highway . . . I'd be fetching you home.* There
was Janette talking about Gurdjieff and
Jerry talking about Jo Carol Pierce. There
was a reel-to-reel tape recorder with no
speaker; you had to plug in the ear-
phones, and the tape was that sweet Flatlanders session cut months before in
Nashville—Jimmie Dale Gilmore's exqui-
site keening voice, pure with youth. (It'd
be another ten years before the record
came out; in fact, it would be years before
any of those singers had a band.) And
there were the fierce bright lights in the
eyes of those women, who were not yet
the teachers and shrinks and designers
and artists and singers and mothers they
would become, and who seemed to me
(and I said so then, didn't I?) smarter than
us men, because they saw farther into us
than we saw into them. And there were
books everywhere that a Yankee like me
had never heard of, books about Sufis and
Ouspensky and Jesus and out-of-body
travel, and there was *The Morning of the
Magicians,* which said, "Men get not what
they merit but what they resemble."

And the songsters seemed to sing not
for the world but for 14th Street, for each
other and for us, and it seemed hardly a
day went by when there wasn't a new
song, sung by Joe Ely or Butch or Jimmie
Dale, sung on the floor in the living
room, a song in which all our secrets
were recited in rhymed code. And there
was the old upright piano, and Ron played

Beethoven all night one night, while we
listened in a kind of daze, and the next
day or the next he and I had the talk
where we concluded: "It doesn't matter if
anyone else ever hears these songs,
doesn't matter if they ever leave this
house—doesn't matter if anyone ever
knows about this house, or how we are
here—doesn't even matter if we forget, or
are never this way again—the beauty of
these songs is *because* of nothing, or
because of the wind, like Joe sang the
other night, and the wind'll take it and be
scented with it, with us, with the songs,
and our tenderness and restlessness will
be felt in the breeze by people who won't
even know why they're feeling it."
Butch'd write me years later from far off:
"No way to pass this on but through
genes and dreams."

Many all over the world know the
songs of that living room now, but that
wasn't a justification anyone sought
then—if we imagined the possibility of
those songs leaving that living room, I
don't remember talk of it. Nothing
needed to be justified, only lived. And
nobody but Charlene and Tommy Hancock was over thirty.

We were confused, scared, searching,
possessed. Some drank too much; most
fucked too recklessly. Someone was
always cracking up; someone was always
taking care of them. Someone was always
laughing, someone was always crying,
and someone was always singing or had

just sung or was about to sing. It's all in the songs.

The rent was $80 a month, or there-abouts, which sometimes came to only $8 apiece, and we'd all eat breakfast at Broadway Drug, sixty-five cents for two eggs, hash browns, coffee, and toast. "Delta Dawn" and "Killing Me Softly" were the new songs on the juke. Nobody had a steady job; nobody kept any job long. At night one of the women would make cornbread and beans, and the table was a door laid down on crates, and we'd all hold hands a moment in silence before we ate. Even now, one of us'll suddenly talk about those silences, when we felt that energy pulse through each other's hands and knew that no matter how lost we were at the time, we were finding something then, or it was finding us, and it would be ours again whenever we really needed it.

We were madly restless—someone was always moving to New Mexico, or moving back from New Mexico, or lost in California, or stranded in New York, or getting religion in Louisiana and return-ing with tales to tell. There was the morn-ing the elephants walked through Lub-bock, and Ely and I joined the circus, and Joe ran off with them (I didn't, because of Kathy), and he came back months later with a song about being locked in a box-car with the Queen of Spain.

And oh, there was Kathy, and how for her I almost killed—came so close it scares me still to remember. And there was Kathy's God, who almost killed me. And how because of Kathy I had to leave 14th Street and Lubbock, because it wasn't love anymore, it was madness, and we two were capable of anything together, any adventure, any crime, and I knew if I stayed one more day I'd do something I couldn't walk away from, so I ran.

But, before that, there was the God that came to town—a God that came as though drawn by all our talk of God. Because, at 14th Street, God seemed all we ever spoke of. All our talks finally came back to God, or gods, Western gods, Eastern gods, gods felt but not named, gods named but not felt, and god-desses, and demons, and spirits. There was the night that Butch and I came to the stunning conclusion (it sure stunned us) that Jesus was a woman with a man's head. "Jesus is a goddess!" we repeated over and over; and we decided that was His/Her power. There was a sense that all of us were daring each other to step closer to that Unknowable we called, for want of a better name, God. And then one of us came back from one of our adventures with word of a new God, and the word spread like prairie fire among us, and everything seemed to split for a while between who accepted that God and who didn't—and you could make a case that it was that new God that broke up that house on 14th Street, which was something I resented but resent no longer. I was a kind of existential fundamentalist then, could accept that God could come in any form but always said the same essential thing: *Change—You're not quite close enough to Me—Change.* And if the change was to leave "14th," as we called it, that too would work for God. I should have known that the real sign was that the songs never stopped, and that every time one of the songsters sang one of their new songs it was 14th Street again, and that would be for as long as we loved each other. And that was all any of the gods were about anyway, loving each other—and loving each other was our key to God and to ourselves, and *that* was something we never needed to say. It seemed to be so obvious. Nixon was still president and America was still in Vietnam by the time the last of us left that house.

I drove there through a storm, after a dream, stayed for two weeks, hitched on to Nashville, then New York, then Boston, where I ran into a friend.

"What are you up to?" I asked him.

"Driving to New Mexico in a few days."

I said, "Drop me off in Lubbock."

Days later, with no money and having told no one I was coming, I walked in. Jimmie and Butch and Janette and Little Debby and Jic and Terry were sitting on the floor in the living room, the songsters had guitars in their laps, and they didn't say hello, they just smiled at me as I smiled at them, and Jimmie said, "Michael! I was just thinkin' about you! There's somethin' I need to tell you." And I was home. That was half my life ago, and everything's changed but the wildness of our hearts and the beauty of those songs.

Kids playing ball in street, San Francisco, California, 1968

A LONG WAY TO LLANO

THERE'S A HIGHWAY west out of Socorro, New Mexico—U.S. 60, a two-lane twisting into the mountains toward the Arizona border. To take that turn I drive past a memory: a Motel 8 where last October I made some bad phone calls after some worse behavior—calls to Santa Monica and Atlanta, the kind of calls that just make things more difficult. And on the tape deck now, passing that motel (with the echo of her voice saying, "I don't know"), Joe Ely sings:

I ran too hard, I played too rough . . . I gave my love not near enough . . . I bled too red, I cried too blue . . . I've beaten my fists against the moon . . .

Last night on a two-lane northwest of Roswell, New Mexico, the moon was so low and close I could see my fist marks on it—mine, Joe's, everyone's. A sign said "Sinkholes Next 35 Miles." I slowed the Chevy way down and my eyes ached to see past the headlights. Sinkholes. Christ. I wondered whether they really had that UFO in a hangar near Roswell. I felt like a UFO myself—an Unidentified Fucked-Up Object. It would be a good night to get abducted like a character on *The X-Files*, but no night's a good night to crash into a sinkhole. Creeping around a tight turn, fearing a crater ahead big enough to eat the car, I saw two large yellow eyes look from the darkness straight at me. And Joe was singing:

Sometimes I follow the fool inside me . . . Sometimes I listen to the song in my heart . . . Sometimes I swear there's an angel beside me . . . Guiding my footsteps on through the dark . . . I saw it in you . . .

Those yellow eyes didn't look like an angel's. They looked more like a cougar's. But you never know about angels—they're changelings. "I'm talkin' about the One that's comin' for you with *healing* in His wings!" I heard Jimmy Swaggart swoon those words long ago on a motel TV down near Laredo. How about healing in *her* wings, Jimmy Lee? Healing wings and cougar eyes. And Butch Hancock singing:

But don't feel so sad . . . You're not doin' so bad . . . You got this far without a clue . . .

I've gotten this far, all right, right off the reality map. Which is fine with me.

Knowing exactly where you are is way overrated. Now I'm taking the road west out of Socorro, past one set of memories and up into the mountains toward others. You crest a hill and make a turn and there's a valley where things get very strange very quickly. There are a lot of valleys like that in New Mexico and Arizona, but this one is strange even for here: twenty, maybe thirty, enormous satellite dishes—actually, they look like what satellite dishes want to be when they grow up. Hard to say how large they are, but I saw an eighteen-wheeler parked near one, and it seemed a tiny widget beside the dish. Ten stories tall, they seemed to me, all pointed into the southern sky at the same angle. The road goes through the center of the valley, those huge dishes are all around you, east and west, and it's as though you can feel the pulsations of their fantastic power. And Joe is singing that love is his only alibi.

There was a sign, thank God—because if there'd been no sign, I would have stayed in that valley for God knows how long 'til I could find someone to tell me what was going on. All these enormous structures, all that power, and not a soul in sight. The sign said they were radio telescopes. I parked and lit a cigarette and just stood there, trying to take in how these things were absorbing information not only from the ends of the universe but from the beginnings of time. The sig-

nals they receive took millions of years, even billions, to reach this valley.

Well, that's not unusual. Such signals bombard us all the time, everywhere. But these telescopes absorb and record them. And Joe sang, *In the cool of the evening she calls me to dance . . . My back's about broken from choppin' the plants . . . My soul is so thirsty . . . I can't sleep at night . . . She walks in my dreams . . . And brings me delight . . .*

And whenever we spoke on the telephone, the good times and the bad, *our* signals didn't stop at the rim of the earth either; they headed Out There somewhere. Maybe someone on Alpha Centauri can decode them better than we did. Love *is* our only alibi.

Healing wings and cougar eyes. Bet those telescopes can't pick *that* up. At least I hope they can't. Somebody'd make a weapon out of it. Everything comes from the heart. Love. Bombs. They exploded the first A-bomb in Alamogordo, about three hours southeast of here. (There's a fine Lisa Mednick song about that. *Every time I come home I'm just passing through . . . I feel the ground I stand on might just spin away.*) The bomb had to exist in the heart before it could explode anywhere. That's why our hearts scare us so. In this valley, all of time and all the stars pulse straight at you. The bomb explodes, love implodes. The bomb destroys whole worlds, love creates whole worlds. And those huge metal things take it all in without feeling, without knowing, just taking.

And Butch is singing, *The last place you look is where you're gonna find it . . . And you don't even know what it is that's hid . . .* And I thought of Jimmie Dale Gilmore singing: *There's something you never lost but have not found . . .*

Back in the car, heading for the Great Divide. West of the Divide, all water flows toward the Pacific; east, toward the Atlantic. How many times did we cross the Great Divide that other summer, in New Mexico, Colorado, Wyoming, Montana, back and forth over the Divide in this Chevy, with love our only map as well as our only alibi?

And Joe is singing, *Burnin' down the highway, lookin' for the truth . . . I saw it in you . . . I'll follow my dreams wherever they take me . . . I saw the light . . . I saw it in you . . .* And the Great Divide between your heart and every other, that you cross over and over, but you can't ever stay on one side or the other, and you can't ever be on both sides at once, not if you keep moving—and there's no way not to keep moving, however much you long sometimes to stop. And even if you try to stop you still keep moving, even in your own house, a house that may seem stationary, but you know better. The Zen poet Bashō said it long ago: "The journey itself is the home."

It had better be. There isn't anywhere else.

And somebody is singing a Jo Carol Pierce song: *Hell on earth made in a minute . . . But Anything can happen in it . . . Heaven on earth was made long ago . . . But, Heaven knows, heaven comes and goes . . .*

Why is it always possible to speak of how miserable you might be, but never quite possible to gauge the dimensions of anyone else's happiness or even your own? To have loved like this, to ride these roads, to hear these songs, to sense that angel accompanying it all—weeping with happiness while a strange light fills the sky, and you don't know what time it is, or where you are on the map, or where your love may be, or what God could possibly be thinking of, except that all of it is always as near as your heart.

I'm writing this in Arizona in the wee hours of the first day of July, near where that coyote stood by the side of the road and stared at us as we passed in the dawn. I'm headed back to the City of Angels. My angel with the healing wings and cougar eyes will no doubt get there before me. And Terry Allen sings, *There oughta be a law against sunny Southern California.* Well, there is, but you can't enforce it. Headed back to the Earthquake Zone where I belong, where the Unenforceable is always in charge.

Joe is singing, *It's a long way to Llano.* I have people near Llano, Texas. They've saved my life more than once. In June we played Joe's songs. He'd made us a tape before the album, *Letter to Laredo*, hit the stands. We drank and talked all night, the kind of drinking that never gives you a hangover because the spirit in the room meets the spirit in the glass. Butch sings, *They say that time'll make it right . . . But time never makes anything right or wrong . . . It just eats away the night.* By the Llano River we fed the night and time our broken, satisfied hearts, and they seemed to like the fare.

I drove off with that tape, and the others, all that love and grief and joy in the songs. But now, in Arizona, with the soft light of morning glowing on the mesas, even the music is behind me, the dawn is quiet but for two birds, and I think of lines I didn't write, not exactly—they just said themselves in the air and there was nobody else around:

Be careful, where you're going.
The right way, the sun's in your eyes.
The wrong way, it doesn't matter what
    you see.

Unknown folks, Los Angeles, California, 1968

FOR YEARS I THOUGHT he was taller than I. He's not, actually. Not so much. Maybe some. But he's more or less my height. Still, for years I thought he was about a head taller. I *saw* him as taller. It wasn't just that he has a barrel chest, a wide face, enormous hands, and big feet, and that I don't have any of those and I'm skinny. (Well, not anymore. But twenty-five years ago, when I met Butch Hancock, I weighed about 125 pounds, *really* skinny.) It was the sense I had of him. I would have sworn on a stack of Upanishads, Bibles, Tao Te Chings, whatever you've got, that Butch was about a head taller than I. It was the way he carried himself. And the way he always seemed to be laughing, quietly, without derision, at some joke I didn't get, didn't even hear. At first I thought he was laughing at *me*. Didn't hold it against him; there's a lot about me to laugh at. But he wasn't laughing at me—at least, not all the time. He was just laughing. Not out loud, necessarily, but laughing. *What* was the joke, dammit? Even now, after all this time, all the roads we've traveled together, all the nights talk-ing over all those coffees and beers—even now I sometimes ask, a little annoyed: *What* is the joke, Butch?

I long ago stopped expecting an answer. Anyway, some of Butch's answers aren't really answers, and aren't meant to be. But then, people have said that about me too. Sometimes we bounce his non-answers off mine, talking about a subject without *talking* about it, talking about it by *not* talking about it, talking on its edges, like making outlines in the air. They're invisible, but we can both see them. Or we think we can. But about the joke. . . .

It's just that the things that haunt me, they mostly make Butch laugh. The things that haunt a *lot* of people mostly make Butch laugh. I know now that it's his inner river of laughter, more than any-thing else, that made my eyes see him as taller.

And, back before he'd recorded his songs, before we'd drifted from the Pan-handle down to Austin and he made a leg-end of himself, it was also the way . . . the way, after he wrote a song, he'd be so eager to play it. Not like he was showing off, not like the song was *his*, but like he'd discovered this strange incredible thing behind the sofa or in the gutter or by the side of the road or in the sky, and he *had* to show it to you, to you in particular. He was amazed and delighted by what he'd found, and he wanted to share his delight. That's what he calls "songwriting" and "singing" and this, too, makes him seem taller.

When we spent that year or so in that tiny town in the Panhandle, by the Salt Fork of the Red River, when it was my job to mix the cement that he would mold into fantastic shapes, and we were tearing down old buildings and using the materials to build a couple of saloons . . . I saw him walk on his hands at the edge of a cliff. Not once, but several times. We'd be walking by this quarry, and suddenly I'd look over and I was walking eye-level with his shins, while he was walking on his hands not a foot from the edge of a five-story drop . . . and he'd do it with absolutely cheerful confidence, so that you were never afraid he'd fall. . . . Well, I'm afraid of heights, and I can't walk on my hands, so *that* made him seem taller.

He once suddenly told me, "The miracle isn't important anyway! It's whether the reason it occurred was absorbed by you or not."

When you have a friend who often comes out with things like that, well, honestly, he seems taller.

Or when he wrote me from the Roman works at Bath, England: "The rocks are worn, corners rounded—colors changed who knows how many times? What? Maybe a couple of thousand generations know. Perhaps a few thousand or a few hundred or maybe only ten or twenty pairs of eyes each generation could remember the fading colors over that generation's span of years—the living wave of consciousness from generation to generation. . . . No way to pass that memory on except in dreams and genes."

I have to smile when I read his interviews with linear-type journalists. He told one hapless writer from some slick magazine, "Stonehenge is a dancehall." The guy quoted him as though he thought Butch was kidding. But Stonehenge *is* a dancehall; we've talked about that for hours. How in Malory's *Le Morte d'Arthur* Merlin is identified as the builder of Stonehenge, and how those rocks got their power from the ancient Dance of the Rings. But where I'd say such stuff portentously, Butch says it with a glint of a laugh, so the reporter thought he was kidding, not seeing that Butch was saying that Stonehenge is one of the roots of rock & roll. Which it is. Oh well.

I'm through being surprised by Butch. Which is a way of saying, I'm so used to being continually surprised by Butch that the surprises don't surprise me. (That's a Butch-type sentence.) Wasn't surprised when he pulled up stakes in Austin and went to live in Terlingua, near the Rio

Grande, to spend most of his days and nights on the river. Well, that inner river of sacred laughter *had* to find a real river sooner or later, and the Rio Grande is just about real enough. (As soon as I write that I can see Butch grin. *"Real*, Michael? And just what is *that?"*)

Butch sings about what the river is telling him and what he's saying back. *Just somethin' shinin' over yonder hill*, one song goes, *And I know not to chase it . . . but I know I will.*

The day I got some of his recent songs in the mail (no letter, no note, just Butch's calligraphic handwriting on the envelope) I played them for hours. And that night I dreamed of my death.

It was one of those dreams you don't tell, but suffice it to say that it was very calm, and because it was calm I knew it was (forgive the expression, Butch) real. So real that when I woke I was still in it. In my death. Well. There was no fear in the dream, but, waking, I waited for the fear to hit. It was death, after all. There was no clue in the dream about when— tomorrow, or twenty years from now; but in the dream death had visited, so I expected, on waking, to feel fear. But no fear filled me. I was astonished. I don't mean to give the impression that I'm so fucking enlightened that I don't fear death; I suppose that when the time comes, tomorrow or twenty years from now, I'll be afraid enough. But the dream had found something in death that was

not about fear, and I was still in the wash of the dream. Astonished to feel *thankfulness*. A deep, sweet thankfulness for all that I've lived. And a verse of Butch's came to me as I lay there:

One man lives to die . . . One man lives for thrills . . . One man only lives to live . . . Hiding in the hills.

To be that man who only lives to live. That is my task from now on. It isn't about writing anymore, or finding a meaning, or changing the world, or getting and keeping love, though all of that is important; but it isn't *about* that stuff anymore. The task now is to be that man who only lives to live. For whom life, life, life, is enough.

And the dream continued to segue with Butch's songs. In my heart I heard the quiet joyful way he sings these days: *Ancient mountains . . . chills and fevers . . . empty roads and fields of flowers . . . dusty beds . . . hanging gardens . . . the golden light still in my eyes.* And then the soft lilting chorus: *Roll around . . . Roll around . . . Roll around and sing forever . . . Spread your wings . . . Spread your wings . . . Spread your wings and fly tomorrow. . . .*

There aren't many songs you can bear after a dream of your death. I lay there, full of thankfulness for all that I've lived, and thankful for my friend.

I played those songs all that day: *All of what I feel . . . And for all I see . . . There is no you . . . There is no me . . . Just somethin' shining . . . Way deep inside. . . .*

That was the thankfulness. A way of singing it. And that day I needed to sing it. (Not that I can sing, but I can sing along.)

You coulda leaned into the face of four strong winds . . . 'Stead of drivin' round town collectin' useless odds and ends . . . 'Stead of goin' nowhere you coulda lived . . . a life of . . . Destinations! . . . You coulda walked around the world. . . .

Well. Yes. A life of destinations. I thought of all my destinations. Of Butch's. Of our friends'. It was a good day. And, as the Lakota say, a good day to die. I pray that on the day of my death this feeling will not leave me.

And for that I must learn to live only to live. So. *You might chase dreams . . . You might chase flies . . . You might chase gold . . . You might chase God. . . .*

Some time ago I was describing Butch to some strangers, and a friend of ours at the table said: "Michael, Butch *isn't* taller than you. Not that much." "Of course he is." "He ain't." And he ain't. I suppose. But he is.

Or maybe he *is*, really, physically, actually, taller. All these years of friendship, and I'm still not sure.

And that, my friends, is the measure of a man.

"S UFFERING DOESN'T teach or everyone would be wise."

Exactly when Jodie said those words isn't clear, but I know where I hear them in my memory. We were driving a two-lane near the North Rim of the Grand Canyon. There, at about 9,000 feet, the air was gentle, cool in the shade. I was trying to pay attention to the trees. Trees aren't quite real to me; I've never known why. Plains, rocks, rivers; mountains, mesas, deserts—these speak languages that I can feel if not understand. But it's rare that I hear the trees. A single tree in a field, or cottonwoods by a creek, yes, sometimes; but, driving or walking, I always want to get out of a forest.

Perhaps Jodie was translating for the trees when she said that sentence. I've been repeating it to myself, or rather it's been saying itself to me, insistently and quietly. "Suffering doesn't teach or everyone would be wise." When I hear it I'm back again in that high air, under a bright sky, wondering when we'll get past the trees and be in open country again. (Life arranges itself in metaphors, which is probably why we invented them, and

metaphors laugh at us, don't they? How long have I been wondering when I'll get past the trees and be in open country again?)

The cars in front of us slowed, then stopped. Ahead and to our left a beautiful deer, a tall buck with many-tipped antlers, stood at the side of the road. He seemed scared of the cars

and was looking anxiously over and behind us. I know next to nothing about deer, but something in this buck's tension made me think he was young. His vitality looked untried, untested.

There were two cars in front of us, and two or three stopped behind. Grown-ups started taking pictures, while their kids called out to the buck. I turned to see what he was looking at. At the edge of the forest, not far from our car, was a doe.

She was large and old. Perhaps she was his mother. The buck was nervous, but she was not. The buck wanted very much for her to cross the road and catch up to him, he couldn't take his eyes off her. She looked at him, then looked away, took some interest in the cars, looked back at him. The buck stamped his foot (even when still his knee joints jerked). The doe didn't react. She simply walked, in no hurry, by the highway. She was cautious without being frightened. Her slow step conveyed what I can only call a deliberate mood.

People shouted at her. Arms reached from car windows, offering candy or nuts or whatever. The doe neither ignored them nor showed interest. She just walked slowly.

I don't know if I can get this across, but the pace at which she walked was terribly important. It changed Time (our sense of time, I mean). The doe's steadiness . . . her apparent certainty about this particular moment . . . how she became the center of the moment for everyone, with all eyes on her, ours and the buck's . . . how her motions seemed chosen yet not conscious, willed but without particular intent . . . how she seemed to enter and step through this moment, elongating it by the manner of her step— a manner that was somehow contagious, for it changed the speed of our behavior: of how we watched, felt, perceived. This was the way the pace at which she walked altered Time.

Not for the kids—kids' sense of time is pretty insistent. They shouted and gestured. But they could not distract the doe from her own pace and concern; thus she made the kids seem far away.

The doe was by Jodie's window now, close enough to touch. Yes, she was old.

Her hide had the scars of many seasons' scratches and cuts. Her face too. Her eyes, close up, were enormous. She chose to cross the road in front of my car. Her grace was—the word that comes is: complete. We humans do not spend much time around creatures about whom nothing is lacking (except, perhaps, when we're falling in love). Nothing was lacking in the old doe's beauty, and the sharp, heavy step of her hooves on the pavement cut through the sounds of voices and engines.

Cars were backing up now on both sides of the two-lane. The buck trotted toward the doe but wouldn't step on the road. He climbed a rise and looked down on her. She turned her head and looked directly at me.

I didn't know where I was. Her stare, too, was complete. I mean that a whole world was in those huge eyes. A world kin to me (I'm a mammal, too), but unknown to me. For those moments I got lost in her look. She stepped toward me, and now her head was close to mine. I was in a strange state, and somehow she had walked me into it. I felt tremendous agitation and utter stillness, both. Could it be I was catching her mood? Is that the state of the deer? Activity and stillness close by each other, equally strong at all times?

Then she bent her head and licked my arm. The window was open, my elbow was resting on the car door; she licked my forearm. Twice. Then she turned and walked toward the buck. Then she stopped and looked back at me. A long look. Then she trotted toward the buck and the two disappeared into the wood.

I felt so not-of-this-world that I had to turn to Jodie and say, "That happened, didn't it?" Her answer was a smile of pure joy. It is difficult to write of joy. Words, for some reason, are better at communicating pain. Nevertheless, this was joy. And a sense of newness I don't know how to explain.

The cars were moving again. My Chevy was moving. I was driving, but I was hardly aware of it. There was nothing to say or do. It would have been somehow insulting, to the doe and to the moment, to affix some specific meaning to what had happened. Except to say that what happened, what the doe gave me, was a moment of utter newness that is there for me to drink from when I am too tied to the suffering that, as Jodie says, teaches nothing or all of us would be wise.

My friend Naunie told me later that deer live with their fear every moment and yet are not afraid, and that I needed to remember this. I don't know how she knows about deer, but what she said feels right.

(There are people who kill such creatures for sport. This is called "hunting," and is presumed to have something to do with how our ancestors lived. If it was done with a spear or even a bow, I'd have more empathy; but a high-powered rifle, a telescopic sight, a full stomach, and a beer hangover have little to do with our ancestors' hunts. I've been around too long to be shocked at what people kill or why. Still, I don't think today's hunters are hunting deer. They are hunting grace—eliminating a little more grace from the world. Grace shames a graceless people. But this paragraph won't change hunting, so let's move on, deliberately and without the unessential, as the doe moves on.)

What Jodie said feels right, too. I repeat it here the way it repeats in my heart. Suffering doesn't teach or everyone would be wise. The question, then, is: What does teach? We know how to learn to do what's been done, but how do we learn to do what hasn't been done? For we also know that what's been done is not enough anymore. We are dying, all of us, of what's been done. We are crying out to learn how to do what hasn't been done.

I said that after the doe returned to the wood there was nothing to say or do, but, as I think back, that's not true. We gave a prayer of thanks. Jodie addresses her prayers, "To Those who listen, and to Those who hear." I address mine, "Oh many-beautied, many-bodied One." I feel a light in such words. We offered that light to the place, to the deer.

It's winter now. A hard winter, too. That road near the North Rim is probably impassable. A difficult season for deer. As I sit here writing, I think of all the eyes of deer, and of that doe's eyes. I think of how they live every moment in agitation and stillness, and of how she lives. She noticed me. We noticed each other. She touched me. I feel, now, that she invited me to follow her, not into the woods, where I am no more at home than she would be in my city, but into that place where activity and stillness meet, where we can drink of newness and feel the contour of the unimagined. Feel the mood, the possibility, of what hasn't been done.

It's right there. Right here. I don't know how to reach for it, but I am reaching. I feel many of us reaching. Beyond suffering. Looking into enormous and unknowable eyes that are looking (it is amazing) back at us. We must have something to offer, or why would such eyes look our way?

*Buddy's L.A.'s best shine, Los Angeles,
California, 1968*

HOW SOFT YOU TREAD ABOVE ME

Two, maybe three years ago, in Lubbock, late on a hot weekend night, driving with Deborah on Broadway toward Texas Tech. They haven't repaved that stretch of Broadway yet. It's a wide brick road, bumpy, antique, as you still find in the older sections of Panhandle towns—a style of building from before World War II. Deborah wants to see if Elvis is out tonight. Not the Elvis, but one of his fleshy, missionary ghosts—one of those obsessive, possessed men of indeterminate age whose greatest satisfaction seems to be to look in the mirror and see some trace of Elvis staring back.

He's there all right.

In the empty parking lot of a joint that calls itself a burrito factory . . . the sign in the window says "Closed" but the parking lot sure isn't . . . he's set up two small banks of lights that flash yellows, blues, and reds, like at a disco . . . a karaoke sound system . . . there's one white metal chair directly in front of him, and, several feet behind that, three or four rows of white metal chairs, four or five to a row . . . of course nobody is sitting in any of those chairs . . . he's strung colored plastic pennants overhead, like a used-car lot, and Deborah says he performs at used-car lots sometimes . . . and there's nobody in sight up or down the street, and hardly a car passes . . . but this guy's got the karaoke turned all the way up and he's singing his heart out, or what's left of his heart, to a sleeping city and an empty street, and to whoever he imagines is sitting in those chairs, as maybe he imagines Elvis Aaron Presley looking down from Heaven in gentle approval. (And does it occur to this guy that Aaron was the name of the Bible's first High Priest?)

There's a hand-lettered sign that says you can have your picture taken with Elvis for a dollar. "Come on, Ventura," Deborah dares, "take a picture with Elvis." It's still hard for me to refuse a dare, but I'm not up to this one. We pull into the parking lot but we don't get out. I don't remember him looking directly at us, but maybe he did. Anyway, our presence energizes him. He's a pudgy guy, gaudily costumed, his huge head of hair dyed raven black with every wave cemented in place, and with sideburns more exaggerated than Elvis's ever were. He throws himself into his Elvis moves with the enthusiasm of a little boy. I don't remember what he sang, maybe because he couldn't sing a lick and maybe because all I could "hear," in effect, was the audacity of the man. What concoction of gall and madness could drive anyone to give such a performance, in such a place, on such a night? What unspeakable loneliness? What irrepressible need to identify his entire being, at the risk of mockery, with a figure clearly sacred to him and absolutely beyond his abilities? Not that I felt sorry for him. What he lacked in stature he made up in nerve. At what point had he crossed the line and taken a private obsession, performed secretly before his mirror, and bought those white metal chairs, those lights, those pennants, those speakers, to live his fantasy late on a darkened street? And what did he expect from it? What did he imagine might happen, sometime, somehow, on some night, because of his performance? And who under Heaven did he imagine to be sitting in that solitary white metal chair toward which he directed his ungainly energies?

Just a few miles southeast of where he sang, the Cotton Club still stood, a huge warehouse of a joint where a nineteen- and twenty-year-old Elvis had once gigged—as had Buddy Holly and Roy Orbison before their fame. "I introduced Buddy Holly to Elvis at the Cotton Club," a man once told me in a now-defunct

Lubbock bar called Fat Dawg's. He said it arrogantly and desperately, as he'd been saying it when juiced for years, and whether or not it had ever happened it had become a true thing for him, a short story repeated precisely over and over to strangers. There are many memories like that floating around this Panhandle town, the city of Peggy Sue—artifacts of the past burnished through many tellings, impossible either to verify or deny, from a time when nobody dreamed these songs would still be sung in fifty years and nobody realized (as nobody young ever does) that what today seems so vital and hip would seem to later generations a little comical, a little pathetic, and very strange, though the songs would still find a way to be heard. (Elvis, had he lived, would be seventy-ish now. As Jerry Lee Lewis used to say, leering over the piano, "Think about it.")

And about 120 miles straight north up I-27, in Amarillo, in the summer of '74, not long before he got fat, the actual Elvis sang his heart out and Deborah and I were there. The soundtrack of *2001* blared as he strode onstage, and beams of white spotlights played over the audience—an interesting touch, as though *we* were the show being presented for Elvis's benefit. There he was, embodying the line that Doc Pomus wrote for him in the song "Viva Las Vegas": a devil with love to spare. Or so he seemed in performance. First and greatest of all the Elvis imitators, a forty-year-old man imitating himself as though his life depended on it. Now we know that as he sang that day he hadn't long to live, but then it seemed he would remain forever just as he was, for his singing seemed to have the power both to invoke the future and to keep it at bay. I was twenty-eight, Deborah was twenty-three, and the music Elvis had helped create was (and in many ways still is) at the crux of how we defined ourselves. There he was on stage, in a blinding white sparkly jumpsuit: "If you're lookin' for trouble, you came to the right place."

And a line we passed over when we first heard that song: "My middle name is misery."

Now this darkened street was the place—"the right place" merely by virtue of being the place we two old friends happened to be—and this strange pudgy man was keeping himself alive by echoing that other life that was no more. He couldn't be more alone if he were playing a computer game. But playing a computer game you risk nothing—and that is the danger of such games, not their enforcement of solitude but their utter absence of risk, for there is no risk without contact. People who don't learn to risk can't learn to live. This late-night Lubbock Elvis, he was risking a great deal, because there's no telling what can happen on a darkened street anywhere, especially in the West, especially when you're exposing

yourself so vulnerably. His middle name is certainly misery, that's there for all to see, but there's no denying the precarious dignity of his effort. Dare to laugh at him and you're laughing at yourself, because, from 1956 on, America became an Elvis imitator; and there isn't a performer around without some reflection of a gesture that Elvis initiated, for no singer before him had dared to move so publicly with such blatant sexual defiance. Pity this Lubbock Elvis and you're pitying yourself, at least insofar as the music of then or now has a grip on you. And can you afford to be embarrassed by or for him? There probably isn't an American alive who hasn't jived in front of a mirror, trying to abduct and absorb the quality of some star through the intimate exercise of imitation; the Elvis imitators, and this one in particular, excite our interest and our sympathy precisely because they've transformed our mirror sessions into a way of life.

Mirrors facing mirrors, disappearing into a distance that we might as well call infinity. Elvis, who became for America both the mirror and the person standing in front of it. Love him tender.

"Tender" is the loveliest of words. No, I couldn't bring myself to take my picture with this Elvis for one dollar or a million, that night. Not if he'd paid me. I wish I had. The night I first saw Elvis I was ten years old, watching *Stage Show* hosted by Tommy and Jimmy Dorsey, Presley's first national exposure. And later that very night I locked myself in the bathroom so I could peform to the mirror for the first time in my life, compulsively aping his moves. So this guy on Broadway was not only a reflection of Elvis; without knowing it (or perhaps he did know, and perhaps that's why he could bring himself to this extreme) he was a reflection of me, and many like me, taking our secret fantasies public. On an empty Lubbock street in the dark.

There was no way to leave gracefully. Just start the engine and back slowly away. He doesn't seem to notice, keeps right on singing. The year he died Elvis recorded "Danny Boy" live—that verse sung from within the grave: "And I shall feel how soft you tread above me . . . And then my grave will richer, sweeter be . . . For you will bend and tell me that you love me . . ."

BROKE DOWN IN BOSSIER CITY

THE MOTEL WAS a short walk from the garage. Belinda, the gal who answered the garage's constantly ringing phone, told me to be careful of "*that* motel"—stay in the room after dark, don't stroll about at night. Belinda said it mainly housed "those people from southern Louisiana"—Katrina refugees who had evidently overstayed their welcome in Bossier City, across the Red River from Shreveport. Belinda had a point. The motel was what I call "a felony motel," the sort of joint that attracts folks who have just committed, or are about to commit, felonies. Interesting places, and I've stayed in many, but only when traveling alone. Apparently this dump was FEMA's idea of a fitting place for helpless families.

The motel clerk defined the word "blowsy"—a little drunk or a little high, a cigarette hanging from her lips, heavy, and showing a lot of breast. Her smile had died a long time ago but she mechanically displayed its corpse. She said her motel was almost full, though I'd seen no cars in the lot, just kids on skateboards. These Katrina victims either didn't own

cars or their cars hadn't made it out. I asked for a smoker and was given a small white ashtray to take to the room.

Some room. One dim bulb on a wall fixture. White cinderblock walls. A TV with a few fuzzy channels. The thinnest possible towels, and on the bed a blanket almost as thin. Burn stains on what was left of the rug. Two plastic glasses, one small bar of soap. The toilet didn't flush until I thought to fill the tank from the ice bucket. A family had lived here?! The TV had an FM radio tuned to NPR. On the bet that NPR listeners are people of some sensibility, I tried to imagine such people (or any people) living in this room for nearly five months. One resident said they'd just left, and I thought of Butch Hancock's line, "Where do you go when you're already gone?"

My Chevy had barely made it to the garage. The transmission couldn't get out of first gear and was screaming an awful whine and emitting a horrible smell. When Rodney and Virgil put it up on the rack and took off the tranny pan, out poured a black stinky liquid full of . . . stuff. But the thing about a '69 Malibu

[26]

Chevelle is: mechanics love it. They've owned cars just like mine, and they rhapsodize about their engines, races, and close calls. "Man," Rodney said, "ya c'n fix a car like this sometimes with bale-wire an' a screwdriver." I told him I knew he was right, because a passerby in a pickup had once helped me fix my cracked fan casing with exactly that, some bale-wire. I showed Rodney and Virgil where and how. Maybe that was when they decided to like me.

Rodney wore overalls, a sporty red beard, and the satisfied expression of a man for whom the world makes way— not the whole world but his world. It's his shop now, and when a driver needs a transmission there's no arguing the price. Rodney naturally likes that. His father, Virgil, started the joint around when I was five—which would be 1950.

Virgil was somewhere in the vicinity of eighty, a tall man for his generation. One eye looked off to the side seeing nothing, while his better eye saw just enough. He told me that back before I-20 paralleled U.S. 80, Bossier City, Louisiana, was known as "Little Las Vegas," and this stretch was known as "The Strip." Anything and everything happened here then, when half this building was a garage and the other half was a honky-tonk. "This here's where the stage was," Virgil pointed out. Virgil fronted "a hillbilly band," played all night, fixed cars all day. He called the life of a musician "a sacri-

fice," because you needed so many uppers and downers to keep the schedule going, and eventually that ruined you—though he seemed not to regret it.

When Virgil was a small boy in the thirties he and his family were the only whites picking in the fields. When they got the work they were told "never say 'nigger'" and they'd be all right. The farm boss was a black woman named Amy. Her word was law. She was their family's "doctor" too, and delivered his four brothers. She'd lecture the "young-uns," Virgil remembered, saying, "See deym horses, see deym mules, see deym hogs—dey's equal but dey's different, an' dey don' mix wey-ll. White an' black is equal but different too, an' dey don't mix wey-ll. Best da white boys don' mix wid da black girls, an' best da black boys don' mix wid da white girls." In Virgil's view, Amy was approving segregation; in mine, Amy was trying to save her people a lot of grief. Seventy years later she was still fresh in Virgil's mind, a no-nonsense person, a midwife, a boss, a protector of her own and holding her own, back when a black woman in Bossier City had no rights and no recourse. All this time later, via Virgil's memory, it was a privilege to meet Amy.

I reproduce Virgil's dialect because you so rarely hear a deep accent anymore and the music of his speech is part of the man. To make a point about why his time was better than mine, he spoke of working for a wood-chopper. They'd chop the wood, load it on a wagon, haul it to the railroad depot, and report to "the depot man," saying, "'Dayr's fah [four] staycks [stacks] of fay-ar-wood [firewood], ayn [and] two of [railroad] ties.' Ayn dayt [that] depot, man wouldn't'ah thunk t'go out ayn check, he'd pay rayt [right] dayr, 'cause'n deym days a man told *the truth*."

Virgil said, "We worked sun-up t' sun-dowyn in deym days, but know whut? It made *people* of us." Then he said, "It was a *culture*. We had a *culture*."

Virgil understood that a culture is built upon assumptions shared so deeply that they require no discussion. And Virgil was right: we don't have that anymore. I don't miss the culture he had; I doubt Amy would miss it either. But we've not replaced his culture with a functioning culture of our own, and that's what much of our conflict is all about. We're a fragmented people living out our fragments without much chance for one fragment to talk to, and listen to, the other personally. Unless my transmission conks out in a place like Bossier City, a guy like me hasn't much chance to hear out a guy like Virgil.

Virgil was for capital punishment "'cause the Bible says 'an eye for an eye.'"

In the Bible Jesus also instructs [Matthew 5:38–39], "You have heard that it was said, 'An eye for an eye and a tooth for a tooth.' But I say to you, Do not resist one who is evil. But if any one strikes you on the right cheek, turn to him the other also." That was a point hard to make on that stretch of U.S. 80 in Bossier City under the flight path of Barksdale Air Force Base. Every ten minutes or so our conversation was drowned out by the screeching engines of a B-52 rising into the sky.

On 9/11 George W. Bush touched down at Barksdale just long enough to tape a message that was aired after he took off again. Bush assured us we would be safe, though human beings have never been safe. My transmission had conked out at an intersection of the past and the present, Katrina and 9/11, war and peace, Amy and Virgil, Virgil and me—the intersection, too, of people trying to hold on to a capital-s Something against the onslaught of the aggressive capital-n Nothing that we're afraid our future might be. I thought of Dylan's line: "Now it's that day of confession and we cannot mock a soul, for when there's too much of nothing no one has control."

G. A. Barber's backyard after tornado, Lubbock, Texas, 1970

Betatakin, Navaho National Monument,
Arizona, 1970

SORRY WE MISSED CHURCH

DRIVING 19th Street in Lubbock, alongside the sprawling edifices of Texas Tech, the little tin-can car in front of me sported quite a bumper sticker:

SORRY WE MISSED CHURCH, WE WERE
BUSY LEARNING WITCHCRAFT AND
BECOMING LESBIANS.

That bumper sticker won't cost you in Los Angeles or Austin, but it takes rare nerve to paste those words on your tail in the Bible Belt. (Lubbock has, I am told, more churches per capita than any city anywhere.) The tin can had Texas plates, and any Texan knows that sticker won't be taken lightly around here. I *had* to see who was driving that car. I pulled up alongside. The driver and her passenger were women of about eighteen, maybe twenty. They wore tractor hats or maybe baseball caps, with brims pulled backwards, and they were laughing. They didn't notice me salute them, and they couldn't know that I was thinking, *Next to these kids, I'm a wuss.*

I write under the ever-flimsier protection of the First Amendment. They drive

around a famously right-wing town daring anyone to say them nay.

Those young women surely know that cops may pull them over on any pretext. And they must know that—coming out of a movie, say—they might find their car surrounded by a gaggle of repressed guys in desperate need to prove themselves real men. To the surprise of many, *Brokeback Mountain*, a movie about gay cowboys, is playing in Lubbock—the sight of a cowboy hat will never be quite the same, will never quite mean what it used to mean. There are lots of cowboy hats hereabouts, many no doubt a little less sure of their image because of *Brokeback Mountain* (they won't see the film, but they'll see the previews). Insecure cowboy wanna-bes won't take that sticker lightly.

But, unlike most Americans these days, those young women weren't letting fear set their limits.

Your freedom may be backed by law, but your freedom can't be given you by law. You give it to yourself by how far you're willing to go. You give it to yourself by what stakes you're willing to play for. Do your loved ones—or your town,

[31]

or your country—limit how free you are by what they can and cannot tolerate? How much of that are you willing to take? Is your freedom limited by your own fear? In this case the freedom we're talking about is basic: the freedom to be oneself. That's what these women were putting to the test—testing themselves, testing their society. And risking all kinds of hell to do it. East and West Coast writers pontificating about "the red states" don't imagine that those very states are also places of the purest rebellions, where rebels walk their talk on tightropes.

I wear a hat, a beat-up kind of fedora, and I took it off to those women—and said a prayer for their protection. (They may miss church, but church shouldn't miss them.)

During World War I, the hunchbacked piano-playing intellectual Randolph Bourne was hounded literally to death for wondering such things as whether, in a time when all the bullying forces of society were bent on useless destruction, there were any "desperate spiritual outlaws" with "a lust to create." That question is still important, and here were two spiritual outlaws making a desperate move, standing up for creativity as well as lust, through a medium more immediate—and hence more dangerous—than any essay or e-mail: the bumper sticker.

It is the signature of our era that we live in a world so unstable that its limits

may be tested merely by a bumper sticker—or, as in Europe and Islam right now, by a cartoon.

There were other bumper stickers on that street, bumper stickers I see wherever I drive (which is saying a lot, because in the last nineteen months I've driven forty of the contiguous forty-eight states): USA #1, UNITED WE STAND, SUPPORT OUR TROOPS, PROUD TO BE AN AMERICAN.

But many of us can remember when we never saw such stickers, and for good reason. When the United States seemed *really* united (give or take someone's ethnicity or race), the average person felt no need to bray "United We Stand." When the United States was *really* dominant you never heard people proclaim "U.S.A. #1!" The whole world knew we were #1, the Soviet Union was #2, and nobody came in third. When we *really* supported our troops—giving combat soldiers and vets all they needed—you never saw stickers pleading for their support. A country convinced its wars are righteous doesn't have to convince itself to support its troops.

And PROUD TO BE AN AMERICAN? For many that phrase has become an incantation to ward off the demons of our time and deny the darkness in our national identity. I *am* proud to be an American, and always have been, because, more than most nations, our history is the record of demons we've battled within ourselves as a people; win or lose, the courage, dignity, and nobility demonstrated in these struggles is something to be proud of. Like any nation we've been as bad as we've been good, but unlike any other nation we have been *original* from the start, in our form of government, our engineering and inventions, our arts, and the never-before-tried experiment of mingling ethnicities—that's a lot to be proud of. But hiding or ignoring our sins behind PROUD TO BE AN AMERICAN is merely shame turned inside out.

Our national self-doubt and self-conflict are nothing new; they've been going on, in one form or another, since before 1776. What is relatively new, in the last forty years or so, is a state of confused and conflicted values that leave us, as a people, with no shared means by which to measure our actions. Now we actually *argue* about whether torture is justified, or whether it's right to spy on Americans without warrants, or whether it's right to invade a country that has not attacked us. The answer to those questions—no, no, and no—would have been obvious to nearly every American fifty years ago, right and left alike. Now, in an increasingly complex world, what is obvious to one faction is blasphemy to another—which means that nothing is obvious.

Stirling Silliphant saw this dissolution of values as early as 1962, writing a *Route 66* episode, "Go Read the River": "Do you know what's right, what's wrong? Somehow, somewhere, a simple beautiful

thing, a single morality, a single set of standards, was smashed like an atom into ten million pieces. And now—now what's right for a man can be wrong for his business, what's right for his business can be wrong for his country, and what's right for his country can be wrong for the world." We are being torn apart by this state of uncertainty. Most people simply can't stand it—and, unable to stand it, many insist fanatically upon their proclaimed certainties in order to bear their unadmitted uncertainty.

Those brave lesbian/witchcraft gals in their cheap tin-can car sporting their bravado bumper sticker—if they can drive unmolested for even a block down Lubbock's 19th Street, their very existence (regardless of what price they may pay) testifies to a tectonic shift in the solidity of what Americans can assume is real or normal. The more you must enforce a dictum of normality, the less that normality actually exists. Those gals are saying to Lubbock, "Your idea of normal is *over*. Now it's normal for you to have to deal with *us*. However threatening we are to you—that's the measure of how little you really believe in your own reality, and that's the gauge of your desperate clinging to notions that no longer work. If you were sure of your beliefs, you wouldn't be threatened. Nice cowboy hat—free tickets to *Brokeback Mountain* anyone?"

If these gals are—as they clearly are—as much a product of Lubbock as Buddy

Holly, then there's a crack in the world, and what's breaking through that crack is unpredictable and not to be tamed. You might kill it, but that's not the same as taming it. The very fact that you need or want to kill it, proves its dominance over your psyche. If I obsess you, I own you— even if I'm dead. (So Islam and the West now own each other.) What we may fail to recognize in our fear is that this state of almost unbearable flux is a state of *becoming*. Something unheard of, for good and/or ill, is steaming out from the cracks of what we thought was our world. It is still unformed, so no one has yet been able name it convincingly. But every end is some kind of beginning. We are at an end *and* a beginning, but most of us are too scared and distracted to recognize that. Well, we don't have to. It will present itself in its own time, when it's gathered sufficient force and form. Only then will our chaos reveal its true nature by what it has birthed.

L ET US CONSIDER Lubbock,
Texas.

In 1973, January through Sep-
tember, I lived in Lubbock—not a resident; a drifter, taking my time passing
through. The Lubbockians I got to know
all were Texans, mostly born and raised in
Lubbock. Ethnically, most were some
mixture of Anglo-Saxon–Celt, often with
Cherokee stirred in a few generations
back. Many traced their American ances-
try to well before the Civil War. As for
Lubbock—socially (to state the obvious
and put it mildly), Anglo-Saxon–Celts,
Hispanics, and African Americans did not
mix much and tended to keep to their
own neighborhoods (the Anglo-Saxon–
Celt neighborhood being most of Lubbock). Once or twice, at the Cotton Club,
I saw an African American male dancing
with an Anglo-Saxon–Celt female; I
admired his guts and feared for his safety.
The only Jew I was aware of was Irene,
the Long Island–born friend who'd driven
me here, and she didn't stay long. Lubbock's cuisine in those days was limited—
lots of Texan diner food, some Mexican, a
Chinese restaurant, an Italian restaurant,

and that was about it. Back then, Lubbock
bragged about having the most Christian
churches per capita of any city in the
world. (Was it true? I never knew.) And all
the Texans had Texas accents.

(Footnote: My newfound friends
were—and are—among the smartest,
most original, generous, multitalented
people I've known. They changed my life.
Long story.)

It's thirty-odd years later, and I've been
a Lubbock resident for several years now.
Lubbock has changed. To understand
America today one must understand the
scope of that change.

Now many who've grown up here
have barely a trace of Texas in their
speech, sounding sort of San Fernando
Valley with a lilt. Now the best supermarkets in Lubbock are identical in look and
products to the best supermarkets in Los
Angeles. Note: they have kosher sections
and sell *challah* on the Jewish sabbath.
There's an Asian market; also, a "Ghandi"
market, serving families from the Indian
subcontinent. Lots of good food—Texan
and Tex-Mex, plus the chains, plus Thai
eateries (run by Thais who've been here a

generation), a Vietnamese restaurant, two French restaurants, Japanese, Chinese, New Orleanian, a fancy Italian restaurant run by a New York Italian, and the old Italian restaurant now has two outlets and is Lubbock's most popular eatery. There's a mosque. The synagogue has a female rabbi. One of the first people I met when I resettled is an Iraqi painter who's lived and raised a family here for twenty-odd years. As in L.A., it's not rare to see people of indeterminate ethnicity, Asian–Hispanic, Middle Eastern–Celt, Euro-Asian, African–Middle Eastern, etc. On my street, in a down-at-heels part of town, there's every sort of race, and no trouble that I've seen. It's not unusual, in any part of town, to see interracial couples of all ages and mixes, with no fuss, no self-consciousness, and no one but me seems to notice (because I take notes). Not that there are *many* interracial couples, it's just not unusual and it's no big deal. The other day, at a Mexican café, I saw a classic well-dressed West Texas Anglo-Saxon–Celt old lady, her blue-white hair in a firm bubble 'do—her old-timey accent rang through the room as she happily played with the child on her lap, her half–African American granddaughter. No one took notice but me and my notebook.

When that West Texas lady was born, every school, restaurant, and bathroom in this state was segregated, and most Anglo-Saxon–Celtic Texans meant to keep it that way. (Lest we forget, most of

them were passionate Democrats—not so much because of FDR's New Deal as because Abraham Lincoln was a Republican.)

Thirty-five years ago Lubbock was *Texas*—the old-timey image of Texas. Now a strong Texas accent is as unusual as a cowboy hat. Now many (especially women) look less like Levelland and more like Santa Monica. Lubbock is still a family-values town, still very conservative, very Christian. Until recently, you still had to drive across the county line to buy package booze, and Lubbock still advertises itself as a pure creation of the pioneers of the Great High Plains. Over 100 miles from any city its size, and 400-ish from any city one might call "major," yet Lubbock has become—there's no other word for it—cosmopolitan! Comparatively. When compared with Lubbock '73, *positively* cosmopolitan. True, Lubbock has special demographic circumstances—Texas Tech University grows by leaps and bounds and requires a sophisticated faculty and staff; also, Lubbock is a medical center for a large area, its hospitals and clinics staffed by people from all over the world. (My doctor is Kenyan.) My point is that if a place like Lubbock is no longer classically "Texas," then Texas is no longer what once was meant by the word "Texas."

And that is no small matter. In 1973 the Texan self-image, the Texan reality, and the world's image of Texas, were roughly the same. Not an accurate image even then (no such image ever is). That image didn't include the likes of Bill Moyers, Butch Hancock, Jo Carol Pierce, Terry Allen, Molly Ivins, John Henry Faulk. But there was still plenty of room in that traditional image for a poseur like George W. Bush to hide, cloaking his spooky lack of identity with a Texas oilman's façade. In 1973 Texas still took its basic image from its small towns and ranches. Now its small towns are falling apart, its ranches are subsidy addicts, and Texas no longer has an Anglo-Saxon–Celt majority. Many urban Texas kids talk like they do in the San Fernando Valley.

The same is happening all over the country. I know young people reared in Atlanta who have no trace of Southern accent. Last time I was in Manhattan, it was almost a full day before I heard someone speak with a strong New York accent. When I first hit the road in 1972, accents, attire, and behavior were markedly different in different parts of the country. There was some ethnic diversity in the big cities, but almost none anywhere else. All that has changed, and the traditional images of a Southerner, a New Yorker, a Texan, are fading further and further from the reality "on the ground," as they say. This is especially true of the middle class and affluent.

California and New Mexico also have nonwhite majorities, while New York, Arizona, Maryland, Mississippi, and Georgia are 40 percent nonwhite. The state with the fastest-growing Hispanic population is none other than Arkansas (so reported by BBC World News America, Nov. 8, 2008). All of which reveals a surprising, utterly unanticipated fact: We don't yet know what an "American" is! We don't yet know what an "American" even looks like. That identity—an "American"—has not yet been settled by history.

From about 1930 to about 1980, the question of American identity seemed settled; but history didn't accept that era's definition of "American." History moved on, though America's self-image lagged (and still lags) far behind our historical reality. Think of Lubbock, this supposedly right-wing city, in the middle of nowhere. If so much drastic ethnic and social change has happened here in merely one generation, try to imagine Lubbock one or two generations from now. You can't. No one can. The same holds true across the country. The American identity is in flux, undefined, and no one knows what it will be in another generation, much less in two.

Nothing so disorients an individual or a people as an identity undefined, threatened, in flux. When George W. Bush was president, his core supporters were people clinging to his imitation of an antiquated American identity. The vitriolic irrationality of anti-immigration frenzy is fueled by a panic of identity. (Irrational, yes. As *Austin Chronicle* editor Louis Black pointed out, just *how* do you round up twelve million human beings? You'd need prison space half again the size of New York City, and more buses than are on the continent, not to mention an extra army.) Americans no longer look or sound like, and will never again look or sound like, this country's rigid image of an "American." Many are unhinged by that fact; their pent-up panic, caused by myriad changes, is unleashed upon one or another comparatively minor change: "illegals." But what changed Lubbock? Not illegals. Lubbock is changing because of tidal shifts in economics, culture, technology, and perception.

A panic of identity can sway politics, but politics can't legislate identity. Such questions get decided by forces more inexorable. Lubbock, Texas, 1973, would never have agreed to become Lubbock, Texas, 2009. Rather, its changes were and are irresistible. What many cannot admit is that change never stops for our convenience. History never picks *you* to be its exemplar, because history is never satisfied with you or me or anyone. The forces of history are never a matter of the past, but of what comes next. History never goes backwards and never remains static. When history repeats itself, it does so in a different language. Or, at the very least, in a different accent.

Crowd, Palo Duro Canyon amphitheater,
Texas, 1970

RED STATE BLUES

U.s. 62 in the Texas Panhandle is a two-lane road with no shoulders, a straight line on land as flat as the palm of God's hand—so flat the skyline on all sides is below eye-level and you have to look a bit down to see the horizon. The sky is contradictory, a clash of delicacy and enormity—as light a blue as can be, but massively so, all-enveloping. The flatness and the sky distort space. Without a farmhouse or a windmill to judge by, it's hard to tell one mile's distance from five. Miles of plowed fields, but there's more prairie grass than there used to be, less cultivation. Then you come upon an almost ghost town, one of hundreds across the West and Midwest.

Just a few homes, and some are empty. A historical marker announces, "Village of Cone—Named in 1903 for J.S. Cone—Town Once Had a School, Stores, and Churches." No trace of anything now but the school: red brick, two spacious wings, windows boarded. Engraved in stone over the front doors: "19 Cone 23." That sign speaks of pride and hope. They expected

something here that never happened: a future.

Floydada, the county seat, is a few miles north of Cone. Like most county seats in such places, a proud well-built courthouse in the center of town marks where the action used to be. Driving the four streets that branch off from the old courthouse, I counted fifty-five defunct stores. Floydada, founded in 1890, has an official population said now to be almost 4,000. Try and find them. Wherever they are they're not downtown, they don't frequent these stores, and they don't go to the long-closed picture show. The people who built this place did not expect this to happen. They didn't found this town to see it all but dead by the time their grandchildren were old.

Continue north on State Road 207. There's a marker where the town of Della Plain has disappeared. Once, on this immense expanse, there stood "a school, church, post office, stores and a newspaper." Now there are not even any ruins.

Up the road is what used to be a farmhouse. Just its corner remains, gray bent wood, beside a tilting gray privy. You see a lot of that in the middle of nowhere, all over the West and Midwest. Down in Terilingua on the Rio Grande, Spider Johnson and I sat on an old porch from which we could see what was left of several long-abandoned homes. "Toil and dreams," Spider said. "That's all that remains of their toil and dreams."

Further up 207 is Silverton, population 771. Another county seat, founded in 1892, its proud and all-but-empty courthouse built in 1922. A website reports that in 1984, Silverton had twenty-seven businesses. That was around the time when Dixie and I would drive fifty-ish miles from Clarendon, across the Red River and up the Caprock to a café in Silverton that baked terrific pies. We'd have our pie and coffee, then enjoy the beautiful miles back to Dixie's. That café still stands, empty, like most of Silverton, where there are no longer twenty-seven businesses. More like seven, if that. In ten or twenty years there may not be anyone in Silverton or Floydada or many another site of toil and dreams across the lands that commentators dismiss as "red states."

Between Silverton and Clarendon you see more ghost-houses and ghost-gas-stations and a tiny ghost-store, and every year they crumble a little more. Clarendon sits on four lanes of U.S. 287, the main highway from Dallas to Denver. The road and a junior college keep the town alive, but I counted thirty-three empty storefronts. The proud county courthouse hasn't been active for many years. Sonic Drive-Ins, Pizza Hut, Lowe's, Dollar General, Best Western, and Napa/Shell franchises siphon their profits somewhere far away from this town that once boasted two first-rate hotels for railroad men (one long empty, one now the site of a struggling local restaurant). Drive north of Clarendon on State Road 70 across the Salt Fork of the Red River to I-40. Not far south of I-40 is a marker documenting the first burial ground in "this area of Donley County, 1895." It was the town of Jericho. It had "a station of the Chicago Rock Island and Gulf Rail Line" in "about 1902." There was a town and a rail station here! They left no ruins, just graves. This road follows the route of the cattle drives on their way to Dodge City, Kansas, in a time when people thought they were building a way of life that would prosper, in a place where they expected their kin to live for centuries.

In Paducah, miles south of Clarendon, I counted again: forty-four empty storefronts, and what looks like an abandoned factory, plus the old county courthouse, the dark picture show, and the hollow railroad hotel. Drive any direction for hundreds and hundreds of miles and you see the same thing. I know. I've driven every state in the West and Midwest these last several years, and everywhere you see the same thing: barely alive towns, ruins of toil, ruins of dreams, ruins of a future that people worked hard for—a future that never came.

A year ago November, I drove Kansas and Nebraska with Dave Johnson (no relation to Spider). We'd read that in many counties there were now fewer people than in the late 1800s and we wanted to see for ourselves. Prairie grass swayed in the wind where there'd been farms. Town after town looked much like what I've described of the Panhandle. The architecture is different, but always the beautifully built and long-abandoned county courthouse and dozens of empty stores. In Kansas and Nebraska you don't see the diversity that you now see even in small Texas towns. Instead, you see mostly large white people of a certain ilk, the great-, and great-great-, and great-great-great-grandchildren of those who pioneered these plains. And many of these folks disliked me on sight.

I forget the name of the Kansas town where we stopped for lunch. It was like a scene in an old Western: we walk in, everybody looks, everybody stares as we take our seats. Dave, he could be a businessman from down the road (as, in fact, he is)—distinguished looking, tall, gray hair, casual clothes. He walks into this diner alone and he's fine. Me—maybe it's the hat, the gray ponytail, how I walk, I don't know. But the people in that Kansas diner, in particular—they looked at me

with naked, livid hatred. (So did old women in Nebraska the next day. As I passed, one said to another, "Well, *he's* different." She spat "different" as though the word meant something vile.) In the diner, one farmhand couldn't take his eyes off me. Sitting with his friends at lunch, he stopped eating and stared at me. His face was trembling—trembling!—with rage and hate. I expected something nasty to go down, but all he did was stare. I was baffled. Why me?

Perhaps this is why:

These people are watching their towns die. Watching their way of life die. They are living the end of their dream, and they didn't believe that could happen. Like their ancestors, they've worked hard and hard and hard. They've played by the rules, believed the right things, worshiped the proper God, lived as they deeply felt life should be lived, *and they're losing everything that matters to them.* And there's nothing they can do about it except to keep working hard, because that's all they know. They're losing a way of life because of forces beyond their ken. Giant agribusiness, globalization, politicians selling them out, a tidal wave of history sweeping them away. Republicans and right-wing demagogues play to them, so they vote for Republicans. But it doesn't help. Liberals and Democrats rarely to talk to them, and still more rarely talk *with* them—why, then, would they vote for liberals and Democrats? "Blue state" snobs make jokes about the stupid "red states." These rural people are not stupid. They're furious. Time has passed them by and they don't know why. They've done and been everything that they were taught to do and be, and it's come to nothing. That's what liberals don't get. These people are furious, and they've got something to be furious about, however much their fury may be misdirected. They want somebody to blame—a useless but human need.

So I walk into their Kansas diner and in my differentness I become an instant symbol of what's pulling them down. Their kids are leaving town, their towns are dying, their leaders are failing them, they're helpless to stop it. They expected to live prosperously in these places for centuries—their courthouses were built to last centuries. They're losing it all, and there's no one to give a damn. They didn't believe this could happen—could not conceive that their time would be so short and their toil would be futile and their dreams would die so hard.

IDLY LEAFING through old travel notebooks I came upon aged Verlie, who sat beside me on a Greyhound from Muskogee to, eventually, Wichita. It was very late; she couldn't sleep; she seemed in pain on that bus seat but didn't complain. You could smoke in buses then and we were smoking. At the last stop I'd gotten her a coffee, not knowing if she'd want one; she was glad to take it and started talking. She told me of being a girl on her family's farm in Arkansas, 1905-ish, grinding coffee beans by hand. Coffee came in fifty-pound bags, "Green beans, roast 'em yerself, grind 'em yerself." She asked where I was from; I told her, and spoke of my travels. She said (very satisfied to say it, too), "I just been to four states my whole life, Arkansas, Oklahoma, Kansas, an' Texas"—she spoke as though even four was too many, and offered the opinion that a young man like myself "shouldn't be wanderin' aroun' so far from family." Birthed her first child in Arkansas at the age of fifteen. Bore six kids before her fifty-one-year marriage was done; she'd been divorced now fifteen years. (I didn't ask why she

divorced after half a century. I wish I had. I was new to the ways of such people and didn't know that Verlie wouldn't have mentioned such a thing if she didn't want me to ask; but, since I didn't ask, Verlie wouldn't volunteer.) She'd worked as a cook twenty years in Hominy, wherever Hominy was; I didn't ask that either. "My sons like Tulsa real well 'cause they have inside jobs in Tulsa. I'm so proud they have inside jobs." Inside jobs. Anything was better than slaving on a farm.

She said "t'oth'un," meaning "the other one." She said "the beautifulest thing"—about what, I neglected to write down. She asked what I did; I told her I was writing a screenplay. She asked what that was and I told her. "I never cared much for shows," she said. Hardly ever went to shows, though her kids did. The show in her town finally closed a couple of years ago. "I liked t' go t'dances, jus' didn't like shows." Verlie's kids got her a TV but she never watched it "'cept when they visit." Didn't watch TV, didn't read newspapers. "Papers, they're jus' 'bout trouble."

I wondered (not aloud) about Franklin

Roosevelt, Woody Guthrie, Martin Luther King, Jr., and further back to Thomas Jefferson, Thomas Paine, Abraham Lincoln—leaders, artists, and thinkers who could talk to Verlie. I wondered if we'd ever again have a liberal-ish politician or artist or thinker who could be bothered to speak to the Verlies of this land about the big things, the issues important to many of us. No point getting mushy about Verlie, no point seeing her limitations as virtues in themselves; still, Verlie's world was a world of the hands and the heart, and you can't *do* anything, on a large or small scale, without people of the hands and heart.

If you can't somehow include Verlie, there's a lot in your program that will not get done, no matter how highfalutin your intentions. Verlie is of those who, in her phrase, "do the doin'." College kids and urban intelligentsia aren't enough; until a cultural innovation makes its way to Verlie, it doesn't stick.

Which is what John Adams meant in his letter to Jefferson when he said, "The revolution was in the minds of the people."

Our bus stopped someplace called Durant. A teenager boarded; he wore a Cheryl Ladd T-shirt. People started talking across the aisles. The large lady bus driver. The old Chicano discoursing of bad kidneys. Verlie announced I was writing a "show." They all wished me luck. And all the while I was thinking, Who

speaks to these good people? Right-wingers seem to know how, but who on the left?

A crusty old farmer, work boots, creased and bony hands, sunburned neck and face, was reading a pamphlet titled, "Government and God"—somebody was speaking to him and it wasn't me, and it wasn't anyone I knew or valued. How do you expect people to go your way if you don't even deign to notice them? That farmer was *interested*. He was reading a pamphlet. If I'd written a pamphlet directed to him, in terms he could understand, chances are he might be interested and read it. If we ignore him, why shouldn't he ignore us?

"You want some gum?" another old fellow said to me, on the bus back from Witchita. It meant he wanted to talk. "Sure." I thanked him and chewed. He was from Quartzsite, Arizona. Well, it just happens I've had several important nights in Quartzsite, and a state patrolman almost jailed me there; I described the patrolman and this old fellow knew him and didn't like him any more than I. We talked about the sexy older ladies who ran Quartzsite's donut shop—fleshy, funny, savvy women. He said, "You could set your compass by gals like that." In the course of our conversation he mentioned that you can't buy a daily paper in Quartzsite anymore. "They had a shortage of newsprint, so they cut out the outlying areas. They gonna come back, they said they will, soon as they have the newsprint. By that time we'll be so used t' doin' without, we won't want it." We've cut out "the outlying areas" and left them to radio demagogues.

Another old travel notebook, from about that same time, describes a bar in Midland–Odessa and an older salesman named Tony. He said he knew the gangster who blinded labor journalist Victor Reisel with acid. "The guy [the gangster] got killed the next day." Tony sighed. "I shoulda been a hit man. I think about it a lot." He stated this dubious ambition in a wistful, dejected voice; Tony wasn't dangerous but he wanted to be. Instead, he was regional sales director of his company and that's as high as he would rise because "I don't have an Anglo-Saxon name." Then: "I always get the feeling I shouldn't be doing what I'm doing; I should be doing something else."

If I had a dollar for every time some stranger on my travels has said something just like that, I could pick up the check for a large party at a very expensive restaurant. In a more or less free country, where (theoretically) you can more or less do what you please, many feel "I shouldn't be doing what I'm doing; I should be doing something else." They're told from grade school that they can go as high as they aim, while at the same time they see from the cradle that this usually is not so. But they can't help believing in the American Dream. When they fail its expecta-

tions and their own, they usually blame only themselves—then they lay their old high expectations on their children, who disappoint their parents and themselves in turn. This longing, pain, and disappointment—this sense of "Oh my god, I've failed the dream!"—are basic to our way of life. Politicians, advertisers, and the entertainment industry play on these feelings for votes and profit, but for many people nothing alleviates their secret sense of having failed. Edward Hopper is the most American of painters because he painted solitary Americans whose wistful sadness and preoccupied expression say exactly, "I shouldn't be doing what I'm doing; I should be doing something else." Underneath America's manic activity, that's the saddest song on the Great American Jukebox—a song mostly sung to strangers, because if you say to someone you love "I should be doing something else" it would be too threatening, too disruptive.

And this at Old Smokey's in Winslow, Arizona: an old working man in a tractor hat said to another old man wearing a similar hat, "I don't know much. I don't understand anything I know, let's put it that way."

Beneath all our competing soundtracks and rhetoric, this is the true and secret American discourse. There is the cacophony of the "Public Discussion" (as a friend calls it in capital letters) and the longing and bafflement of the private discussions in our bars and diners and public conveyances. The craziness of this country is that the public and private discussions have almost nothing to do with each other.

But I also think of Butch Hancock telling me, "My granddad drove the first car to Lubbock"—drove it on a dirt road from Wichita Falls. Janette saying, "My granddad lived in a dugout in Palo Duro Canyon and built the first road in Palo Duro Canyon, from Claude to Wayside." Debby recalling talks with her grandmother who came to the Texas Panhandle in a covered wagon. Or old Ruby, in Sweetwater, whose father was a trail boss and twice employed Billy the Kid on cattle drives. Perhaps that's why we're so confused—as a country, we're still young enough to know someone who drove the first car, built the first road, arrived in a covered wagon. One generation builds a way of life and before they die the next generation changes it utterly, so we remain congenitally young, eternally immature, baffled but pretending not to be, except maybe with a friend over morning coffee when we say, "I don't understand anything I know, let's put it that way."

THE VOLUME was purchased for
only six dollars in an odds-and-
ends store in Los Angeles. Its
cover was water-damaged and faded, so
you could barely read the title; the cover's
illustration was impossible to make out;
but all its 224 pages were intact, though
stained, and its paper and ink had been of
such high quality that the print was still
clear and easily read and its once-white
pages hadn't faded much—they were a
light beige; the binding was badly
cracked, but because of the old practice
of binding not only with paste but with
high-quality string, the pages still held in
place and were easily turned. (The string,
amazingly, hadn't rotted at all.) You could,
with effort, make out the title: *McGuffey's
Eclectic Second Reader*.

The inner title page read, in more
detail: McGuffey's Newly Revised Eclectic
Second Reader: Containing Progressive
Lessons in Reading and Spelling. Revised
and Improved. By Wm. H. McGuffey,
LL.D. Cincinnati: Sargent, Wilson, & Hin-
kle. And on the next page: Entered,
according to Act of Congress, in the year
Eighteen Hundred and Fifty-Three.

On the inner side of the cover, two
names were printed in pencil in a child's
hand: "Irene K," "Louisa Van Waters." On
the next page, in an only slightly more
mature child's script: "Louisa Van Waters,
May 30th 1860."

From its first edition in 1836 (the year
of the Alamo), *McGuffey's Reader* was the
standard textbook (often alongside the
Bible) in America's schools for the next
100 years—in every part of the continent,
my reference book says, except New England (no reason for New England s rejec-
tion is given). You can see, or rather hear,
the successful application of McGuffey's
methods and curriculum in Ken Burns's
documentary *The Civil War*. Burns's nar-
ration consists largely of quotes from letters written by all classes of society and
from all regions of the country. The language is alive, clear, vivid, and utterly
absent of jargon. The grammar is sometimes fanciful and colloquial, but always
rooted in experience; the usage is rhyth-
mic with local inflection but, North and
South, lower- and upper-class alike, black
and white, you hear a shared American
written language that is marvelously

expressive. Most of these letter writers, from the wives and soldiers and runaway slaves and aristocrats and officers, would have had little formal education by modern standards; and most would have learned to read and write through a *McGuffey Reader*. Nothing like that had ever been accomplished on such a wide scale before. McGuffey's enthusiasm and care for education is transmitted on page eight in his "Suggestions to Teachers":

> *The great object of the intelligent teacher should be to awaken the attention of the pupil to the subject of the lesson he is reading. The conversational mode of imparting instruction, and of training the young mind, is believed to be the true and only means of attaining this end. . . . Let the teacher be assured that the hour of the reading lesson is one in which he must tax his powers to the utmost, if he expects success. It requires no ordinary application on his part to fix the attention of the pupil; to enable him fully to understand what he reads; and to make this exercise more a pleasure than a task. The teacher, who devotes himself to the attainment of these objects, will be more than repaid for his own labor and exertion, by the rapid progress of his pupils.*

On every page you see McGuffey's conviction that reading is an explicitly moral act. That is, he saw reading not only as a means to impart and learn

morality, but as an act through which morality is fixed, rooted, and stored. I would define morality as a fundamental respect for the rights and needs of others. The best expression of this, for me, is Rabbi Hillel's, early in the first century: "Do not do to others what you do not want done to you." McGuffey would agree, though his instruction is steeped in the assumptions of his era: religion—specifically, Christianity—is worked into many of the *Reader*'s lessons; so are imperialism, sexism, a classification of Native Americans as "savages," and a glorification and idealization of (white) American history. It was McGuffey who invented the tall tale of young George Washington's cherry tree, which was still taught as fact (and in McGuffey's version) when I was a boy. But for all the objections I have, it would be perversely politically correct not to admit the idealism, however flawed, that is implicit in every line and in the book itself. For McGuffey had created a textbook for a "public education"—the education of the general public—in which largely working-class children, who had never been taught on a mass scale before, would be given the tools to open any book of any kind in their language. With decent instruction, anyone could master McGuffey's highly entertaining *Reader*. Educationally, its standard was high: anyone who successfully learned *McGuffey's Reader* could read anything. Obviously, the teaching methods of today are not nearly as successful. The very last lesson in the book is the Ten Commandments, as usually listed in America; but McGuffey adds, as an unnumbered eleventh commandment, the same words from the Torah that Jesus cites as the most important commandments, and that are not usually included in America's ten; it's the last sentence in the book: "Thou shalt love the Lord thy God with all thy heart, and with all thy soul, and with all thy mind: and thou shalt love thy neighbor as thyself."

No, I'm not advocating reinstituting McGuffey's blend of education and religion into public schools. His *Reader* helped establish education as we know it (or knew it); but for most of his students it didn't inoculate against committing genocide, slavery, Jim Crow, child labor, the suppression of women, bigotry of all kinds . . . the list goes on and gruesomely on. I believe it is not only legitimate but necessary to expect education to be at least an antidote to, and a means to fight, atrocity and oppression. Yet it is also true that most of the people who learned how to fight these immoralities, from the 1830s into the 1930s, were people who developed, in large part, through reading; and who had, in effect, learned to read at McGuffey's knee, as part of an educational movement, unique in history, of which the *Reader* was a crucial element. And this result was implicit in the *Reader* from the start. McGuffey was a mixed

blessing, to be sure, but a blessing nonetheless. Hannah found the book in a dingy antique shop. When she gave it to me and I read the copyright date, 1853 . . . and saw the child's script: "Louisa Van Waters, May 30th, 1860" . . . I thought: This book was published three years after *The Scarlet Letter*, two years after *Moby-Dick*, one year after *Uncle Tom's Cabin*. In the year of its publication, Congress authorized the survey for the first transcontinental railroad. One year later, *Walden* was published; and a year after that, *Leaves of Grass*. Not long after little forgotten Louisa wrote her date, Lincoln was elected and the Civil War began. The Native Americans west of the Mississippi were still strong. Commerce and farming in America were still largely individual and comparatively free enterprises—more free than anywhere else in the world. America had yet to be conquered by corporations.

Reconstruction had yet to fail so miserably, so disastrously. America didn't yet require a large military. We had committed the ineradicable sins of genocide, land theft, and slavery, but it was not yet too late to expiate and even correct those sins; those sins weren't yet so deeply ingrained into the structure of America that we could never escape them. There was still time to be just to the tribal peoples of the West. There was still time to free the slaves and give each his 40 acres and his mule, which every slave had more than earned. There was still time for America to be America . . . to be more like the America of *Leaves of Grass* than the America of the *Wall Street Journal*. The volume was printed, and Louisa wrote her name and date, at a hovering, transitional, all-important moment when there was still time . . . a moment that Whitman understood, and Lincoln, and Frederick Douglass, and a precious few others . . . aptly, as I write, the tune playing happens to be Crosby, Stills, Nash & Young: *Find the cost of freedom . . . Buried in the ground.* . . .

Louisa, Louisa . . . Louisa Van Waters . . . who were you and where were you? Were you perhaps ten years old in 1860, when America still had half a chance? Did you live to be, perhaps, seventy? Were you finally allowed to vote before you died? By 1920, a hypothetical year of your death, we were a world power on a technological binge that has yet to spend itself. I hold the book you held. I'm a citizen of an America that never was. It's the only America I care about. I live in two Americas: I confront the America that is with the America that could have been. That confrontation is, now, what it means to be an American.

Cotton clouds and overpass, near New Deal,
Texas, 1970

AN ANGRY READER challenged my statement that during the first half of the twentieth century an African American man was lynched in the South at the rate of roughly one every three days. Now that the Confederate flag is again an issue in American politics, with hot debates as to whether it is moral to officially fly that flag atop the statehouses of the former Confederacy, it is time to answer that reader's challenge and to face what the Confederate flag really stands for. The South did not keep official records of its lynchings, but others, like the Tuskeegee Institute and the *Chicago Tribune*, tried to. Figures vary, but on January 13, 2000, the *New York Times* quoted the following, which is one of the lower estimates that I've seen: "Between 1882 and 1968, an estimated 4,742 blacks met their deaths at the hands of lynch mobs." Do the gruesome math: 86 years times 365 days divided by 4,742 equals 6.6—or roughly one lynched black person per week.

However, this is a skewed figure, because few (if any) were lynched after 1955, for by then this nation had grown

eyes (television cameras) and its eyes were focused on the South by the Montgomery bus boycott and the movement that followed. So revise the figures to 1955: 73 years times 365 divided by, say, 4,700—which averages to about one lynched human being every five and a half days, or 5 or 6 a month. Such figures should make any decent person furious, but the fury that many white Southerners still feel, when faced with these facts, is one of raging denial. At least two states still sanction the flag that symbolically flew over these atrocities: South Carolina flies it on its state house; Texas displays it on plaques in its Supreme Court; worse, Texas allows the Confederate flag to be displayed in many public schools, though it should be obvious that no children of color should be compelled to receive their education under the banner of their ancestors' murder and enslavement.

Lynchings weren't always backroad affairs carried out by a crazed few. Many African Americans were lynched right in the center of town before large crowds—a fact for which there is ample photographic evidence, as can be seen in a new book by James Allen, *Without Sanctuary: Lynching Photography in America*. These pages are mostly reproductions of postcards. Yes, postcards—for the communities that perpetrated these horrors were proud of them and wanted distant friends and families to see. Roberta Smith, in the *Times*: "What takes the breath away is the sight of all the white people, maskless, milling about, looking straight into the camera as if they had nothing to be ashamed of, often smiling. Sometimes they line up in orderly fashion, as if they were at a class reunion or church picnic. Sometimes they cluster around the victim, hoisting children on their shoulders so that they can see too." Anyone who doesn't find this fully as horrible as the Nazi atrocities is living in a moral vacuum.

But a moral vacuum is what one often encounters when speaking to white Southerners about their history and their war flag. The Civil War may have ended many decades ago, but the propaganda justifying that war is still so virulent that good, intelligent, generous people will still parrot that the war and the Confederate flag were and are not about racism and slavery but about "states' rights," though the only "state right" in contention was the right to own slaves.

The facts are these: In 1860, Abraham Lincoln was elected on a platform stating that, while slavery would be allowed to continue in the South, any territory in the West that wanted statehood must be slave-free. The slave states were afraid that under Lincoln's policy free states would outnumber them in Congress and would eventually abolish slavery. So the Southern states seceded. Their purpose was the defense of slavery; "states' rights" was merely the excuse. In 1861, this was admitted by no less a Confederate than Jefferson Davis's vice president, Alexander Stevens, who said: "Our new government is founded upon the great truth that the Negro is not equal to the white man."

Why was the "states' rights" canard politically necessary? The leaders of the Confederacy knew the technological and numerical superiority of the North, and knew they could only win their rebellion with the recognition and aid of England and / or France, who might have an interest in stymieing the growth of Northern power. But those countries had outlawed slavery decades before and were not likely to consider a slave state worthy of recognition. The "states' rights" concept was a ploy to win European approval on, as it were, a technicality. It failed.

The oft-resorted-to statement that "most white Southerners didn't own slaves" is only a way of saying that most white Southerners weren't wealthy and didn't control the Southern economy. But the health of the Southern economy depended upon cotton, which in turn depended upon slavery. Most white Southerners didn't own slaves, but all depended for their prosperity upon the wealth that slavery created. The white South was fighting for its economic system, a slave system, so in fact the Confederacy was defending nothing but slavery, whether an individual Confederate owned slaves or not. The proof of this is that for the century following the Civil War the entire white South kept African Americans in bondage through viciously enforced Jim Crow laws in order to keep essentially the same economic system in place. There would have been no need to do that if the war had been merely about "states' rights." Which is why we don't hear about states' rights again as an American political issue until the 1950s, when the South once again bleated about states' rights in defense of segregation.

The moral vacuum that still curses the South is evident in its treatment of those whom it chooses to call heroes. For instance, Nathan Bedford Forrest was a slave trader before the war—the lowest moral degradation to which a human being can descend. He was certainly the most brilliant cavalry commander of the era; he was also a war criminal. At the battle of Fort Pillow, his troops shot and bayoneted 300 black Union soldiers who were trying to surrender. Forrest said: "It is hoped that these facts will demonstrate to the Northern people that nigra soldiers can't cope with Southerners." After the war Forrest became the first Imperial Wizard of the Ku Klux Klan. This infor-

mation isn't recorded on his statues.

Or take that sacred cow of the Confederacy, Robert E. Lee—a brilliant general, he was also a hypocrite whose brand of hypocrisy was particularly vile. Before the war he was said to disapprove of slavery, yet, like Thomas Jefferson, he didn't free his slaves—i.e., his money was more important to him than his morality. When Lee invaded Maryland in 1863 he ordered all free blacks shipped back to the South as slaves. Where was his disapproval of slavery then; and what had such a decision to do with states' rights? When Confederates massacred black Union troops who were trying to surrender, Ulysses S. Grant demanded that black soldiers must be treated like whites or he would cancel the practice of prisoner exchanges that until then had been one of the rules of North–South engagement. Lee refused. Lee sank deeper into the depths of hypocrisy when, early in 1865, with the South losing badly, he petitioned the Confederate Congress that slaves be allowed to serve in his army. The carrot was that any slave who fought for the South would be freed after the war. The Confederate Congress, in an act so barren of pride and consistency that "hypocrisy" hardly suffices to describe it, passed a law approving Lee's request. One Confederate senator, Howell Cobb of Georgia, was honest enough to state, "If slaves seem good soldiers, then our whole theory of slavery is wrong."

Another fact that Southern mythmakers have obscured is that there were many white Southerners who, to their great honor, refused to defend slavery and fought against it. Ken Burns, *The Civil War*: "In North Carolina, the pro-Union Heroes of America had more than 10,000 members. By the end of the war Unionists from every Southern state, except South Carolina, had sent regiments to the North." This proves that the defense of slavery was not an automatic or inevitable response for Southern whites. The defense of slavery was a conscious choice, and those who made that choice must answer for their acts in the judgment of history.

Can Americans truly transcend our institutional racism if the white South doesn't discard its self-serving myths and face its history? I doubt it. That's why it's so important that the flags come down and the myths be shattered. That such a mass cultural transformation is possible has been proven by postwar Germany, which has rejoined the more-or-less civilized nations by facing and rejecting the demons of its past. Until the South rejects its "rebel" hypocrisy, white Southerners must bear this disgrace: that the descendants of the Nazis have lived a greater honesty, have more deeply atoned for their crimes, and have displayed incomparably more moral courage than the descendants of the Confederates.

PIT STOP IN SHOW LOW

Show Low is the name of the town, and I have no idea why. It's not far from a place called Fool Hollow. Founded in 1871, it sits on Route 60 in the mountains of eastern Arizona at an elevation of 6,331 feet. Brutal winters, cool summer nights. This used to be Apache country—their reservation is just to the south. Show Low goes its unnoticed way surrounded by some of the wildest geography anywhere. Thirty miles north is the Petrified Forest, a lush, dense wood turned to desert stone. The Hopi Mesas are 110 miles northwest, vistas of surreal formations, where the eyes of a Salvador Dali or a Georgia O'Keeffe would be at home—hardly a tree anywhere, and the arid ground catches the light so delicately that colors appear and disappear on its surface at the slightest change in the sky.

Draw a fan from Show Low west to east for 200 miles, and you map dozens of extinct volcanoes, lava fields, ice caves, ruins of ancient cities, and a crater where a rock came burning from the sky and left a hole a thousand feet deep and a mile wide. Its impact killed every living thing around. Less than a two-hour drive east from Show Low is the Great Divide— near which, on a cliff face, is a message carved in an ancient dialect of Phoenician about 2,000 years ago. A sailor too exhausted to run anymore wanted it known that he was the only man left of his crew, and that Indians would kill him soon.

In a land of so many wonders, I didn't think to ask why that little town was named Show Low, but at the Chevron I did ask where you could get a good hamburger. One guy had just moved from Iowa City, and he didn't know. I asked why he'd come. He didn't know that either. He had a scared face. Whatever he was running from, Show Low wasn't comforting him any. The others had lived in Show Low all their lives. They recommended the McDonald's. When they saw my credit card they said something I hear a lot in such gas stations these days: "Any relation to Ace Ventura?"

"He's my son."

Used to be, I'd stop in a little town, ask where to eat, and the gas station guys would point me toward So-and-So's Café.

Greasy food, but you could strike up a conversation at the counter. Once you got the locals talking, the suspicion in their eyes would usually soften. The younger ones among them would be thin and almost anyone over thirty would be fleshy, except for a certain kind of waitress who would always be skinny, as though eaten from within by something that wanted to get out of town and never would.

There aren't many of those cafés left. Lately the locals point me to the Denny's or the McDonald's. Even the young are chubby now; and for some reason people in fast-food joints don't talk to strangers. Maybe it has something to do with how the money spent at So-and-So's Café would stay in town; the place belonged to them, there was a strength in that, so they had their pride. The same folks work and eat at the McDonald's now, but they don't know the names of the owners far away, and their money leaves the town just like the strangers'. Their sense of strength, their sense that their little town is unique and their own, is gone—and with it, a capacity for hospitality. Now the *Wall Street Journal* reports that, along with the Christian cross and the Muslim crescent, McDonald's golden arches are the most recognized symbol in the world. Is it possible to measure how many fewer conversations there are between strangers?

And let's remember that when the McDonald's opened, nobody put a gun to anybody's head to go there instead of to So-and-So's Café. Choices were made, a way of life was betrayed, and nothing was ever the same.

It was dinnertime; the McDonald's was hopping. Orders flew for "ten Chicken McNuggets," "six Big Macs." Route 60 is not a major road; Show Low isn't a tourist town. These were local families out for supper. But there were odd touches. The joint served Bigelow teas: Earl Grey and all the herbals, just like big-city coffee shops. And jazz on the speakers! A sound you never used to hear on any road between L.A. and Austin. I wondered about the manager. What longing for a world beyond Show Low had selected tony teas and jazz to gentle the degradation, the sameness, the greasy odor, of sixty-hour weeks (a manager's lot) in a McDonald's.

There was something else new in Show Low, and all over the Southwest this trip. Many women over thirty wore the severe, close-cropped haircuts that in big cities you usually see on butch lesbians. I'm not going to touch that one, except to say that something is changing out there.

The place was crowded with fat folk of all ages. Their pastiness was a uniform that said, "I am of these people." And it was also a camouflage that said, "You must get past this look to know me."

Only two weren't fat, weren't saying, "I am of these": a dark-haired boy and a blonde girl, both about fourteen.

They were ahead of me in line. He said to her, "I pled not guilty to two charges and guilty to one."

"They'll send you to AA," she said.

"I won't go."

"If a judge orders you to AA, you'll go."

I didn't catch what came next, but then he said, "I have a six-pack. It's ugly when a girl has a six-pack."

"You owe me so much alcohol!" she laughed. "You owe me four beers."

They got their Big Macs and went to a booth. I got my McChicken and sat one small round table away from them. The boy was telling what had happened.

"'Where are you going?' the guy says. 'Are you gonna hurt me?' He says that to five guys with knives!"

I liked his face. Hers, too. He was intense, intelligent, quick. She was savvy and had an easy, I-can-handle-you way with him. I doubt they were lovers. Teens aren't that loose with each other when they're lovers. They seemed blessed with that lovely boy-girl bond that can happen at that age, two kids gentle and confident and reckless with each other, able to say anything and everything, an intimacy fueled by dammed-up sex. They spend months skirting the dangers while relishing the feelings (usually the first real closeness they've known), then lose it all when they finally kiss.

These two were "bad" in their town. Tough. And, from his story and the way she relished it: dangerous. Yet they shined. It would be a mistake to minimize the danger they put us in (in return for the danger we've put them in), and a mistake to minimize their glow. With four of his homeboys he'd pulled a knife on some guy. He didn't say why, or if he'd cut the guy; but he'd gotten caught. I suppose in his mug shot he looked as cold and dead-eyed as all the pictures of kid-thugs you see in the papers. But here he was fresh and alive, lost but not yet ruined. And here she was, loving the danger of him in a land that tried to teach her that to be safe was to be good—when she could see, right there in her Show Low McDonald's, that to be safe was to be fat and smell of fries.

They spoke too softly for me to hear for a while, and then she said, mocking, "Don't talk about Dylan, Bob Dylan!"

"You ever heard 'Knockin' on Heaven's Door' by Bob Dylan?" He said it quietly, almost desperately.

Come put my guns in the ground, I can't use them anymore . . . I feel I'm knockin' on Heaven's door.

Extinct volcanoes. Meteor craters. Apache wastes, and wasted Apaches. The words of an ancient Phoenician way off course. Forests turned to stone. A kid telling his friend that his life is over, he's knocking on Heaven's door.

I finished my coffee and left that town. Eight hundred miles down the road, near the Llano River in Texas, the son of a dear friend—Vincent, age thirteen—said to me: "Our soul is the only key to the gate." He had gotten that sentence from his solitude and his deepening integrity. I said to him: "You haven't wasted your time. On that foundation, you can build anything." His eyes looked far beyond me, far beyond himself, and deep into the enchanting and frightening mystery of the world. With the same audacity that one reaches for a knife, another reaches for the truth.

What separates them? The luck of good parents? Fate? The thought that it's all arbitrary is crushing and probably true. All the more reason to recognize the possibility that the reach for the knife began as a grasp for some kind of truth, however mistaken, however terrible. How else can we save them, or even speak to them, if we do not honor the root of their impulse?

I thought of that boy knocking on Heaven's door, and that girl on a dangerous journey all her own. ("You owe me four beers!") And Vincent's eyes and words. I remembered the words of a Boris Pasternak poem: "The root of beauty is audacity, and that is what draws us to each other."

Vistas so sensitive to light that they change color all day. Murderous rocks falling from the sky. The soul is the only key.

Typical Lubbock elephant scene, Lubbock, Texas, 1971

IN THE MUSIC of the Southwest, one image is constant: the road. Whether it be blues, folk, rock, swing, conjunto, country, or those unclassifiable singers who combine and transcend all categories—if the road isn't invoked directly, its presence is felt; somebody is always arriving, always leaving, and there's always something immeasurable just past the outskirts of town. For there's no place in the Southwest where you can't get from downtown to open country in a half hour or less. And then   you can drive a thousand miles in most directions and still have more distance to cover before you reach a glacier or an ocean. Unlike urban music, the music of the Southwest is alive with the possibility of unfettered movement. Walt Whitman, who never actually saw it, imagined it well in his "Song of the Open Road": *Here a great personal deed has room*. Which can make the lack of a great personal deed all the more galling. The road is an inspiration and a joy, but it also dictates the terms of despair: for to lose one's sense of possibility where the very landscape beckons you to possibility in all directions

is to feel trapped not by the world but by yourself. The endless sky mocks you. In terrain where the concept of infinity cannot be ignored, you're never sure whether your argument is with society or God. And under the great Southwestern sky, it's possible to feel very, very small; but also to feel, as you hear so often in Townes Van Zandt's songs, an undercurrent of wonder no matter how bad things are.

The road is such a powerful universal symbol in Southwestern music precisely because each road is specific, real, fateful. No way to tell you how but to focus on a particular road. For instance, U.S. 84.

Eighty-four begins in southern Colorado, at Pagosa Springs—near Summit Peak, which is more than 13,000 feet high; and near the source of the Rio Grande, where that great river is just a deep, swift stream. Eighty-four winds down into New Mexico, southeastward, crossing the Great Divide not far past the state line. Here 84 curves, climbs, and descends through mountains, and every time it crests a hill the vista takes your breath away. On this stretch, not more than twenty or so miles on either side of the road, are the cliffside ruins of the Anasazi, which means "ancient ones"—tribal people who lived in a continent untouched by Europe, a continent without horses or guns, an (in this terrain) arid vastness, subject to extremes of heat and cold, which could only be dared on foot. Then, at Española, 84 divides the two greatest extremes of human behavior:

About a half hour to the east there's Los Alamos, where atomic bombs were first perfected, and, in the name of fighting evil, human beings raised a godlike ax of radiation above their heads and have since waited for it to fall; to this day, weapons of mass death are invented there. Almost the same mileage to the west is El Santuario de Chimayó, a small adobe church to which thousands make a pilgrimage every Easter, some walking miles on their knees, a few carrying crosses, to worship at the shrine of a crucified Jesus clad in a blue dress. The chamber of that Jesus has a dirt floor, "healing dirt," they say, and it is claimed by many that they've been cured of all manner of disease by rubbing that dirt upon them as they pray. Crutches line the walls outside that chamber, left by cripples who walked away. Where else in the world are Hell and Heaven juxtaposed in such absolute terms?

About a half hour's drive south, 84 becomes St. Francis Boulevard as it passes through Santa Fe, the oldest inland Euro-pean settlement in North America, founded 400 years ago. Most of the Hispanic people here are not Mexican; they're descendants of the original Spaniards, with four centuries of marriage with the Pueblo peoples, who are in turn descendants of the Anasazi. They barely get by these days, for affluent Texans, Californians, and Yankees buy their land and hike up every price tag. They can't afford to live and can't afford to leave; they have been here longer than any of us.

From Santa Fe, 84 becomes I-25 for an hour or so, heading east. Then, at Romeroville, near the headwaters of the Pecos River, 84 turns sharply south, then directly east for a little while as it joins I-40—old Route 66, the *Grapes of Wrath* highway—until it cuts southeast again at Santa Rosa. Santa Rosa's Main Street is old 66 itself; the Club Café has been closed for years, but the building and its sign are still there, where Woody Guthrie and Cisco Houston once ate their biscuits and gravy. And at Santa Rosa, 84 crosses the Pecos for the last time—hundreds of miles southeast on the Pecos was the hamlet of Langtry, where Judge Roy Bean meted out justice, of a kind, on the porch of the Jersey Lily, the bar he named for an actress whom he worshiped and never did see.

(Yes, that story's true, more or less.)

Now you're out of the high mountains in terrain of rolling plains, mesas, arroyos, where you can see for miles and miles unobstructed in every direction. Here 84 heads south until Fort Sumner, where Billy the Kid is buried. His assassin, Pat Garrett, was himself assassinated years later, not a long drive from here. Now 84 heads due east to Clovis and becomes the main drag of that town. The building in Clovis in which Buddy Holly and the Crickets recorded some of their greatest tunes still stands—in fact, I'm told it's still a recording studio. No one could have guessed in Buddy Holly's day that the most historically worthy thing ever done in Clovis was being accomplished by some Panhandle kids playing what many thought then was "the Devil's music." And soon there's the Texas border, where just off the road a billboard used to advertise Holly's hometown thusly:

"Visit Lubbock—For All Reasons."

For whatever reason, you're driving now where Holly drove many times, a hundred and more miles into Lubbock, where the land is flat as the palm of God's hand, as they say there. Once the prairie grass was horse-high here, and buffalo roamed by the hundreds of thousands a herd, hunted by Comanches. As 84 goes through Lubbock, it becomes Avenue Q. About midway through town on Q, there's a big statue of Buddy Holly holding his guitar. And as you continue past town, there used to be a big warehouse-type building on the plains, the old Cot-

ton Club, where a not-yet-famous Elvis Presley played his music, as well as Holly and Roy Orbison; and, years later, the legendary Flatlanders—Joe Ely, Butch Hancock, and Jimmie Dale Gilmore; and where I don't think Jo Carol Pierce performed (she wasn't doing that in those days), but where I know she danced. South and east you drive now, through Abilene, through Brownwood (a stomping ground of gunfighter John Wesley Hardin's), then 84 heads due east: Waco. The immolation of the Branch Davidians—the terror that made for the final twist of Timothy McVeigh's mind, and would result in another terror, the bombing of the Federal Building in Oklahoma City. The American Dream on fire. The American Century in a millennial panic to find some kind of certitude, some kind of meaning, at any price—the higher the price, the more absolute (and useless) the meaning. If you can't live in the City on the Hill, blow it up or burn it down, praying for deliverance with every lick of the flames. Somewhere long ago and far from here, some people wrote us a Constitution, a document that tried to include everything on U.S. 84; we read it now in the light and heat of Waco's flames.

It's a long drive on 84 east from Waco to the Atlantic, from the dry Texas plains through the steamy lush growth of Louisiana, and just before the Mississippi River (which is to rock & roll what the Nile is to Egypt), you go through Ferriday—84 is its central street. Birthplace of Jerry Lee Lewis and his cousin Jimmy Lee Swaggart, demon-driven men, great balls of fire, whose whole lotta shakin', for the beat and for the Bible, embodied every contradiction in beat and Bible both.

You cross the Mississippi into Natchez. You can still smell slavery in the air in this country. Sites of old plantations. Civil War graveyards. Fiery Ku Klux Klan crosses. The sad brave eyes of the first black children who dared their way into the "white" (i.e., public) schools. And Alabama the same. And crossing the Chatta-hoochee into Georgia, the same. A sense of historical suffocation that, like the thick humidity, make it equally hard to breathe. Until finally, just south of Savannah, 84 ends near the Atlantic.

In the music of the Southwest, song after song invokes the road. The people who make the rules in this country, and most writers who interpret its meanings, mostly fly. They miss it all. But musicians serve their apprenticeship on the road, driving gig to gig, learning, as Townes put it, that "you can't count the miles until you feel them."

Álvar Núñez Cabeza de Vaca was born in 1490 and died in 1557. Today's media enshrine the cliché that our era has seen the greatest change in human history, but judge for yourself whether or not the changes in Cabeza de Vaca's lifetime were equally transformative: Columbus opened the Americas to European exploitation, beginning the greatest mass migration in history, a population shift that ended up creating no fewer than forty-five new nations; 800,000 Jews were expelled from Spain and the Inquisition was instituted; Cortez ended two civilizations, the Aztec and the Inca; Michelangelo, Leonardo da Vinci, Hieronymus Bosch, Dürer, and Brueghel revolutionized Western art; the first modern clock was built, beginning a transformation in our perception of Time; the German priest Martin Luther and the English King Henry VIII broke from the Church of Rome, ending a 1,000-year dominance; Machiavelli wrote *The Prince*, initiating the modern view of politics; Copernicus developed the theory of the solar system that inaugurated con-

temporary science; the African slave trade began; the first insurance policies were written, the first surgical manual was published, the first theory of germs was formulated; and, in England, theaters became the first European public space not under direct control of church or state.

So Cabeza de Vaca lived as we live, in a time of terrible violence and sweeping innovation during which centuries-old certainties dissolved. At the age of thirty-five he was appointed second-in-command to Pánfilo de Narváez for what was intended to be the conquest of Florida. Narváez had won power by such acts as ordering the slaughter of 2,500 Native Americans who'd come bringing his (earlier) expedition food. That Cabeza de Vaca accepted a commission with him tells us that, at this point, he was quite willing to be your average murderous conquistador. But quickly something changed him. In his *La Relación* (the first important book written about America), he tells of the Florida expedition's stop in Cuba for provisions and gives the first description of a West Indies hurricane:

All the houses and churches went down.
We had to walk seven or eight together,
locking arms, to keep from being blown
away. . . . We wandered all night in this
raging tempest. . . . Particularly from mid-
night on, we heard a great roaring and the
sound of many voices, of little bells, also
flutes, tambourines, and other instru-
ments . . . till morning, when the storm
ceased.

His record for clear-headedness as a sol-
dier argues against fancifulness; rather,
this account shows that in extreme situations some strange inner sense opened in
the man. Catastrophes that brought out
fear and worse in others caused Cabeza
de Vaca to experience a deepened, wild
spiritual awareness. In the midst of a hurricane, while fighting for his life, he could
hear music. This is the signature of the
man.

Florida was a disaster. Narváez made
stupid, vicious decisions. Disease and
needless warfare with the Florida tribes
decimated the Spaniards. Most, Cabeza de
Vaca included, became separated from
their ships and were lost. "You can imagine what it would be like," he wrote, "in a
strange, remote land, destitute of means
either to remain or get out."

On the west coast of Florida, the sur-
vivors built huge rafts to try to make it
around the Gulf Coast to Vera Cruz,

though they had no accurate idea of the
distance. The rafts quickly were separated. No one knows what happened to
the others, but Cabeza de Vaca's raft
inched its way around the coast; these
were the first Europeans to see the Mississippi, and in *La Relacion* Cabeza de Vaca
was the first to write of that river. Finally,
storms blew them to what they called the
Isle of Doom and what we call Galveston.
These first Europeans to set foot in Texas
were by now "so emaciated we would
easily count every bone."

What happened next went against all
their expectations. Tribal people found
them. "The Indians, understanding our
full plight, sat down and lamented . . . in
compassion for us." The native people
cared for them. Now he records the first
known instance of cannibalism in North
America. "Five Christians [as he refers to
his people] came to the extremity of eating one another. The Indians were so
shocked . . . that, if they had seen it sometime earlier, they surely would have killed
every one of us. . . . Then half the natives
died from a disease of the bowels and
blamed us." Not surprisingly, some
sought to kill the Spaniards. "The Indian
who kept me" interceded, saying that if
the Spaniards were sorcerers they would
not be dying of the same disease. Reason
prevailed. Cabeza de Vaca had come to
conquer Indians. Now he owed his life to
one. For the remainder of his time in the
Americas, he would never kill, or initiate

battle with, another Native American.

Time passed. Eighty Spaniards had survived the raft voyage; under a dozen were left. Then things took another extraordinary turn. The tribe "wanted to make us physicians . . . we scoffed . . . at the idea we knew how to heal." The tribe denied them food until the Spaniards complied. They had come to subdue; now they were commanded to heal. "Our method . . . was to bless the sick, breathe upon them, recite a Pater Noster and Ave Maria, and pray earnestly to God our Lord for their recovery." No one was more surprised than he when his method worked. "God willed that our patients should directly spread the news that they had been restored to health." Here Cabeza de Vaca passes the point where history is prepared to accept him (which is why he is the least famous figure of the exploratory period). He ceases to be a conquistador and explorer, and journeys beyond category.

More time passed. Finally, only four of his party remained: Cabeza de Vaca, Alonso Castillo, Andrés Dorantes, and Dorantes's slave, a Moroccan Moor converted to Christianity named Estevanico, the first black man in North America (a century before the Pilgrims). They lived a strange, difficult life. By now able to speak the native tongues, sometimes they healed, with Cabeza de Vaca's ministrations being especially effective; sometimes they were treated as mere slaves; some-

times Cabeza de Vaca served as a kind of traveling merchant between tribes. By various adventures they made their way west across Texas—remaining for a time in what is now the Austin area, the first non-natives to live in this country. Now, wherever they went, the four would be housed with the tribal shamans, a fact indicative of their status and function. "Since the Indians all throughout the region talked only of the wonders which God our Lord worked through us, individuals sought us from many parts in hope of healing. . . . If anyone did not recover, he still contended he would. What they who did recover related caused general rejoicing." There is corroboration. Years later, when Coronado's expedition went north of the Rio Grande, tribal people told them stories (as a contemporary account relates) of "four great doctors, one of them black, the others white, who gave blessings and healed the sick."

When, after nearly eight years, Cabeza de Vaca and his companions met up with conquistadors pushing north from Mexico, the Native Americans would not believe Cabeza de Vaca was of the same race as these who murdered and enslaved.

We had come from the sunrise, they from the sunset; we healed the sick, they killed the sound; we came naked and barefoot, they clothed, horsed, and lanced; we coveted nothing but gave whatever we were given, while they robbed whomever they found. . . . To the last I could not convince the Indians that we were of the same people as the Christian slavers.

Cabeza de Vaca tried unsuccessfully in "hot argument" to stop the terrible actions of his countrymen. "When the Indians took their leave of us they said they would do as we commanded and rebuild their towns, if the Christians let them. And I solemnly swear that if they have not done so it is the fault of the Christians." In *La Relacion* he wrote to his king: "They are a substantial people with a capacity for unlimited development. Clearly, to bring all these people to Christianity and subjection to Your Imperial Majesty, they must be won by kindness, the only certain way." It would be centuries before any vocal Euro-American would share this view.

It was only when he was once again among his own people that Cabeza de Vaca was truly lost. "I could not stand to wear any clothes for some time, or to sleep anywhere but on the bare floor." If he retained or ever again used his shamanic powers, he made no record of it. In 1540, he was appointed governor of a South American province, where he prohibited the slaving, raping, and looting of Native Americans. His soldiers had come for booty and they resisted his strictures; they finally deposed him, imprisoned him, and sent him back to Spain in chains, where he remained in prison for eight years (almost as long a time as he'd wandered in Texas). Finally his wife bribed away the better part of her fortune to free him; he died in 1557, at the age of sixty-seven. When the great raconteur Lord Buckley retold his story in the early 1960s, he summarized Cabeza de Vaca's truth like this: "There is a great power within. And when you use it, it spreads like a living garden. And when you do not use it, it recedes from you." The inner history of our country is outlined in those sentences. Álvar Núñez Cabeza de Vaca. Remember him.

Irene at 14th Street, Lubbock, Texas, 1972

ON I-40 you drive past Groom, Texas, in seconds—a tiny town barely managing to be a town anymore, like many of its kind, clinging to the highway for dear life. Just west of Groom stands the second-highest cross in our hemisphere (there's one slightly larger in Illinois). Its massive, shiny metal glints in the sun, nineteen stories high, visible for miles in that flat land. One may wonder whether something so large is a monument to faith or to unadmitted doubt, or some of both; but one may be sure that nothing so expensive is created in a county so poor without deep need. This is thunderstorm country. On many nights Groom's cross must be lit and struck by lightning like the lightning announcing Yahweh's presence in Exodus 19:16—a light show counterpointed quickly in 20:21, where Moses draws near "to the thick darkness where God was." The vast plains of the Texas Panhandle are an apt setting to depict the lights and darks of the divine.

Surrounding the Groom monument in a wide oval are refreshingly, earnestly human statues: the Stations of the Cross.

Groom's Jesus is Anglo, not Palestinian, shorter than today's average height but taller than Jesus likely was. (The Gospels never suggest his appearance was unusual, so his height was likely average for the time, about five feet.) Groom's cross dwarfs us, but its statues silently convey what feels almost like an appeal: "See, we were much like you; it isn't so hard to understand our sins, our faith, and our sufferings, not if you look into yourselves."

Day and night there are always a dozen or so trucks and cars in the parking lot and people looking up at the high cross and, more accessibly, into the eyes of the statues. I am neither Christian nor anything else, but I revere Jesus as a teacher and as a fighter for the poor—for Jesus, like other Jewish prophets, distinguishes himself from Buddha, Lao Tzu, and the great Islamic mystics by his absolute insistence that the poor and destitute be included in his Kingdom (or, as Caroline Casey says, his "kin-dom"). I find these humble statues a sweet relief from the bombast that passes for public Christianity these days. There are some wise

Christians in Groom, Texas, who have not forgotten the Nazarene's humility and humanity.

Their stone memorial of the Ten Commandments proves it. Let's be generous and call it an oddity that the American conception of the Ten Commandments excludes the two Jesus insisted were most important. Plaques, plates, and T-shirts all over our country display the familiar thou-shalt-nots. But in Groom, near the huge cross, the American Ten are inscribed in stone and then, beneath them, we read the answer Jesus gave when asked (Matthew 22:36–40), "Teacher, what is the great commandment in the law?" He answered, "You shall love the Lord your God with all your heart, and with all your soul, and with all your mind. This is the great and first commandment. And a second is like it, You shall love your neighbor as yourself. On these two commandments depend all the law and the prophets."

Interesting: Jesus is quoting from Deuteronomy 6:5 and Leviticus 19:18, but neither passage includes the phrase "with all your mind." That's his addition. He wanted the mind to be involved. He wanted us to think. In any case, the American Ten exclude the *love* of God and the *love* of neighbor, though Jesus said clearly that all else rests upon such love, and to love our neighbor "is like" loving God. To underline the point, his last public teaching in Matthew (24:35–40) states

without ambiguity that if you have not cared for the poor, the ill, the stranger, and the imprisoned, then you are no friend of his. "As you did it to one of the least of these my brethren, you did it to me. . . . As you did it not to one of the least of these, you did not do it to me."

In light of this, when people call the United States "a Christian country" one can see a Jesus very much as he's depicted in Groom, saying humbly and in great pain, as he says in Luke 6:46, "Why do you call me Lord, Lord, and not do what I tell you?"

On I-27, not far north of Lubbock, on the southern edge of Abernathy—another town of mostly empty storefronts—is another, stranger Jesus. Constructed beside St. Isidore Catholic Church (Isidore was a fifth-century Egyptian ascetic), a narrow two-story structure fronted by glass displays a crucified Jesus of terrific proportions who leans far out from his cross like the figurehead on the prow of a sailing ship. Carved in the grotesque yet beautiful style of Mexican icons, this Jesus bears a peasant's face of no specific ethnicity, but universally peasant, with dark reddish-brown hair, light eyes, and bad teeth—a strangely disturbing detail, those teeth. Imagine the Sermon on the Mount delivered not by the handsome Anglo Jesus of the movies, but by a broad-faced peasant with bad teeth. Would we listen as attentively?

The structure is open night and day;

you can light electric candles, and there are scraps of paper on which you may write prayer requests to be honored at the next Mass. In summer the air is thick and hot in that high narrow room. You stand at Jesus' bloody feet. You look up, and his pained eyes look straight down into yours, as he looms over you so that you imagine for a moment he may fall upon and crush you. That, certainly, is the Jesus of my childhood, the Jesus the nuns and priests dinned into us—not a teacher but a sufferer, who suffered (they said) for me (though I hadn't asked him to), and to whom I therefore owed a debt (which I'd never agreed to). Yet I have always honored the unflinching endurance of that sufferer. It is no small thing for a religion, or for anything, to teach you to endure.

There's an iron stairway up each side of his cross, and the point seems to be that you walk up one stair, pass in the space between Jesus and the cross, and down the other stair—a ritual I've not heard of. On the right stair is a small sign: "I, Your Christo de Mi Paso, Ask You to Promise a Change of Life Before Going Up and Passing Through." That sounds like Jesus. To be a true supplicant you must promise to change. Change what? That's not specified. Which is what I admire about this depiction: The nature of the change is up to us.

At night this Jesus is brightly lit. Driving at seventy miles per hour on I-27 (old U.S. 87, which is, as Terry Allen sings,

"that hard-assed Amarillo highway"), suddenly you see this terrible and terrifying Sufferer out of the corner of your eye. You pass in an instant, wondering did you see it or not, and what did you see? Perhaps that night you return there in your dreams.

Then there's the Jesus on Texas Route 114, some twenty-five miles west of Lubbock, not far past the Wal-Mart as you're coming into Levelland. At St. Michael's Catholic Church, fronting a large parking lot, stands a metal crucifix maybe two stories high. Again, the Jesus is not generic. The face, hands, and feet are rather abstracted, but the arms, chest, and thighs are beautifully suggestive of a pained, strained body. Guano streaks his shoulders and chest, implying the birds and flies that no doubt tormented anyone crucified. The oddest thing is that, yesterday, sticking out of each nostril was a long strand of straw. The work of birds, kids, the wind? A stone's throw down the road is—alas, was—the Mean Woman Grill, where Miz Ayn served excellent hamburgers and sang the blues, a café fronted by suggestive metal cutouts of dancing women. Straw up Jesus' nostrils, sexy dancing gals—a Texas Panhandle collage. Texans have told me that Panhandle religion drums two lessons into its young: 1) Jesus loves you, and he'll send you straight to hell; 2) sex is filthy, dirty, and sinful, and you must save it for the one you love. Welcome to Levelland.

And welcome to Clarendon, on U.S. 287, some sixty miles southeast of Amarillo. West of the highway, but not in its sight, on graveled Leroy Street, a sign tells: "Welcome/The Silent Teacher/Prayer Walks and Healing Walks/Meditations/Encounters." (Encounters? I'm interested.) No pictorial depictions, but a captivating park of crosses and stones arranged in unusual ways over maybe an acre of land. One cross is tipped on its side. There's a gate in the middle of the field. Stairs to a white platform. A sunken bench where you sit at ground level to view the upright cross. Chairs here and there. At night, solar-cell lights glow without glare, illuminating gently. You know it's a special place, but you don't know what it is. It took much work and strength to move these stones, build these crosses. Everything seems unfinished, but so are you unfinished. "The Silent Teacher." I thought of something Saint Francis is supposed to have said: "Preach the Gospel at all times. If necessary, use words." Only if necessary. Silence and example teach better, and so does the wind. Wind blows all the time in Clarendon, where this place seems to say as Jesus did (Luke 17:21), "The Kingdom of God is within you."

THE PRIEST is a very small man, almost dwarfish, with an unusually large head—a head that would seem large even on a tall man. He's in his seventies, I should guess; his hair is thick; he's bowlegged, and walks with small decisive steps; his hands are agile in their gestures, and callused—hands of manual labor. His brown skin is deeply lined, and it's as though he has been carved out of dark heavy wood—a folk carving, crude of feature but marvelously expressive. I am sitting in a pew, watching him. He stands in the aisle and speaks Spanish to several women who are even smaller than he is. He listens intently, talks quietly but with surety, and looks them straight in the eye. The subject seems serious, perhaps urgent, and they speak as though they are the only ones in this small church.

He is not the kind of man one interrupts, and even the gaggle of affluent Anglo tourists knows it—proprietary people who act as though picture-taking confers the right to speak loudly of nothing, even in church. They stand a discreet distance from this priest while he finishes

with his parishioners. When he finally turns toward the tourists they seem suddenly smaller than he, though they tower over him. He is open, smiling—not judging them the way I am. He is charged with upholding the sacredness of this house of God, a sacredness rooted in treating everyone not merely as a welcome guest but as kin in the family of God. I do not believe in this priest's doctrines, but I believe in and pray to God, and I often think of that beautiful phrase, "In my Father's house there are many mansions." I respect the way this priest conducts this house.

One of the tourists, a woman, asks this old priest, "Father, how long have you been here?"

"Forever," he replies quietly.

Right away their conversation turns to other things, but I have stopped listening. His reply has opened my heart, and I am overwhelmed with so many conflicting emotions. I am again a small boy afraid of priests, because they can make you go to Hell—a boy who went to confession only once, before his First Holy Communion, and never, as boy or man, had the courage to go again. And I am again an adolescent, sixteen, who wants to be a priest but knows he cannot; there are too many doctrines he can never accept and too much sensuality simmering in his flesh and too many blockages between himself and God—yet for a season he haunted the churches of New York, which were open twenty-four hours a day back then, praying to be freed from his doubts and even from his sexuality so that he might be allowed to become a priest, and feeling even as he prayed that God's answer was a deep and inescapable *No*. And I am again and again a man of many ages, reading the Gospels as I so often have, and coming to that most poignant line: "Lord, I believe; help thou mine unbelief." And for me the line no longer has to do with the Catholic Jesus or with anybody's Jesus; it has to do with the question that haunts everyone, at one time or another: Why did the Creator create the sources of evil? All of this flickers in my sense of being overwhelmed, sitting in that pew, but mostly:

I want one day to say the word "forever" the way this priest has said it.

Quietly but not casually; with no special or self-conscious emphasis, but deeply; it is as though the presence of Forever is so real to him, so present, that he can evoke it with the mere saying of the word, and it's no big deal, he goes on to other things, for his reference point, his center of gravity, is *Forever*. He lives there,

and so with trust he can die there. All his life he has mediated between the sacred and the everyday, between Forever and our sense of time, and so when he uses the word it's as though I can feel Forever in the room.

I am stunned. How often is one in the presence of a holy man or woman? How often does one feel the substantial day-to-day results of true devotion emanating from a human being?

For me, too, Forever is a felt (rather than an abstract) reality; but I am a long way from it being the reference point, the center, of my life. Yet I imagine that evil is a small thing in the vastness of Forever—and goodness, too, is small; they take their place as small flickering lights in Forever, if that is where one truly lives; and still there is the work of the day to do, the work of this priest's callused hands, and hearing the god-awful secrets of the confessional, and administering the sacraments of marriage and baptism and death, and offering communion with the One for whom even Forever is merely one part of Creation. The concerns of those small earnest women are to be addressed—Forever doesn't trivialize that need, but rather makes it all the more present, present but not overwhelming. Or so I imagine. "Lord, I believe; help thou mine unbelief."

I said to a friend a year ago: "We live *in* God. We call it living in Time." As though Time is the physical body of God, but where that body exists is larger than Time. And I remembered visiting my brother Aldo in a mental ward when he said to me, "We're not the creations of God, we're the result of God's exertion. We are God's sweat." He liked that image and he laughed—and Aldo doesn't laugh often; he laughed again, saying, "And if we are God's sweat—then we are God's smell!"

But Forever exists outside of all such images and laughter—and at their center.

And in that sense, perhaps, are we made of Forever? Is that why God seems so unutterably familiar and yet so far away?

Well . . . I am very much out of my depth in these matters. And now I am pulled further out—out of myself.

One of the tourist women says: "Father, please give me your blessing."

Well, he is a true priest of the Nazarene, for, following the example of Jesus, he doesn't ask this woman for proofs and doesn't seem to care whether or not she's Catholic; the priest simply looks intently at her and gives her the sign of blessing.

Now I have tears in my eyes—which is incredibly surprising to me. But I know what I must do, what I will do, and I can hardly believe it even as I'm doing it: standing, going to the priest, and saying in a voice I hardly recognize, "Father, please give me your blessing."

He looks into me, as we stand in the aisle of that small church, his eyes are very dark and not sympathetic. His is an utterly inclusive stare—as though there are only he and I now in the world. It is a look of intensity and seriousness that pierces me—and makes me a little afraid. When he reaches his hand toward me I flinch. I flinch! Men have thrown punches at me and I haven't flinched (and, at times, I have); but I flinch now from this old priest's gesture. With his large and very callused thumb he presses the sign of the Cross into my forehead. His thumb is so rough it scratches. He presses hard. I have to push my head against his thumb, or my head will just go back and back. I'm surprised at the force.

I say, "Thank you, Father." I return to my prayers. I am sitting in the center of Forever, for a small bit of time-out-of-time, with the sting of his blessing pulsating on my forehead. Something has been opened in me by the presence of this holy person—something that has to do not with Christianity (I am not a Christian) but with reverence.

How long will it take me to live into and truly occupy this new opened place?

All this happened some years ago at the Sanctuario de Chimayó, a small adobe church in the mountains of New Mexico. Behind the church is an outdoor chapel beside which a cold, fast stream rushes down the mountain. Huge old trees shade the outdoor pews and altar, the sunlight reaches through the leaves in shafts of dust-speckled gold, and horses and cows graze in the meadow beyond the stream. It used to be you could wade in the stream, but now they've put up a metal fence at the edge of the water. A sacrilege, you'd think, but people have made a sacrament of it: Everywhere on the fence are handmade crosses constructed of two sticks tied together with strands of the tough grass that grows all around. So the fence itself has become a kind of altar—a sweet and remarkable transformation.

Wondering who was the first to fashion such a cross and fasten it to the fence, and thanking that person, I too made a cross of two small sticks, tied them with a strand of grass, and with another long blade of grass I bound my cross to the altar-fence in an offering of thanks. And the reverence I felt was like a song I'd heard lifetimes ago and was just now remembering. That is the way of Forever in Chimayó.

Dilapidated gas station, U.S. Hwy 84,
Texas, 1976

PERCHED in the main lobby of the Albuquerque airport is a 1914 Ingram/Foster biplane, a craft of elegant simplicity and, to me, astounding audacity. It's just some wood, wire, and canvas, an angular frame that flies, powered by a 6-cylinder, 100-horsepower engine, with a ceiling of about 1,000 feet. A year or so ago my friend and I paused awhile to admire it. In 1914 a man sat in the midst of that frame and flew with nothing to shield him from the wind, on a day when that putt-putt plane was at the forefront of technology. Just thirty-one years later a B-29 with a ceiling of 30,000 feet, its engines delivering 9,000 worth of horsepower, dropped an atomic bomb on Hiroshima. And just twenty-four years after that, people walked on the moon. Such amazing leaps in the space of one life span. And you think of all the other leaps till now, you step back, you stop taking it for granted, and no wonder the whole world is dizzy. We are, every one of us, travelers in a new dimension that keeps expanding itself beyond the power of any person or institution even to catalogue it, much less to exert restraint or control.

That thought sent me driving west on Route 60, along the southern edge of the Gallinas Mountains, in the vicinity of Magdalena, New Mexico. You top a rise at about 6,000 feet, and spread all across a valley is the Very Large Array. That's its official name. Twenty-seven radio telescopes, each nearly 100 feet high (a ten-story building), each with a dish "about as big as a baseball diamond," to quote the explanatory film at the visitor's center. "There are many sorts of light," the film explains, "most of which we cannot see." Something disquieting about that. There's lots to be seen all around us, most of which we cannot see. To know this intellectually is one thing; to feel it for a moment emotionally is quite another. Then I stood under that wide blue sky beside one of these towering white "dishes" through which a kind of dialogue is taking place that, literally, spans the universe. This human artifact reaches out to the edge of what we know of existence, a distance so far beyond human scale that, trying to imagine it, my mind goes blank. I've driven my '69 Chevy some 670,000 miles, so I have some concrete idea of what a round trip to the moon means; but at the Very Large Array I'm so far out of my depth that I might as well be what, I suppose, I really am—a somewhat conscious speck. Yet representatives of our species of specks carry on, in my name and yours, this dialogue with the infinite.

And there's this: Those lights I can't see, beaming into that dish—well, they're not *only* beaming into that dish; some of them are no doubt splashing on me, on all of us, and none (except, maybe, astronomers) have measured or guessed the effect of *that*. If I'm sounding like a little kid, hey, little kids have the sense to know that, as Dr. Who would say, existence is fan-*tas*-tic—which is what anyone must feel at the Very Large Array. But even in my reverie I'm aware that we're a species of troublemakers, marvelous and otherwise, and I can't help but wonder what trouble we'll make (may it be marvelous!) of the knowledge gleaned at the Array.

That thought, in turn, led me to those steep roads up the Jemez Mountains, north of Santa Fe, to Los Alamos—a place of incredible vistas, especially thrilling when horizons of great storm clouds take to showing off.

Los Alamos sits atop a mountain that not so long ago geologically (25,000 years) was a volcano; something's still cooking down in the depths, which is why there are hot springs in the neighbor-

hood. My destination was the Manhattan Project exhibit at the Bradbury Science Museum—but a smaller exhibit there, of the fan-*tas*-tic variety, blew me away first. You know those thousands of terra cotta soldiers buried with the first Chinese emperor in 210 BC? Some were painted with "a rare pigment called Han Purple." Apparently Han Purple contains properties that enable Los Alamos scientists "to study an unusual phase of matter known as superfluid, whose characteristics exhibit capabilities to communicate faster than the speed of light." That's right: faster than the speed of light—which, until recently, was believed the fastest possible speed in the universe. Not anymore. Just thought you'd like to know.

The Manhattan Project exhibit gives lots of chewable information to ruminate about—like, "the average age [of the scientists] was 25," and the majority of them were liberals, who, as one said, "truly believed that by building that bomb there'd never be another war." And you can stand beside replicas of "Little Boy" and "Fat Boy," the cutesy names given to two bombs that obliterated more than 200,000 Japanese civilians in two explosions lasting about nine seconds each. Hiroshima, August 6, 1945; Nagasaki, August 9.

It isn't generally known that Manhattan Project's scientists, even the notorious Edward Teller, wanted first to drop a kind of demonstration bomb where it would do the least harm, to induce a surrender by convincing our enemy of our new-found might. President Truman rejected that proposal. What most Americans "know" is that our atomic bombs forced the Japanese to surrender and spared us an invasion that would have cost (the usual figure is) 100,000 American lives. But the museum exhibits testimony to the contrary, from experts whose knowledge and patriotism are beyond question.

General (later Republican president) Dwight D. Eisenhower, supreme commander of Allied Forces, when consulted by Secretary of War Stimson, expressed "my grave misgivings, first on the basis of my belief that Japan was already defeated, that dropping the bomb was completely unnecessary, and secondly because I thought that our country should avoid shocking world opinion by the use of a weapon whose employment was, I thought, no longer mandatory as a weapon to save American lives. Japan was at that very moment seeking some way to surrender with a minimum loss of face. It wasn't necessary to hit them with that awful thing."

Admiral William Leahy, chairman of the Joint Chiefs of Staff, and Truman's personal friend: "The Japanese were already defeated and ready to surrender; the use of this barbarous weapon at Hiroshima and Nagasaki was of no material assistance in our war against Japan at

all." (Leahy had the guts to say this in public in 1945.)

Major General Curtis LeMay, U.S. Army Air Forces: "The war would have been over in two weeks without the Russians entering [they were to invade Japan August 8] and without the atomic bomb. The atomic bomb had nothing to do with the end of the war."

Why, then, Hiroshima? And why Nagasaki? Probably to prove to Stalin and the Soviet Union that we were smart enough to make atom bombs and evil enough to use them.

It could be argued that—in the short term, at least—Present Truman's employment of horror as an instrument of foreign policy was not stupid. I'd never agree, but there's an argument to be made. That discussion isn't on the public table because many Americans, then and now, crave the belief that their country is what no country has ever been: innately good. So they swallow the propaganda version of Hiroshima's and Nagasaki's necessity. For example:

The exhibit directly facing the testimony by Eisenhower, et al., is in a way the most interesting of all and is presented by an outfit calling itself the Los Alamos Education Group. Their exhibit discounts and denies the generals' testimony and repeats at length the same old lies that Truman told—plus justifying the bombings, by implication, with testimonies of Japanese atrocities, while failing to mention that the soldiers who committed those atrocities were not the civilians of Hiroshima, any more than the civilians of San Antonio were responsible for using the atom bomb. The ferocity of denial is such that, in the face of it, the Bradbury Science Museum compromises its honesty and permits an exhibit that its own researchers know to be false.

Nicolas Roeg's film *Insignificance* came out in 1985, forty years after Hiroshima. In Roeg's film, Einstein's watch stops at 8:15, the hour Hiroshima was bombed. I interviewed Roeg when the film was released. He said, "When something has happened—with lovers, or with the world—it's very easy to think, 'Oh, that was forty years ago.' We think that forty years diminishes it somehow. Hiroshima was forty years ago, so it's all right. But 8:15 comes around every morning. It comes every day, and that moment is *in our lives*. It's in my little two-year-old boy's life. It's here. The act is with us. Everyone in the world now has a little bit of it on him. It's important to know that something that's been done, committed, is *lived with*."

UNIDENTIFIED FRAKKIN' OBJECTS

SAW ONE ONCE. Summer of 1981. It was unidentified, flying, and definitely an object. My brother David and I were visiting friends who lived in an adobe home without plumbing in the mountains fifty miles northwest of Santa Fe, New Mexico. True I'd had a beer, maybe two. I was a little buzzed, but far from drunk; nor had I imbibed hallucinogens, pot, etc. (I never do). Having to pee, I stepped out into a very black night brilliantly canopied by what seemed the entire universe. The adobe was in a small, deep valley, flanked on the east and west by steep, high ridges. I was facing east, contentedly relieving myself under the stars. My gaze panned from north to south—and there it was.

Very close. Maybe a half mile—I gauged that by its relation to the road. Straight up the hillside, near the top. Round—perfectly round, it seemed to me. Rotating slowly like a flat metallic wheel, with small red and white lights near its circumference, it radiated a vague glow of its own. Noiseless. I saw it full for a moment, then, in less time than it takes

to tell, it sank below the ridgeline—down into the next valley, I presumed.

Zipped myself, ran inside, told my dear ones I'd seen something and I was going to look for it, and—having seen way too many movies—added that if I didn't come back in a couple of hours they should call . . . somebody. Alas, I drove up and down that road and found only a deep-rutted truck path over the ridge that my low-slung '69 Chevy couldn't manage. As for hiking up in the dark—for a city-bred tenderfoot, that seemed a bad idea, UFO or no UFO. We all hiked up in the morning but found nothing that looked unusual to our untrained eyes.

The Los Alamos National Laboratory perches in higher mountains about fifty miles south as the crow flies. Maybe my UFO was something from the Lab, we figured—or something interested in the Lab. I gave it no more thought than that. I saw what I saw.

That same year my friend Richard saw what he saw: a long, wide, gray-glowing oblong passing low and humming over a ranch house in which he was a guest, some miles south of Austin. And dear Dixie—who died this year not long before her ninety-first birthday, and who in our long friendship never told a fib—she saw what she saw when, driving a two-lane one night in the Panhandle between Matador and Clarendon, she was accompanied (followed?) for miles by a large glowing disc above and to her left.

I mention these sightings now because, however unusual they may be, they were, in a way, not as unusual as finding an op-ed article in the *New York Times* headlined "Unidentified Flying Threats," highlighted in bold with "Why we should be more curious about U.F.O.s" (July 29, 2008, p.19). The news wires and some good newspapers are not above reporting UFO sightings when witnesses are many and reputable. But a serious UFO article on the editorial pages of "the paper of record"? Was it a joke?

Nope. The article was by one Nick Pope, identified as the author of *Open Skies, Closed Minds*, a man who "was in charge of U.F.O. investigations for the British Ministry of Defense from 1991 to 1994."

Well, that made things slightly more explicable. Americans won't do, but the *Times* will print it if a well-credentialed Brit writes it.

Pope cites several instances. On Nov. 7, 2006, in broad daylight, "pilots and air-port officials at O'Hare International Airport in Chicago saw a disc-like object hovering over the tarmac for several minutes." Radar didn't pick it up, but Pope's point is, "Stealth planes are designed to be invisible to radar, and many radar systems filter out signals not matching the normal characteristics of aircraft." He sees UFOs as a national security issue, questioning whether our government can afford to ignore the phenomenon. (Why presume our government ignores it? Official U.S. investigations ceased in 1969; secret investigations may well continue. Richard told me that the military was all over the county the day after his sighting, and certain areas were, for a short time, closed to public access.)

Pope writes that "Britain and France . . . continue to investigate U.F.O. sightings, because of concerns that some sightings might be attributable to foreign aircraft breaching their air-space, or to foreign [read: U.S. and Russian] space-based systems of interest to the intelligence community." For instance, on Dec. 26, 1980, "two American Air Force bases in England reported seeing a U.F.O. land. An examination of the site turned up indentations in the ground and a level of radiation in the area that was significantly higher than ordinary. . . . The deputy base commander reported that the aircraft aimed light beams into the most highly sensitive area of the base." And there have been enough near-misses "between U.F.O.s and known aircraft . . . to prompt the Ministry of Defense and the British Aviation Authority to advise pilots, if they encounter anything, 'not to maneuver, other than to place the object astern, if possible.'"

Nick Pope isn't alone in his call for the U.S. to investigate UFOs. Reuters online, Nov. 13, 2007, reported that "an international panel of two dozen former pilots and government officials" agree. "'It would certainly, I think, take a lot of the angst out of this issue,' said former Arizona Gov. Fife Symington, who said he was among hundreds who saw a delta-shaped craft with enormous lights silently traverse the sky near Phoenix in 1997."

Lessen the angst? I wonder. At the O'Hare sighting "mechanics, maintenance workers, and a pilot all saw the craft, which made no sound as it sat motionless in the sky for minutes, and then shot up out of sight, leaving a perfectly circular opening in the cloud cover" (*The Week*, Jan. 19, 2003, p.3, citing the *Chicago Tribune*). "[One] employee was so shaken by his otherworldly vision . . . that he's experienced 'some religious issues.'"

Believers the world over would experience "some religious issues" if ever an official, public consensus was reached that UFOs exist and that they ain't from around here. Just for starters, whether you believe the Quran, the Tanakh, or the

Bible, your creation stories would be pretty well shot to hell in terms of anything but metaphor—and no one should be flip about the undermining of faith on such a mass scale. Our universal use of the term "aliens" for interstellar life forms is a giveaway that we believe we are the center of creation. However we may cherish *Star Trek, The X-Files, Babylon 5, Doctor Who,* or *Battlestar Galactica* (whose writers coined the useful usages "frak" and "frakkin'"), proof that there are technologically advanced species who can fly rings around us might be unsettling, to say the least. Some people would be thrilled, but most would be frightened.

Given the variety of Unidentified Flying Objects seen by reliable witnesses, one may justifiably speculate that a variety of Other Folk are interested in us. Why so many sights in the last sixty-odd years? Astronomer Carl Sagan gave a cogent reason in his book *Intelligent Life in the Universe*: Since the commercialization of radio in the 1920s, our planet has emitted an increasing intensity of electronic signals. To electronic telescopes elsewhere, it might be as though a blank space in the galaxy suddenly became incredibly bright, and keeps getting brighter. That would be worth investigating. Thus, twenty years after the advent of radio, UFO sightings began to be reported worldwide. Makes sense. Somebody—"aliens"—might want to know who's new in the neighborhood.

When Barack Obama was running for president, a nervous local newsman—from, I believe, the Midwest—asked whether, if elected, Obama would reveal the existence of "aliens" if he had "positive proof." Said Obama, "It depends on what these aliens were like—and whether they were Democrats or Republicans."

EVERYBODY NEEDS A RIVER

WHAT IS SANITY? The *Oxford* definition has got to be tongue-in-cheek: sanity is "the state of being sane." In other words: "How would *we* know?" Its second definition is merely British: "tendency to avoid extreme views." (Sanity is a *tendency*? What could that possibly mean?) *Webster's* isn't any better: "soundness of mind," whatever that is—which is how the *Oxford* defines "sane." The pocket *Webster's* doesn't attempt a second definition, as though to admit, "What's the use?"

I can't do any worse as a definer, so why not try?

Sanity is a balanced, symbiotic relationship between the heart and the mind. Since such a relationship, like any relationship, must always be in flux, one person's sanity on one day, in one situation, would be different from that same person's sanity on another day in another situation—for different situations call forth different qualities of heart and mind, different emphases between the two, though their essential balance remains the same. (When balancing on a rail we lean from one side to the other.) By this definition,

your sanity might sometimes seem to a casual or even trained observer not sane at all. Sometimes, for instance, it's sane to be extreme—for extreme situations may require extreme reactions. Someone who behaves within the limited range traditionally defined as "sane" (logical, temperate) in *any* situation . . . that person might lack the flexibility that my working definition implies, and so in some situations this "sane" type would be unsane, yes? As you can see—and as the *Oxford* and *Webster's* lexicographers obviously fear—to go at all deeply into a definition of sanity is, sooner or later, to call your own sanity into question.

Or to quote my friend Stanley Crawford: "Begin to explain something, and you end up having to explain everything."

So when I say that Crawford's book, *The River in Winter: New and Selected Essays* (University of New Mexico Press), is exquisitely sane—is, in fact, the sanest book I've read or expect to read in these mad times—I mean that on his pages you experience a balanced, symbiotic relationship between the heart and the mind, a heart-mind relationship constantly in flux but always consciously focused. It is a wonder to behold.

For several decades Stanley and Rose Mary Crawford have worked a small farm an hour's drive northwest of Santa Fe, near the Rio Embudo (the river of his title). Now and then he takes time off to write a book: nonfiction (*Mayordomo* and *A Garlic Testament*), fiction (*Some Instructions* and *Log of the S.S. the Mrs. Unguentine*), or essays of the sort collected in *The River in Winter*. Other novels, before the days of the farm, are the prophetic *Gascoyne* and *Travel Notes*, which contains the sentence that could summarize *The River in Winter*: "All landscape is moral." Those who know these books also know that I've not exaggerated when, several times over the years, I've written that Stanley Crawford is (with Steve Erickson) the finest prose stylist in the American idiom. Read this passage from the title essay (it must be quoted at length for you to receive the gentle cumulative effect of Crawford's force):

> I can remember the shape of the cottonwood, the texture of the lump of basalt, the darting trout, or the call of the killdeer. But the river, that sly and elusive presence, flows wordlessly through my memory and then surprises me again when I return to its waters each day. When I bother to listen carefully, its movement always sounds different, perhaps as tuned by temperature, humidity, depth,

> speed, air pressure, and my own mood: sometimes soft, a flat washing sound as over gravel, and sometimes a hearty roar. When low, it issues distinct notes, musical. Higher, at a certain stage of flood, it hisses past. At full flood, six feet or more deep, boulders unloosen and bounce along the bottom with muffled bangs. . . .
>
> When I go each day on my walk and gather up these images of water, tone, and feather, twig and wood, and the sounds they make, and feel the gravel underfoot, I know I am a little safer. In their granular disorder, in their flow, in their thickets, they are the emanations of the power of a place studied and absorbed in daily habit; they are the grains and spores and seeds of a place, whose shapes give no hint of what ultimately may spring from them, in understanding . . .

But *The River in Winter* is no rhapsodic invitation back to nature. "Woe to he," Crawford warns, "who would move to the country seeking peace and quiet." He writes, in a contrapuntal rhythm of grave and humorous detail, of the endless chores and tensions and duties and frustrations of rural village life—"the larger reality is that the small places of the world are run on the backs of the unpaid, the underpaid, and the volunteer." He writes of the do-or-die grinding political struggles against developers and against callous government and of struggles between the villagers themselves.

The village can also offer a useful lesson: that the man you may quarrel with today may have to help put out the fire or repair the acequia [an irrigation system] next to you tomorrow. And he will probably be among those you shake hands with at a funeral. At the very least, you will run into him again and again at the post office or the village store. The village says: Deal with it.

He reminds us that "these days most cities live with only a three-day reserve of food-stuffs on hand." In this era of imminent catastrophe—whether from human motive, climate change, or primeval force—that's a scary realization for us city folk. And, speaking of city folk, Crawford asks: "What is the lifetime of our industrial civilization? . . . What vast suffering are we storing up for the future in our unthinking ways?"

That question echoes in me: "What vast suffering?" The question plays between the lines of *The River in Winter*'s every page, like the sound of something rustling in the darkness beyond a campfire. For Stanley Crawford, born in San Diego, knows cities, too. His *Gascoyne* is a masterful satire of the L.A.–San Diego megalopolis. He's disturbingly well informed about issues like soil depletion and water scarcity. These essays are, in part, a record of how he's fought—up close, nose to nose—the arrogant ignorance of governmental land management. He doesn't rant, he isn't afraid; he is simply, and deeply, experienced. Out of his experience he offers proposals that would be politically feasible if enough of us could bring ourselves to give a shit. He also knows that most don't and probably won't. This grieves him but doesn't stop him. He does his part. This book is, above all, the record of a man who does his part.

Watching him do his part, you question how you're doing yours. That, and its beauty, its graceful sanity, are what makes *The River in Winter* matter to someone like me, a city guy who recoils at the daily manual toil that a man like Stanley assumes as a natural part of life. Stanley Crawford is an intellectual who has chosen to be a peasant, not sentimentally but because he loves the job, loves its harshness and its surprises and the sounds of the river. He represents the best of what we were and what we might become, while making his stand amidst the paradox of what we are.

Mickey boots, Luckenbach, Texas, 1978

SMOKING A CIGARETTE in the parking lot of a Super 8 motel north of Seattle. Across the street, Ronna's Video for Adults—Private Video Booths—Open 24 Hours. It's about noon, a chilly day. An old car and then a new car pull up at Ronna's. Out of each, an average-looking guy gets out and walks quickly into the joint. Private Video Booths. What loneliness. Jerking off to porn in a closet-like space on your lunch hour, then going back to work. Or maybe you told the wife you were going to the store (one of the guys was older, probably retired). And who wants to imagine how those booths smell?

Beside Ronna's, an old motel has been converted into cheap apartments. You know they're cheap because the cars outside are little tin-can putters—just enough of an automobile to get you to and from work, where you make just enough or just less than enough to keep the car running and live in the cheap apartment, with its minimal construction, thin walls, scant insulation. A phone, a bed, a little table, a TV, probably a microwave and a waist-high fridge. Car engines revving at Ronna's next door 24 hours a day. And the constant sound of the highway, tire-rasp on the pavement, trucks rattling the windows, motors, motors, motors.

Next door to the motel, a KFC chicken joint, cars idling at the drive-through window, engines puffing. The parking lot smells of KFC grease. The motel halls and rooms smell of KFC grease.

The motel, the KFC, Ronna's, the cheap apartments and me, about 4,000 miles into a long roundabout ten weeks and–8,000-miles journey—one tableau of what it means to live in the Age of the Car.

I asked a high school class what was the most important human invention in their lives. Almost with one voice the class said, "Computers!" I said, "Naw." They argued fiercely about the importance of the computer, the Internet, how it's reorganizing everything. I said, "Naw." They started to wonder if it was a trick question. "I don't do trick questions, you know that." Finally I said, "How did your computer get to the store where you bought it? How do your parents get to work? How do you get to school? How does every single thing you wear and use get to where it is? By computer? No, my beauties. By car and truck. The most important invention in your life is the internal combustion engine, encased in steel and fiberglass, propelled by oil and various chemicals, sold by any means necessary, and insured to the hilt. Imagine your life without self-propelled vehicles fueled by gasoline. There would be no suburbs. There would be no air transport. No goods would be delivered by truck. It would take days to traverse where now you can go in an hour. Your life *is* your life by virtue of car and truck. If computers disappeared it would be a major hassle—we'd have to adjust to living as we lived ten to fifteen years ago. But if the internal combustion engine disappeared, in many ways we might be living as we lived a century ago."

Like most of us—me too, usually—the class had taken the automobile for granted the way fish must take water for granted. The automobile is just . . . there. Everything is organized around the fact that it's there.

I'm writing this nearly 2,000 miles down the road from Ronna's and that Super 8, in a nearly identical Super 8 on the edge of Lake Superior near Duluth, Wisconsin. What a fantastic assumption, utterly new in human experience: that I can go anywhere on this vast continent, and anywhere I go there'll be a fairly

cheap decent place to sleep, an OK place to eat, a Staples to buy fresh yellow-pads to take notes on, a Circuit City to replace the surge board I forgot in the last motel—and highways filled with people not unlike me, going from here to there, mostly alone, separated from each other in encased vehicles. We take it so for granted, yet people have been living like this only in my lifetime, and, when this era exhausts itself, people may never live like this again. What will they think of us, I wonder. Will they think us lucky? Will they think us unbelievably unrooted and frantic? Incredibly wasteful? Amazingly free? All of the above?

In the magazine *DESIGNER/builder* (July–August 2004), my friend Stanley Crawford wrote a stunning piece titled "Driver's Ed: A Million Miles Later." He figured he'd driven about 20,000 miles a year, "probably typical . . . for most westerners and rural and suburban residents"—a million miles in his lifetime. Then he did the math. His conclusions are startling and deserve to be quoted at length:

> I have owned cars and pickups whose fuel consumptions ranged from 11 to 50 miles per gallon. At 25 miles per gallon, my likely average, I burned 40,000 gallons of gas and diesel over the course of one million miles. . . . A million miles requires 250 oil changes adding up to 300 to 400 gallons of oil, plus fifty transmission-fluid

changes, another 50 or 60 gallons of fluid. I have worn out some 133 tires, assuming I have averaged 30,000 miles per tire . . . My cars have required batteries every five years on average, for a total of 100 (I have usually owned two cars at a time), weighing about two tons. In antifreeze, add another 100 to 200 gallons. . . . Assuming most vehicles can reach 200,000 miles with reasonable care before being junked, I've been responsible for the manufacture of five cars or about 20,000 pounds of steel, glass, plastic, paint, and other materials, for which I have paid approximately $140,000, plus another $10,000 in interest. Another 400,000 pounds of fuel and resources were used up in the production of those five new cars. I estimate that repairs and maintenance, some of which I am able to do, have cost $500 a year each for my vehicles, or $50,000. In my fifty years of driving with no serious accidents I have paid $60,000 in insurance. . . . Those are back-of-the-envelope figures we million-milers might more or less agree on. . . .

In sum, my out-of-pocket costs for my million miles will be in this range: Cost of vehicles, including interest: $150,000. Gas, oil, fluids: $50,000. Repairs, including tires, batteries: $50,000. Insurance: $60,000. Total: $310,000.

Calculating from his own more-or-less average driving life, Stanley estimates we spend about "twelve years of eight-hour

days driving our one million miles, assuming we have averaged about thirty miles an hour." Gasping at that, I did some rough numbers: We work eight-hour days from, let's say (for college graduates), twenty-five to sixty-five—forty years. Add twelve years of eight-hour days driving, and that comes to: fifty-two years of eight-hour days driving and working. For people who work straight out of high school, fifty-nine years.

It's hard to imagine that anyone in the future will admire that. Or be nostalgic for it. Or think we were anything but out of our minds.

Yet, Stanley continues,

[T]his is just the beginning. Every automobile generates costs which are externalized out into society and the environment Tailpipe emissions are a major source of air pollution. Our cars contribute about a pound of carbon per mile toward global climate change. To a lesser degree they distribute particulate matter from brake shoes and pads and metal parts and tires . . . The effluvia from leaking oil pans and transmission and power steering and bearing seals and grease fitting and radiator hoses and the soluble portions of asphalt pavement itself pass into storm drains and foul waterways and beaches. . . . As automobile users, we will be billed for some of these costs through taxes and the health effects on ourselves and our families, but on the whole most of

them will be passed on to the environment, which will ultimately bill us in other ways.

Plus:

A large portion of our income tax payments goes toward covering the cost of wars and other military expenses needed to keep sea lanes open to support repressive oil-producing regimes in order to maintain a reliable supply of petroleum. Our right to drive is assured by the largest military budget and the best-equipped military force the world has ever known . . ."

[For many of us,] *"in the act of driving we vigorously oppose everything else we believe in."*

Back at Ronna's (Open 24 Hours), someone has just pulled into the parking lot to sit in terrible loneliness in a Private Video Booth. He will leave Ronna's, still terribly lonely and just as isolated, in his incredibly wasteful private transportation booth. A few more miles of a million-mile commute. He is one of us, desiring, wasting. He is our brother, for the future will make no distinction between him and me and you, desiring, wasting.

DRIVING IN SIN

THE ONLY TIME I saw my father truly happy and almost free was on a winter night when I was ten. We had driven, for obscure reasons, from New York City to Albany to see a couple whom I would never see again. In those days my parents had nothing but obscure reasons—some political (they were Communists when it was illegal to be Communist), some psychological (they were kind of nuts). Why was it suddenly important to drive to Albany? Why was I included? Who was that couple? I'll never know. (I hear my mother saying what she often said when I was ten: "*Why* is a crooked letter.") Whatever the "why," suddenly that night an awful weight lifted off my father; it would descend again, and remain all his days, but for this one night it relented. And there we were, on the newly opened New York Thruway, the widest, fastest highway built to that date in America, and Pa was speeding and happy—unguardedly and utterly happy.

On that road we seemed alone—in those days, when people didn't drive constantly night and day, a highway in the

wee hours was a lonely place, distant from daily concerns. Our swift movement alone together in the darkness felt like freedom. Illusory, yes, but sometimes illusion can be enough for a forty-year-old man and a ten-year-old boy to find a moment beyond their lives, a moment that can stand apart from their lives for all the rest of their lives—a moment to return to in memory, never needing replenishment, always new.

Pa started to sing. It sounded like, "Cheyyyy Ma-rieeeee —" Then he shouted, "HIT 'IM WITH A BRICK!" Then again, "Cheyyyy Ma-rieee . . . HIT 'IM WITH A BRICK!" Then some melodious lines in Italian, and again, "Cheyyyy Ma-rieeeee. . . . HIT 'IM WITH A BRICK!" And we laughed and laughed as the car sped as fast as it would go.

It was a 1940s Hudson—fabric covers on the seats, a musty smell mixed with Pa's chain-smoked cigarettes, a smell like a long-closed room in an old house. Sometimes he'd let me work the gas pedal. Sometimes I'd sit on his lap and take the wheel, going fast into the dark.

We were free. Anything could happen. Anything might. And anything was enough. What happiness!

No moment like that ever appeared again for us, as father and son. Nor was my father strong enough to create that kind of moment again for himself. For to create happiness, and to dwell in it, takes a strength few possess. We scramble to shape our lives, acquiring what we believe valuable—knowledge, fame, security, love, a perfect home or family or whatever we fancy, whatever might make us happy sometime in the future. It does little good. The future is always different from what we expect. Despite our efforts, happiness usually catches us unawares, by chance. I am no expert on happiness (what an understatement!). But sometimes I've had the strength not to run from the present moment, whatever that moment offers, and to allow the moment to blossom in such a way that there is no thought of happiness or unhappiness; it's more a matter of grasping the freedom inherent in any instant, where anything (always) can happen—to join with that freedom, to allow it to shape and change the next moment and the next, to allow life to *be* life, rather than impose my pet notions of what "life" should be . . . That, for me, has been happiness.

For me, beginning with that night-drive with my father, I would forever associate unbounded happiness with a car

and a road. My car, and any road. I have been lucky enough to find many kinds of happiness—for I've had a *good* time, a really good time. (Often accused of being "a romantic," as though that's a bad thing, my reply is, "I can't help it if I have a better time living my life than you have living yours." Put a better way: I once met a jazz bassist who'd played with greats like Charlie Parker and Lester Young, and I said, "I envy you." He said, "Don't envy me. *Join* me.") Anyway, "happiness"—for me it always comes back to a car and a road.

Of course, that's left me unsuited for the more settled varieties of happiness. And that, in turn, has caused much unhappiness. But that's another story. This story is: the first happy time I consciously remember was that night with my father when I was ten. Four years later I read Jack Kerouac's *On the Road*. Re-reading it in my late fifties, I found it a sloppy, gushy book, overwhelmed by the influence of a far greater writer, Thomas Wolfe. But when I was fourteen, *On the Road* was *the* book; it clinched my association of freedom and happiness with cars and roads. (What disillusion, later, to hear that Kerouac never learned to drive.) Then, from 1959 to 1964, I watched *Route 66*, a TV show about two guys who drive around the country looking for the meaning of life. That finished me. When asked in high school what I wanted to do, I said

I wanted to drive around the country, working here and there, writing, looking for meaning, never stopping. I was told that was immature. I suppose it's still immature, but, immature or not, it's been my life. Underneath it all, even when I've stayed in one place for years, it was always what I was *really* doing—and few years have passed when I haven't spent some months on the road. All told, I've driven from Tijuana to Bangor, from Seattle to Key West, from Calgary to Tampico, and many a place in between, under the banner of Bashō's poem: "The journey itself is the home."

What crap. Not Bashō. That Zen poet was right. And not the road—the road, in so many ways, is all there is, all there ever is. Asphalt or metaphor, the road goes on forever. Dirt road or rail-road or forest trail, the road goes on forever. The crap is: the car. My beloved car. A '69 Chevy that I've driven for many, many years— the only car I've ever owned. But I know that every one of our miles has cost the world dear.

We're screwing up Iraq because of me and my Chevy. We're polluting the environment because of me and my Chevy. We've paved an enormous chunk of this fantastic continent because of me and my Chevy. Exhausted our resources, our land, our liberty, and our future, because of me and my Chevy. Blotted the continent with suburbs and malls to accommodate me

and my Chevy and Pa's Hudson and every other car that any of us have ever driven.

But there we were, Pa and me, cruising the New York Thruway, speeding and singing and laughing, oblivious to the geopolitics that made our happiness possible. And here I am, still in love with the feel of an open road before me, content to enact an American maxim: Drive on.

But happiness costs. Costs someone. In the case of this particular happiness, it costs everyone.

I know better now than to indulge this happiness, but I also don't care—not really, not where it counts, not in action. I know the cost but I drive on. In this last year I've driven the West, Midwest, East, Northeast, South, West again, Northwest, North Midwest . . . nearly every state in the continental forty-eight. I can't/won't stop. Somebody or something will have to stop me. Stop us.

Because it isn't right that me and my Chevy, and you and your car, eat up the world's resources at the rate we do. We're driving in sin. It's time we paid, and we will. But still I sing my sin, letting others pay the cost. And the song, the poem, goes something like this:

This '69 Chevy Malibu, sweet of line, lime-green,
Is the only car
I have ever owned. She's gone nearly

700,000 miles, and I will do
Everything I can, I will not hold back
Anything
To keep her going. I need her. I love her. People
Joke me about this, but gingerly, gently, they're
    careful
Not to go too far. Because they know: I may be
    crazy
But I'm not kidding. I love her. So they joke
    about how
Having a relationship with me means having
    a relationship
With my car—because if I meet someone I like
    very much
I will take them to my car, and will say, of my
    car,
"This is one of my dearest friends." Some
    think
I'm just trying to be charming, or eccentric;
These are people
I've been mistaken about. I rarely see them
    again.
Some criticize me for not being ecologically
    sound.
I respect this point of view
Twelve miles to the gallon is not ecologically
    sound.
I point out that my Chevy
And I
Have no air conditioners, so as to save
The ozone. I ask

About their various
Air conditioners. I ask about the relationship
    between
Beauty
And ecology, and whether something as
    beautiful
As a '69 Chevy Malibu
Can be resented
By the Goddesses
And Gods of the planet. They think I'm being
    evasive. I'm not, I'm truly not,
I really do believe that my '69 Chevy,
With her graceful line and her strong spirit,
Is welcomed where we pass
Among the spirits of the earth. But let's say
All that's malarkey, let's say
We're sinners, my Chevy and I, driving in sin.
Then we will claim that last refuge of honor:
We have the courage of our sin. The beauty
    we feel
In each other's company
Is better than being
Right
Or good—and that,
Lady,
Is love.
In case you were wondering.

Sin never apologizes. Not really. And being right and good is never really enough.

IT WAS A SEASON of volcanoes. For me it was summer, a summer when there was no job but there was somebody holding my hand, the car was in good shape, and we went from here to there for a few weeks—from volcano to volcano.

It began in Albuquerque, at the Museum of Natural History. There is a dark hall with glowing walls that diagram one version of the beginning of life. The earth is molten, the crust cools, the molten core breaks through the crust, gases rise, an atmosphere forms above the steaming surface, the revolution of the planet ("revolution," indeed) creates changes in temperature, those changes swirl the gases into storms—incredible lightning storms. It is an atmosphere of gases that would kill us, it is lightning that could destroy cities, but we and our cities are billions of years off. The lightning ignites the gases and creates the elements from which, one day (when there's such a thing as "day"), life begins.

I probably have that theory garbled, but it appealed to me: life beginning with volcanoes and lightning. For days, some-times with the woman who was holding my hand and sometimes not, I returned to that dark hall with its glowing walls and their violent story; then I'd walk out into the bright, windy light of Albuquerque and drive up that long rise west of the city to the ancient volcanoes that overlooked the valley. Five nubbed cones—all that remains of the forces that shaped this place long ago.

I would sit and stand in the crusted remains of what had been cauldrons, my boots and pants dusty with lava millions of years old, reading books from the museum and the library. The process wasn't over, it hadn't stopped. It was one thing to read this in one's room, or see the information in a museum, or hear it in a classroom; it was quite another to sit in the wind on the remains of a volcano and to read that the freshest lava flow in North America was just a few hours' ride south, and that the hot springs an hour's ride to the north could be harbingers of the volcano that would one day sweep away the city below me.

We are still in the midst of the Creation. The Book of Genesis is a rough notation, a wild hope that God has finished the work of making; but the volcanoes are still active, the work isn't finished, human beings live between the lines of a work in progress—fragile, erasable creatures awaiting the next volcanoes.

The woman whom I'd been leaning on so heavily, she just smiled when I told her I had to see more volcanoes. She'd been reading the books too, and now read them aloud as we drove west, past volcanoes to the north and south of I-40, and through the Petrified Forest. Once the Painted Desert was a forest of thick huge trees—trees that were turned to stone in a cataclysm of some kind (the theories change every decade or two). The mesas of the Hopi and Navajo—some of them are the cores of ancient volcanoes. Flagstaff, a frontier town turned now into a sprawl of malls, McDonald's, and gas stations, is like a bit of lichen fastened to the slope of what once was an enormous volcano—much, much higher than the mountain is now, a volcano out of which Arizona poured.

Time began to collapse for me. As we read, as we drove, as we stopped for hours and gazed, the present landscape seemed a hasty design sketched upon an ancient yet recurring violence.

We headed north, through Nevada, Utah, and Wyoming, to Yellowstone. All the people scurrying around with their children and their camcorders, bored and

disappointed with Old Faithful and the hundreds of other geysers that steam upon the hills and in the forests—most don't know they are walking on the top of one of the hugest volcanoes in the world, a volcano larger than anything that has exploded in the memory of human beings. Not what we think of as a "classic" mountainous volcano, but a dome volcano—the very thing that we're driving, hiking, and camping upon *is* the dome. Every 600,000 years or so it explodes. No one knows when it will go again. Sometime in the next 10 to 100,000 years? It will rip the American West, cause chains of earthquakes all across the continent, belch measureless clouds that will darken the landscape and change the weather, and if there's anything that's still called "America"—well, those people will be writing an addendum to Genesis, won't they? If they're not swept away.

We drove west, then, and south, to Idaho—Idaho, which is only a great lava field. There's a place called Craters of the Moon, where the lava is still fresh, glistening, sharp. That's a fissure volcano. Not a mountain that erupts, nor an exploding dome, but a place where the earth simply splits, and from that split lava oozes. It last erupted only 2,000 years ago. The time of Jesus and the Romans, the time of civil upheavals in China when millions died in wars and famines. Sometime in the next couple of centuries, if it obeys its rhythms (or what they now think are its rhythms—they're often wrong), it's due to erupt again. There very well might still be something called "America" when it does, maybe even something called "the United States," maybe with some of our present constitution still intact; people may still be trying to elect presidents here, manage health care programs, investigate scandals, or live quietly in Pocatello, Idaho, when the lava oozes over the farmland.

We drove west and north, then, to Mount Rainier—which looks, today, very much as Mount St. Helens looked before it blew. There are so many volcanoes like this, all up and down the West Coast. People hike in their forests, fish in their streams, boat on their lakes, camp, take photographs, sell vegetables and gasoline and magazines. All those volcanoes are active. Unpredictable. No one knows when they'll blow.

The transformations of Genesis, or of the Hopi creation tales, seem like children's stories by comparison. The preoccupations of our newspapers and our literature, of our television and our talk radio, and of the tawdry and ineffectual exercise that we call "government," occurs quite literally on the sides of a volcano, a series of volcanoes, of which few are aware and about which fewer speak. It may be that tribal people are right: when you live upon a volcano, there is nothing to do but sing.

We drove to Mount St. Helens. A horizon of felled trees lying in gray dust. The occasional fly. A few yellowjackets buzzing about the molds on the rocks. Our footprints in the ashes. Silence, except for the wind, and the sound of engines on the highway far below. Huge forests were knocked to the ground, stripped of their bark, in instants. The geologists had set up a station about eight miles away. Those geologists, with all their knowledge of such things, or what they thought was knowledge—they expected to live. They were dead in less than ten seconds. Yet compared to Yellowstone, Mount St. Helens is a tiny volcano.

There is nothing to do but sing. Sing as we pass our laws, sing as we make our money, sing as we hold hands and try to depend upon and trust one another, sing even as we kill each other, because nothing is going to stop the volcanoes that we live upon; this century or some other century they will continue the Creation, the great unfinished, never to be finished work, a Creation that occurs to the accompaniment of our frail but persistent singing, the singing of beings whose knowledge is as incomplete as our position is temporary, and whose fate is to witness beginnings and endings that cannot be controlled, but can only be sung.

Three days after a tornado, Clarendon,
Texas, 1981

A FANTASTIC TABLA drummer, Marcus Wise (check him out, see for yourself if he ain't fantastic) cut red paper into a heart and wrote upon it: LOVE IS A DOG FROM HELL. Then he tied string to that red-paper heart and hung it around my neck. No, he wasn't making a pass, and it wasn't Valentine's Day. Marcus just thought I should wear that truth around my neck, and I did, in a public situation, for the remainder of the evening. (It hangs as we speak from a doorknob in my apartment.) Neither Marcus nor I could guess, at the time, that in 2008 Jo Carol Pierce would release her first recording in twelve years, *Dog of Love*, addressing in song those very truths and issues which Marcus hung around my neck, to which she added inflatable dolls, carnivals, cars, drunken rain, nudity, barbed wire, a baby smiling over her mother's shoulder as Mama's on the cell phone, prayer, a rock in one's shoe, the nature of truth, and the Blessed Virgin Mary Magdalene. For instance:

Parts of *Dog of Love* are spoken, and in "Criminal Thinking" Jo Carol says: "That night I dreamed a new grammar rule: Any personal pronoun can be replaced with the phrase 'a pair of your panties.' The example given was: 'A pair of your panties just robbed that liquor store.'"

Wearing a LOVE IS A DOG FROM HELL heart would hardly impress a woman who did this bit, expressed in dialogue on Jo Carol's *Bad Girls Upset by the Truth* (on many a Top Ten list in 1995). The guy (David Halley) says, "Jo Carol, I heard you drove through the Hi-D-Ho take-out window naked today after school!" High-school-age Jo Carol answers, "Oh, God, I'm so relieved! I was afraid I'd made that whole thing up in my head and was turnin' out crazy like Mama. . . . I'm so relieved that somebody besides me thinks that happened!"

Dog of Love (spoken by female people who are maybe seven): "We're carnival girls even when there's no carnival."

There's often no carnival. But a real carnival girl doesn't let that stop her. Which is a problem Jo Carol's dealt with the hard way (same way she does most things). *Dog*'s slow and wistful "Naked and Home" tells the story of more married carnival gals than I know how to count: *"Took my vows and went to sleep / so deep so I could keep them . . . Naked and home / I find you in the music . . . I'm naked and home / in a world of my own/ with you . . ."* How many carnival girls have had to put themselves into a waking sleep to keep their wedding vows? Jo Carol's song makes how many husbands shiver?

Now we need the take of a woman, the writer Jazmin Aminian Jordàn— knocked out by *Dog of Love,* she wrote an e-mail to Jo Carol, copied to me:

All your songs are NAKED and I listen to you sing and I can't believe Eve ever wanted to put clothes on. And something inside it all tells me Eve's God is all right with her having other boyfriends cuz you sing and make music that goes back before woman was virgin or mother, wife, angel or queen—this is music that is before wild . . . it's woman waking up with Dog-of-Love ability, the see-you-in-me ability, it's woman that sings east, west and smack inside of Eden. It's a woman who knows the ins and outs of Paradise that can write music like this. Ending with "Barb Wire Crown" is perfect—who else but the Blessed Virgin Mary Magdalene can hold all the shattering after Mary has shattered too?

You need to hear *Dog of Love* to make

sense of that, but, believe me, Jaz talks true.

How's this for "Love Is a Dog From Hell" paradox? From *Dog of Love's* contemplative "You're So True": *"You're so true / not that you don't lie, you do / But you're like a door always flying open / You're so true / like a story in a book / for truth mistook / though it probably / never happened / Truer than true / as opposed to / the merely agreed upon."*

This woman should be a legend. Among some of us, she is—and has been for years. There was a "Jo Carol" in my mind before I ever met her, instilled in me by many a story told by mutual friends. Surely she's had one of the stranger careers in music. For instance, she didn't exactly participate in her first album, though that album was the Austin Music Awards' Best of the Year in 1992, when she also won Best Songwriter. The album was *Across the Great Divide: Songs of Jo Carol Pierce,* on which (except as songwriter) Jo Carol herself is absent. Led by Michael Hall, Austin musicians rallied 'round Jo Carol and cut an album of her stuff. Some of those artists were famous (Terry Allen, Joe Ely), some weren't but deserve to be (Lisa Mednick, David Halley), and many are forgotten now; even though the album displays many styles and conceptions, its remarkable consistency results from Jo Carol's unique vision.

Her rhythms, timbres, and shadings are pure Americana, especially when delivered in her breathy, sexy Texas accent. Melodically, however, Jo Carol takes big risks (like she does in most things): She'll sing long lines of many syllables, or short lines of clipped syllables, which don't always scan but always work. Melodically, in many songs her closest equivalents are European art and cabaret music, as in Bertolt Brecht and Kurt Weill or Jacques Brel or even (amazingly) Noël Coward. I don't know if she's listened to these people, but sometimes she writes in forms they use.

From *Across the Great Divide,* as sung by Michael Hall: *"Heaven on earth was made in a minute / but Anything can happen in it . . . Heaven comes and goes . . . When I'm living in Heaven, sometimes I know / that Hell's as close as my own shadow . . ."*

Often she doesn't exactly sing a song—she *does* a song. It's just as good.

Her second album was 1995's *Bad Girls Upset by the Truth.* A spoken-word, sung-from-the-core, spiritual-sexual, coming-of-age account of a daring woman realizing herself in Lubbock, Austin, and points unknown (unknown, that is, to the rest of us—until Jo Carol explains). For instance:

"Loose Diamonds": *"And I know that God means well / Will you please tell Him / I've been to Paradise / And I'm amazed that I survived."*

"I Blame God": *"He's the only one original enough to make a mess like this / and even He can't clean it up / I didn't do this by myself / I had divine assistance / You'd have to be a deity to be this mean / You know that's just not me."*

And the song with one of the best song titles ever, "Vaginal Angel": *"Prepare a place for another bad girl / to grow up and do what bad girls do / They give their bodies to the music / 'cause the music knows what to do / for the bad girl who's forgotten / who she is and who to give it to / the music knows what to do."*

This, from her new *Dog of Love's* "I've Got Your Eyes": *"Old coyote paces down / the edges of his cage / looking to get free / like you and me / Always thought we were / the same one / or are we just missing the same parts? / Same broken heart."*

Those questions aren't asked, they're lived—and if you've got to dive down the rabbit hole to find the answers, well, that's what you do . . . if you're of Jo Carol Pierce's tribe.

Gone with the Wind's Scarlett O'Hara stands as our culture's standard of a certain kind of Southern belle—determined, charming, flirty, tough, ruthless, manipulative, seductive, impossible to truly know, and impossible to stop. But only in the songs of Jo Carol Pierce and the performance pieces of Jo Harvey Allen (both reared in Lubbock) can be found the expression and embodiment of a distinctive type, a woman of the West, wild, down to earth, mystically metaphysical and lustily physical, witchy (in the best sense), "bad girls" who demand strength and wildness and weirdness in their men, men whom they meet on their own terms. Such a woman of the West believes, as Jo Carol sings, that *"holy nights like this / are meant for burning down."*

Burning down to what? What Jo Carol's music says is: Go the distance, baby, and find out—find you.

That dog from hell is your dog.

Ely bonfire, Texas, 1984. Standing, left to right: Jo Harvey Allen, Terry Allen, Joe Ely, Butch Hancock. Seated, left to right: Janet Gilmore, Jimmie Dale Gilmore, Sharon Rae Ely (holding baby Marie Ely), Michael Ventura

DRIVING INTO Minnesota through Fargo, the land was flat and moist and green. The sky was wide as the Texas Panhandle's, but in the dry air of West Texas the sky seems to go on forever, while Minnesota's humidity somehow brings the sky down close. I was headed for a conference in Wisconsin, but I'd allowed myself a day's detour to mosey through a place I'd always wanted to see: Bob Dylan's hometown—Hibbing, Minnesota.

Dylan says he doesn't know how a guy like him came out of a place like Hibbing. In *No Direction Home* he says, "I was born very far from where I was supposed to be," and that in Hibbing he sometimes felt "that I was maybe not even born to the right parents." He's been saying things like that for forty years and I don't know a rock critic who doesn't take him at his word. But I also don't know a rock critic who's been to Hibbing. I wanted to see for myself.

Driving north on U.S. 75, a two-lane, the land was peaceful but the towns were desperate—towns like Shelly, population about two hundred, with its pleading bill-

board: FREE LOTS FOR HOUSING CONSTRUCTION. In the midst of our greatest real-estate boom they were giving it away around here, or trying to. I turned east on U.S. 2 and crossed the Mississippi River—here it's no wider than a good-sized creek. The road was cracked and bumpy with filled-in potholes, very dangerous in winter, but clearly the county can't afford better. Then on U.S. 169 I passed villages that once meant to be towns and are now barely hanging on: Taconite, Pop. 311; Marble, Pop. 675; Calumet, Pop. 383; Nashwauk, Pop. 935. Hibbing's a big city around here: as you enter, the sign announces a population of 18,046 (the number is 17,000-and-change on Hibbing's website, on which it's noted that the city is 97.33% white). All along that road, huge ugly mounds of earth rose on either side. They were manmade, but I had as yet no idea that I was driving through an enormous open-air mine.

On Hibbing's main drag, American flags hung from the lampposts. The picture show Robert Zimmerman attended as a boy is now a deli. The old railroad hotels are abandoned or worse—in the sinister, shabby Delvic Hotel, people still reside. The once-fancy Audroy Hotel announced in all-but-faded paint on its brick wall, "Hibbing's FINEST Supper Club"—now long defunct.

Photos of Dylan were in the drugstore window. And then there's the high school, built in 1920, a classic: wide steps, pillars, fine red brick and—the high school is on Bob Dylan Drive! ("I got out of high school and left [Hibbing] the very next day," Dylan says in *No Direction Home*.) "Irony" is a word I steer clear of because it's so often misused, but that the high school Dylan hated, the high school where the principal drew down the curtain on his first band's first performance—that his high school is now on Bob Dylan Drive, *that's* irony. It's also clever: a sure-fire way to make most of those high school kids dismiss anything Dylan ever sang.

Then a sign interested me, quite apart from my interest in Dylan: it pointed the way to the Greyhound Bus Museum. I wondered, Why is that *here*? In the museum, a half dozen very old people were *very* glad to see me. I was the only visitor. They asked me to sign their guest book and told me stories. In 1914 the Hibbing Transportation Company was formed to transport workers to the mines. The company purchased what passed for buses in that day, but those buses kept breaking down, so they perfected the long drive shaft, weight distri-

bution, etc., and invented the modern bus. The company expanded and changed its name to Greyhound.

The old folks shooed me into an enormous, hangar-like room and let me have the run of the place. There were many, many old Greyhounds from 1927 on; some, like the '56 Scenicruiser, I'd ridden as a boy. I went from bus to bus, sitting behind the wheel and in the seats, seeing my adolescent self with a bus ticket and the whole country down the road, in days when $250 bought a Greyhound pass with which you could travel as much and as far as you wanted for one month—$350 for two months. That came out of Hibbing.

I went from bus to bus remembering my youthful adventures and thinking maybe it wasn't so strange that Dylan (who probably left town on a Greyhound) came out of Hibbing. In its heyday Greyhound was the cheapest ride from anywhere to anywhere—"anywhere" is a big concept, and it can't help but imply "anything." So Dylan wasn't the first "anywhere and anything" energy to come out of Hibbing.

Those old men at the museum had worked in the mine, and they asked, eagerly, with pride, "Have you seen it yet?" "Sir, I don't even know about it." "Kid,"—it's fun to be called "kid" in your sixtieth year by someone who has the right—"Hibbing is *still* the largest open-pit iron mine *in this world*." The almanacs back him up. Little Hibbing is still ranked as "the iron-ore capital of the world." Iron, the metal of metals, the metal most essential to constructing the twentieth century (a metal needed by our bodies, by our blood)—Hibbing was its central source. Greyhound ("anyone can go anywhere") and iron: they represent two different but interlocking elemental energies, and they're the very reason for Hibbing's existence. When Dylan was a boy, Hibbing's Greyhounds roamed everywhere and Hibbing's ore was in damned near everything. A boy sees the obvious, and the man remembers what the boy saw: that Hibbing's culture was, to put it mildly, limited. But a young genius's psyche takes in far more than the obvious, and Hibbing's secret was that, almost anonymously, it's had more impact upon America than any town its size that I am aware of. In *No Direction Home* Dylan says Hibbing "looked like any other town out of the '40s and '50s." That's how it looked, but that's not what it was. Hibbing emanated rare and potent forces.

So has Dylan. I doubt that's a coincidence.

The old folks told me how to find "the Grand Canyon of Minnesota"—the viewing place from which one can see the great mine. "Grand Canyon" is an apt description. At the viewpoint, you stand at the edge of an abyss: they've dug ore so deep out of this earth, you could stick an Empire State Building down there and not touch its tip from where you stand.

Beside the viewpoint was a gift shop, and in the gift shop was a friendly old woman who had one bad eye. She asked me to sign the guest book, smiled, and said, "You're here about Bobby, aren't you?" She just knew. We talked a while. I asked permission to quote her. The knowing lady was Nonnie McKanna and she'd been telling me of a golf date with "Abe" (that's Abraham Zimmerman), and how Mr. Zimmerman pulled out his wallet, showed Nonnie a check for $10,000, and said, "Bobby sent this for my birthday—and I thought the kid would starve to death!" Nonnie laughed, "We *all* thought he'd starve to death!" And she added, "He had wonderful parents. He comes from good stock. *Very* good stock." Nonnie McKanna hoped one day "Bobby" would return to Hibbing and give a concert. She said that wistfully.

I stood looking down into that gargantuan iron pit for a long time, astonished by the elemental energies that have emanated out of Hibbing. Dylan seemed to me an expression of those energies. By definition, you can't explain a mystery. How could young Dylan, who'd had a fairly uneventful youth, very quickly write songs of which it could be said (as he said of Woody Guthrie's), "You could listen to his songs and actually learn how to live."

One becomes a great artist not through the expression of oneself but through the expression of forces greater than oneself. The deep cold of Hibbing's winters, the deep pit before me, and whatever made Hibbing generate the most accessible transportation from the mid-'20s to the mid-'70s—it may well be that Dylan's sensitivity to what's elemental *here* gave him the foundation needed to be the greatest artist of my generation. For what has distinguished him more than his capacity to express the elemental, the mysterious core, of what he sang about and of the very medium of song?

Standing at the edge of the iron pit's abyss, I thought of what an old miner said at the museum.

It went something like, "One of the prettiest things I ever saw was at the mine on the night shift when the sun was coming up—there was a mist, you see, and the sun was shining through the mist on that red ore, mist and earth glowed red like the glow was coming out of the ground—I can't tell you, I can't tell you how pretty that was." Sounded something like a Dylan lyric.

WHY DOES a young woman carve a swastika onto her leg, sometime around midnight, a few days before Christmas, while the snow is falling prettily on Portland, Maine?

I never learned the answer to that question, but learning to ask it, and not to forget it, was my discovery of America—a wider, wilder America than most people were aware of the night I saw that woman in the winter of 1962.

I was only a few weeks into the age of seventeen and had just boarded a Greyhound in Waterville, Maine, for what was then the longest drive I knew: the night run from the snow-quiet streets of Waterville, that modest Yankee town, down through Augusta and Portland to Boston, Hartford, and I-don't-know-how-many little New England villages that still looked like models for a very expensive electric train set. My destination: the Port Authority Bus Terminal, a brisk walk from Times Square, New York City.

Times Square in 1962 was decades from the Disneyesque gaudiness of today,

nor was it yet the mecca of skin flicks and sex shops that it became for a while. Between 7th and 8th Avenues, 42nd Street was a full block of twenty-four-hour-a-day movie houses showing mostly Westerns and those murder ballads of the '40s. Continuous shows. Admission fifty cents. A good place to run away from home to. Just don't sit next to anybody who keeps his overcoat across his lap. And if you plan on staying all night, find an aisle seat and spill a Coke on the seat next to you so it'll remain vacant. My film school.

On 7th Avenue, just north of Times Square, the Metropole Café hadn't yet switched to topless go-go dancers and bad pop. The bandstand was behind the bar, and you would hear the jazz of Woody Herman or Pee Wee Russell and, one glorious night, the man they called the Onliest Louis, Mr. Armstrong himself. Unless the weather was really bad, they left the doors open and you could see the bandstand from the sidewalk and hear as clear as anything. A continuous clot of listener-gawkers formed and re-formed a step from the open doors, most just glancing in and moving on. But some of us stayed hours. That was the first great live music I ever heard. My music school.

When I got tired of standing up, and wasn't in the mood for a movie, I would go to a bookstore up near 42nd Street—well, part bookstore, part sex shop, but the bookstore part stocked real books. I would sometimes buy, sometimes steal a book, then go to a diner and drink coffee and read as long as I could stay awake. The first book I stole and read, at the age of fourteen, was e.e. cummings's *Selected Poems*. I had no idea who he was, it was just the easiest book to steal. Highly recommended for young or old who do their reading at a table next to a booth of chattering prostitutes.

As for what I was doing at that age roaming the streets and shuttling between Maine and New York—suffice it to say that the whereabouts of my parents was often, at best, problematic, and that children can't be raised by good intentions alone. I'd been raised as much by New York City as by my parents, and with Mama in a mental hospital and Pa god knows where, my guardian angels—or pure dumb luck—had landed me with a Unitarian minister's family in Waterville, from which I'd Greyhound back to Times Square every chance I got.

In America, circa 1962, even Times Square—a raunchy, dirty, and genuinely unsavory place—was, by today's standards, relatively tame. Almost no street

people. No runaways (unless you count me). Drugs hadn't hit the streets full force, as yet, and were mostly (as far as I saw) the purview of short-order cooks, whores, and musicians—and, in a way, I only witnessed that in retrospect, for back then how did I know what marijuana looked or smelled like? As far as I was concerned, the working girls just smoked cigarettes that smelled funny. Occasionally some man would ask me to his room "to see something," and I'd scare him off because my street sense flashed red, not because I had any idea what he wanted me to see; I wouldn't hear the word "homosexual" for almost another year, and I had but the haziest idea of what a "faggot" or "fairy" was—1962 was like that. I carried a knife because it was sort of expected and it gave authority to one's slouch and one's walk, but in my case it was more a comfort than a weapon. If I posed with it before a mirror it was because I'd seen too many movies, not because I expected to use the thing. Perhaps I walked under a lucky star, but those seamy, sin-stained streets seemed to me more like a painting by Brueghel than a film by Scorcese. Yet Times Square was touted, in those days, as America's worst.

Anyway, I'd gotten on the bus in Waterville, bound for Times Square, after watching my favorite program, *Route 66*. For me and my friends *Route 66* was not a television show. It was a promise. A weekly training film. A way out and through and over. It kept me and would keep me going in the most literal sense, and because of that show I can never feel superior to television or pretend that the tube doesn't offer a genuine lifeline to some of the people some of the time.

Route 66 went like this: Two guys, Tod Stiles (Martin Milner) and Buz Murdock (George Maharis) tooled around the United States in a Corvette, odd-jobbing their way from town to town, looking not for adventure but—and they were quite explicit about this—for meaning. The formula, if you want to call it that, was simple: in each episode they would meet some man or woman or kid who was totally, but *absolutely,* over the edge. It might be Tuesday Weld as a Texas girl who returns to her hometown wearing a ghastly mask and calling everybody's cards. As she's burning rag dolls in a spooky sidewalk ceremony, she says of the quite normal-looking spectators, "Make them take off their masks and I'll take off mine."

It might be Lois Smith playing a woman who, when asked why she came running back to a father who doesn't want her, says, "I didn't come running here. I slipped back screaming."

It might be Julie Newmar riding a motorcycle around Tucson at ninety miles an hour and then telling the judge, as he's about to pass sentence on her, "Isn't there a higher purpose for living than peace of mind? I give myself to

life—I let it take me where it will— instead of asking life to give itself to me."

Remember that this was 1962, when pundits were saying that rebellion was done in America, that dissent was over, and that kids were interested in nothing but conformity and money. So imagine how it sounded when, in an episode called "Go Read the River," an engineer said: "Somewhere, somehow, a simple beautiful thing, a single morality, a single set of standards was smashed like an atom into ten million separate pieces. Now, what's right for a man can be wrong for his business. And what's right for his business can be wrong for his country. And what's right for his country can be wrong for the world."

Buz and Tod would often just watch and listen. Or try to talk somebody out of suicide. Or *not* attempt to follow Julie Newmar as she rides out of Tucson on her own motorcycle to her own uncertain sunset, a strong and wild woman alone and searching. (Where would you find her character now, on any size screen?) Buz would say things like, "That's what understanding is: taking away all the limits." (*What?!*) And: "I can even hear saxophone cases slamming shut at two a.m. and tired sidemen crossing the parking lots and wiping off the windshields when they're wet before they drive home—so, who needs radios?"

There were corny episodes, of course. But the best ones—written mostly by

Stirling Silliphant and occasionally by Howard Rodman—were great. Keep your David Mamet and Sam Shepard. Silliphant and Rodman (who also wrote the great *Naked City* series) took more chances, created more haunting characters, and wrote like everything was at stake every time. With Rod Serling and some very few others, they were the finest dramatists of their era, and no playwriting or screen writing since has gone beyond the territory they charted. Silliphant's output was staggering. He wrote about two-thirds of the more than 100 fifty-five-minute *Route 66* episodes.

Every show was filmed in black-and-white and on location, with the knowledge that, as Michael Corcoran of the *Austin Chronicle* put it, "The road is America. It's Raleigh and Cleveland and Louisville and Topeka. It's Route 66 no matter what the road-sign says." Watching *Route 66* on our fuzzy black-and-white screens in New York and Maine I saw Tulsa, Austin, Reno, New Orleans, Santa Fe, the deep South, the High Sierras, and the Mojave Desert. Silliphant would go to a town, hang out for a few days, then lock himself in a hotel room and turn out his script in a day or two—with the aid, as Howard Rodman later told me, of ample booze and local ladies. And that's how those scripts played, as though written in frenzy, impassioned by a young writer's ruthless need to live it all fucking now.

We didn't know that Silliphant had based the show on Jack Kerouac's *On the Road*—that, in fact, he'd tried to buy the rights from Kerouac, who wouldn't sell, and who later felt ripped off by the show; nor that George Maharis had been hired for his resemblance to Kerouac. (Their voices were practically identical.) We didn't need to know. We lived for that one-out-of-five *Route 66* that was a masterpiece of the genre the show itself had created, waiting for an actress like Susan Oliver to come up to Milner in a bar and describe daily life as "a kind of a game in which you substitute one cliché for another."

So it was 1962 and almost Christmas and I'd boarded the Greyhound in Waterville, Maine, after watching a particularly crazy *Route 66* with a title from a Carl Sandburg poem, "Where Is Chick Lorimer? Where Has She Gone?," in which Vera Miles played a broken-down stripper trying to come home. Her credo: "Onward, with guts and dignity."

In an hour or so we pulled into Portland.

Which is where *she* got on. Pale faced, eyes circled dark, she had blue-black hair cut unevenly at her shoulders, wore the tightest black sweater, had large breasts, and her brassiere had hard-pointed nose cones. Tight black chinos cut halfway up her calves. No coat, and it was ten degrees outside. She threw her suitcase up on the rack and sat down in an aisle seat and said aloud to no one, certainly not to me, "This is the craziest thing I've ever done in my life."

She needed to say it badly enough to say it again: "The craziest thing, I swear."

She was, as far as I was concerned, an older woman. She may have been all of twenty-two. As I'd suspected, Silliphant had been telling the truth all along. There his truth was, sitting across the aisle from me, and I wouldn't dream of saying a word to her. For I had learned from Tod and Buz something about the power of being a witness—it amazes me still that I learned this from a television show, but one shouldn't be choosy about where one learns the important stuff—and somehow I had learned that one of the most important things we can do in this world is stand as witness. To look, to feel, to wonder. Even if the possibility of action is remote or nonexistent.

A witness *cooks,* just by being there. The raw elements of everything cook under the pressure of one's witnessing silence, and when they cook long enough something nourishing is concocted simply by the power of our attention. *Then* there's something to be and to give.

I was her witness, and she didn't have to know it. She was grandstanding like that in order to be witnessed, whether she knew it or not. And what I witnessed was that just above her ankle a swastika had been knifed into her leg.

Not deeply. Just enough to neatly peel off the top layers of skin. Had she done it

herself or had someone done it to her? And if someone had done it to her, had she wanted it done or not?

It had happened very recently; the wound, no longer bleeding, was still raw. The swastika was about the size of a quarter and straightly done. It would form a small, precise scar. She kept rubbing at it, unthinking, all the way to New York, in and out of light snows that fell straight down, whirled in the wind only by the passage of our Greyhound. It would take the whole length of road from the midnight of Portland to the dawn of New York for her wound to form its scab.

Her message was very clear to me. Without speaking a word, in a Greyhound that smelled of cigarettes and sleep, she was telling me, lecturing me, by her very presence, "They're lying, kid. Except for Stirling Silliphant and Howard Rodman and a bunch of musicians, they're lying. The schools and the ads and the movies, they're lying. I have big tits, tight pants, and a swastika on my ankle, and you can call me America. I got on this bus in the straightest town in the sanest state in the country, and look at me. According to your school and your church and your newspaper and your government, I don't exist. But let me tell you something: The rest of this century will be as over-the-edge as me in no time. It's going to be the craziest thing we've ever done."

She'd be how old now? Probably gone to fat. If you saw her today she wouldn't seem so strange. The country has caught up to her. Her swastika scar has probably swelled up and thinned out as that bony ankle bulged with age. It probably doesn't look like a swastika anymore. A sinister possibility knifed into America's sexy ankle. And sure, I was just a horny kid tripping over any excuse for an epiphany. But the phrase "Miss America" would never be innocent for me again, and she was my proof that the truths of Silliphant's *Route 66* were out there, alive in human form, demons and angels, no matter who lies, who denies, or who disappears into the dark.

Ouch, Colorado, 1985

LITTLE FLESHLETS ON THE RUN

IN MY BACK-POCKET black notebook I wrote the date numerically without punctuation: *111999*

The first day of the last year of the last century of this millennium.

Then I wrote the place and time: *Terlingua—Texas—2AM.*

Terlingua's a stone's throw from the Mexican border, near the Rio Grande. It calls itself a ghost town, but take that as a metaphor: It's a place of spirits, all right, and it's true that the people there have left the so-called "normal" life behind, and there are ruins of old adobes and abandoned mines—the remains of toil and dreams; but in Terlingua flesh and blood dances and sings, and paints, writes, prays, imbibes, and stares for hours at the desert vastness all around—a jagged, dangerous labyrinth of mountains, canyons, arroyos, and mesas, cut through by the great river.

In the wee hours of New Year's Day, 1999, the moon was full. I know no whiteness like the harsh yet soft gleam of moonglow on that land—a strong enough light to read by, it cast delicately etched black shadows from every rock and shrub.

The outline of my Panama hat and leather jacket made my shadow seem bigger and more powerful than I (as one's shadow-side so often is). The only sounds were the rustle of the breeze in the shrubbery and the murmur of my friends talking not far from where I stood. And I thought:

The voices of friends and the song of the wind, surely that is more than enough to evoke and confirm one's faith—that, and a pulsation in the air which might be the heartbeat of God, with the clouds in strangely quilted pattern above, such as I'd never seen, translucent under the moon. I offered a prayer: "Thank you, dear God, that I am included in the spectacle of Your Creation."

It felt like a night of passage, a night when the whole world moved one step closer to the end, not of civilization, but of the power of this civilization to imagine its future—the end, then, of imagination as we've known it. For when you get requests from several magazines to submit your prediction for "life after 2000," then you know that we as a culture and as individuals are grasping at straws, trying frantically to imagine the unimaginable, to manufacture visions, to exert just a little control over the future by anticipating and predicting it. My friend Spider Johnson had been speaking that day of "the mind, that nattering entity," and how the mind "hankers after some kind of understanding—'cause it's the gatekeeper." It seemed that, like myself, everyone dear to me was trying to walk through the gate of their own minds and expectations into something we can't quantify or qualify; for we will be the future as we are the present and the past, and if there is to be true newness in that future it must be within us. So I replied to only one of those editor's queries: "No matter what we think or imagine or predict, something unexpected will change everything—it always does."

One unexpected thing, on this particular journey, was how difficult it was for me to speak—though the difficulty didn't stop me from trying (which may have been a mistake). My words either weren't getting out at all or were garbled in transmission. My heart felt like a darkened room in which you know there's furniture but you don't know where it is and you're afraid of tripping over it. I was remembering a time long ago when I'd read a poem by George Seferis to a then-fourteen-year-old student named Stenya, and had asked, "What do you think makes a person write a poem like that?" Stenya replied: "Long long periods of indecision and suffering, when you don't know which life is your own."

At times like this I've always remembered that sentence. Standing there under the moon, after writing the date— *111999*—I felt the urgency to write something that would be, for me, absolutely real. Something that would be a letter to my loves, living and dead, with our relationships changeless and changing. For my faith in writing is just this, and it applies even more to the writer than to the reader: An honest sentence should look you straight in the eyes and leave you nowhere to hide. Only when we have nowhere left to hide are we true.

Slowly three sentences formed within me, and I inscribed them with this punctuation:

> *The paradoxes are singing—*
> *The truth doesn't take sides—*
> *What is as ruthless as love?*

After sunup, Spider led me up a steep slope that he called "Fossil Hill." Everywhere were rocks of every size in which were etched the outlines of ferns, sea shells, tiny fish—for at one time this desert, these mountains, this mesa, had been the bottom of a sea. How many upheavals, how many apocalypses, had been necessary to change that ocean floor into this mountainous desert?

What is as ruthless as love?
Time.

Time is that by which oceans become deserts, which will, one day, again become oceans. And I remembered that the top of Mount Everest, earth's highest point at 29,035 feet, is made of marine limestone. The rock of Everest's peak was molded in the depths of the sea, and through a remorseless inexorable movement of Time that undersea rock made its way high into the air to become a mountaintop. And it hasn't stopped moving. Will it continue up or head back down? Will this happen in moments of cataclysm or in an endless series of earthquakes or both? I remembered that people behave that way too. And I remembered a fragment of correspondence from my friend Jill Neimark. I'd written her last fall about sitting by the banks of the Chattahoochee River in Atlanta when a simple and inescapable sentence said itself to me as though it were the river speaking: *Life makes no deals*. She'd written: "About 'life makes no deals'—you really see it when you're in nature. Supreme beauty built out of a remorselessness we'd better not forget. It's the remorselessness that builds the beauty."

What will "life after 2000" be, and what will happen to each of us? Make lists of predictions, compare your lists, argue them, broadcast them, print them—but go sit on Fossil Hill in Terlingua and you'll know what's going to happen: The oceans will become deserts and the deserts will become oceans. Some slab at

the bottom of the sea will become the highest peak of all, and the place where you live will become a ruin, a ghost town; it will crumble, or be buried, or be flooded, or be taken by the wind. The history you make will be forgotten. The art you create will disappear. The technology you're so proud of will rust to dust. And the great new concepts that go so far beyond all the old ways of thinking—they will become intellectual antiques that a future generation will discard without a qualm. The globe will warm and then will chill. Oceans will become deserts. Deserts will become oceans.

"Why do a damn thing, then?" one of my favorite students asked me later, when I'd spoken of Fossil Hill.

"'Cause you can't help it. Even trying to do nothing, or checking out altogether, is, in fact, doing something—because it has an effect on everyone else, and that effect ripples out, the butterfly causes the hurricane whether it intends to or not, whether it wants to or not. So why not do what you love? Why not stop listening to assholes and discover the nature of *your* love and go on from there? It'll just take all your life—but so will everything else. Yeah, I know it's corny. Do you think it's not embarrassing to say this shit? But I didn't invent it—you can't invent the truth—so it's corny but it's true. And I didn't come this far to lie to children."

The remainder of that New Year's Day in Terlingua was spent in sweetness and strangeness, closeness and distance, music and silence, with friends on whom I depend to be my touchstone, as they depend on me. And then there was one of the weirder sunsets I've ever seen, colorless yet bright—the sky pale, spooky, calm. And sometime after dark Butch Hancock showed up, and, as though he knew what we'd been thinking about all day, he said, "God is everything, and the only attention *is* God's. We say 'we're paying attention,' and it's horseshit; the Universe is made of attention!" What is humanity? "Just a wave of energy housed in these little fleshlets."

And I thought of two "little fleshlets," Deborah and I, dancing the night before as 1998 became 1999, a dance of celebra-tion and defiance, two old friends accepting the dare of the new year. And I thought of Lora, who had gone for a long walk down the dry creekbed and brought back a rock that she handed to me, and which, when I returned home, I put on my altar—an altar practically made of the art and stones that Spider, Deborah, and Lora have given me over the years.

And there was something else I put on my altar when I got home. On Fossil Hill, Spider had picked up a small, gracefully curved piece of ironwood and said, "It's gotta lotta starlight stored up in it." He gave it to me later, but only after he'd carved a delicate spiral upon it, and he said: "To remember that you're made of starlight."

I WRITE THIS a little under protest. My writing-self says, "Write about your practice. *That* is your subject tonight!" But another self cringes: "I don't want us to write about that, it'll screw things up." Yet another (rather stuffy) self chimes in: "To act, or to fail to act, out of fear—only creates more fear." I don't know what they're fussing about, the writing-self always wins anyway (though sometimes that second voice is right). So it seems that after years of enacting my practice, it's come time to write about it. (I don't know why. My writing-self never tells me that.)

"Practice" is what Buddhists call it. The usage suits me, though I'm not Buddhist. (I'm not any -ist or -ism or -ian.) "Practice," in the modern sense, means to work at something persistently, trying to get it right—which also fits my meaning, my practice: the hour or so a day when I read my "devotionals" (a Catholic usage), then go to my altar to meditate and pray.

I should begin by admitting that I know little of such matters; I do the little I know. My practice refreshes and calms me and helps me feel connection to a larger, more inclusive reality, beyond the everyday and beyond this crazy moment in history. When, twenty years ago, I felt the need for such a practice, my practicality—underneath it all, I'm *very* practical; to get away with what I've gotten away with you've got to be practical—my practicality instructed me: "Form your practice simply, out of simple things known to you, without dogma, and without the grandiose or esoteric. Just a plan to sit and 'pray in your closet,' as Jesus suggested."

Which is how it began. Over the years there've been some modest elaborations. (My practical self is very firm with this instruction: "Don't get too fancy in this realm. Keep it simple.")

From the first I had the need to read "devotionals," as I call them now. I sit with several books and slowly read a page or so of each aloud. First I recite a line from a Zen verse: "This day will not come again . . ." Then another: "When the hubless wheel turns / Master or no master can stop it . . ." Words from Paul Reps's *Zen Flesh Zen Bones*, from which I then read. Then a page or so from the *Tao Te Ching*, Idries Shah's *The Way of the Sufi*, Martin Buber's *Tales of the Hasidim*, Dorothy Day's *Meditations*, Marcus Aurelius's *Meditations*, John Dominic Crossan's rendition of Jesus' sayings, poetry by Hafiz, and poetry by Ikkyu. So: a Zennist, a Taoist, a Muslim, a Jew, a Catholic, a Roman emperor, Jesus (another Jew), another Muslim, and finally the wildest of all Zennists.

It wasn't my intention to be so multicultural. These books were gifts. Butch gave me Idries Shah; Jodie, the *Tao Te Ching*; Mikey, Buber; Dave, Dorothy Day; Hannah, Marcus Aurelius; Karen gave me one Ikkyu book and the other was given by a stranger. There's my practicality's voice again: "Don't go too far out of your natural way for such things. Take what's given."

A kind of personal community of wisdom-teachings, then. The *Tao Te Ching* instructing: "Do your work, then step back. That is the only path to serenity." Buber: "The world in which you live, just as it is and not otherwise, affords you that association with God, which will redeem you and whatever divine aspect of the world you have been entrusted with." In the Sufi book, Saadi of Shivaz: "Make no friendship with an elephant-keeper if you have no room to entertain an elephant." Dorothy Day working for "that kind of society where it is easier to be good." The emperor: "The Mind of the universe is

social." Jesus: "Love your enemy." Ikkyu: "Entrust yourself to the wind-blown clouds and do not wish to live forever."

Hard stuff to live up to. I like to think I am an intelligent and capable person, reverent in my way, doing what I can—but I need help and I'm bad at asking for it or taking it. These voices give it in a form I can manage. My "devotionals," then, are no more than that: listening for help.

Then I go to my altar, where candles are burning. My long messy altar. I like a mess. I like crowded streets and crowded desks. Messy walls with lots of photographs and art on them, and nothing exactly level. Shelves of books emphatically not in alphabetical order. My altar is in that spirit. And again, so much of it is *given*: Deb's shrine, Spider and Lora's box, Evann's cross, George's cross, Daisy's rock, Jenni's candle holder, Brendan's shaman figure, the little shrine Kathleen and Cynthia built, the small wood box that Dave built and the larger box my father built, Andrew's angel, Kyra's leaves, Jazmin's dried flowers, Big's vial of Italian soil, Jo Carol's cards, my mother's books, my cousin's candle holder, my stepmother's incense burner, Hannah's little duck (altars should QUACK, shouldn't they?) . . . and photos of the dead of my blood . . . so my altar is a space that is peopled, connected, no matter how solitary my daily life appears. (I've often gone days without a face-to-face talk with anyone I know.) I'm praying, in effect, in my crowded, peopled, messy closet, so small in the shadow of God.

John Coltrane wrote: "No matter what . . . it's God." A transcendent and awe-ful vision. I don't expect to know what I mean when I say "God." If I knew what I meant, it wouldn't be God.

Joseph Campbell put it another way, saying something like: "God is beyond human category. 'Good' and 'evil,' 'order' and 'chaos,' are human categories. God is beyond all that." (Coltrane's "no matter what.") My brother Aldo used to say to me, "How can you pray to a God you have no personal relation to?" I'd answer, "The Moon doesn't have a personal relation to me, that I know of, but I can still think it beautiful and love it and talk to it." Anyway . . . first, I beg God to forgive all that I haven't the strength to forgive. For Jesus (whom I don't worship, but whom I do revere) instructed that before we pray we forgive all those we have anything against. And then I pray . . . for my beloveds, for strangers, sometimes even for myself, that I may act truly.

There's no need to relate what I say in prayer. We must all find our own words, whether we compose them ourselves or find words from whatever serves our longing. (Kathleen says that there's really only one prayer: "Thank you.") In any case, I pray. In *Tales of the Hasidim*, Rabbi Pinhas says, "The prayer a man says, the prayer, in itself, is God . . . for prayer unites the principles." Unites the one

praying with God. May it be so. I don't know. As I don't know what God is. I simply desire to pray. Realizing it may be: nothing. I seek no comfort. I ask no favors. I can think of nothing more pathetic than to present God a shopping list of one's desires. Insofar as I am able, I attempt to stand naked before the will of the Universe. I always fail. At best, I strip down only to my underwear. Usually, I'm wearing the spiritual equivalent of a tuxedo at the very times I fancy I'm most naked. It doesn't matter. I have to pray for my people or I don't feel that I'm doing my job or even living my life. What God does about that is God's affair.

And then I meditate. Meditation and prayer are very different. In prayer, one addresses the sacred as best one can. In effect, one seeks an audience with God. Which may be impossible   and so, very worth trying. In meditation one enters the realm of possibility. But very carefully. In the tradition in which I was taught, which does not need to be named, one does not teach a meditation to someone one does not know. So I'll say little about it. Over the years I've developed my own meditation, but it's best to start with what's simplest: to sit with back straight for a half hour or so, and breathe evenly, and be as quiet as possible, quieting the mind. This aligns your spirit-body with your physical body. (Let "spirit" stand for that part of you which can't be measured.) It's my experience that when you do this every day you become much more patient. My testimony: only after I did this for years did I really and truly grow up emotionally—insofar as I've grown up, that is. Meditation . . . gives you more space. You live in a larger world.

That is my experience, my testimony.

After I've meditated I say aloud, "Thank you." I'm not sure to what, exactly, except to the calm and connectivity of the moments that have just passed. It just feels right to say it.

And that's it. My practice. Which my writing-self, in its dictatorial fashion, com-manded I tell. We live in a time of "dire beauty" (Caroline Casey's words). At the center of how I face this direness and beauty, is my practice. Perhaps my writing-self decided to speak of it, over the protests of several other selves (including one that said, "This is gonna make us really look silly," and another chirping, "We *are* silly!"), because . . . in dangerous times we owe each other an account of how we survive, for it may be useful to someone else's survival. This practice is at the heart of how I survive.

Off 34th Street, Lubbock, Texas, 1968

RAINDROPS IN A STORM

THERE'S A METAPHOR that's been obsessing me lately. "Just a raindrop in a storm," I keep telling myself. "I'm just a raindrop in a storm." If I say it out loud on street corners I'll get put away, but I can write it here and you can pick it up on a street corner, or wherever, and I get paid—what a life. Now that I think of it, maybe I got the metaphor from Butch Hancock's song, a song I heard him sing in a living room in Lubbock my first days in Texas, half my life ago, years before he recorded it: "If you were a raindrop, you'd be fallin' . . ." "Just a raindrop in a storm." We come from somewhere we do not know, and we are bound for somewhere we do not know, and in between we're lit by lightning, and like the rain, every drop of rain, we are more alike than different, we are important yet forgotten, we are temporary yet needed, we are thirsted for. And life is a long leap through the wind.

And one morning in August, in southern Utah . . .

It had rained the night before: great flashes of lightning ricocheted over Mon-ument Valley . . . I watched from the little town of Mexican Hat a few miles north, the smell of the rain so sweet in that vast and spectacular country, which still has the feel of the ocean bottom that it was millions of years ago. . . . It wasn't a restful rain. I don't sleep much or well, never have, and so I woke in the dark, maybe an hour before dawn, dressed quietly without waking Hannah, and went and sat by the river.

The San Juan River makes a narrow gash through that part of the world, runs fast and muddy toward wherever it joins the Colorado. . . . You sit on the ledge of the rock and look at it about thirty feet below. . . . The storm had passed, there was a big moon, full or just a little less than full, and it made a clear bright rippling reflection on the swift black water below. Strange, and an unexpected privilege, to look down on the moon, a dreamlike moon, for it was in motion, rippling yet still, and I could look down and see all its details, then look up and see that same moon frozen high in the night sky. A night of two moons. And reality parted, a gateway opened up in the darkness, a gateway that would stay open longer than I thought such a gateway could . . .

I decided to sit and watch the river for however long it took the dawn to come and the sky to brighten: I wanted to see the moment when the moon left the river, when the sky would be so bright that the black waters would take on color and blanch out the moon. Most knowledge is temporary, and history seems to change everything faster and faster, but you can connect to all the Time that's past and all the Time that will come by entering a state of silence. Nothing mystic about it. If you can find a silence, or make your own silence in the midst of noise, it's the same silence that was there at the dawn of humankind and will be here when we're all gone. It is the only, or at least the most accessible, connective thread to everywhen and everywhere. And when you find it, it changes Time, or your sense of Time—not so much slows it down as makes it malleable. Time becomes not something that's happening to you, but something you're made of and part of. That's why the sages say that meditation is not passive or still; it's a stillness full of movement, a stillness that moves with true Time and not clock time, still as the reflection of the moon on the river, and moving like the moon on the river.

So I sat in that connective state, and waited.

The day before, in a little Utah town called Boulder, which is so remote that it was the very last town in America where the mail was still delivered by mule train . . . in Boulder I'd seen hundreds of hummingbirds. Yes, hundreds. Hovering and darting over a swampy pond. When there are hundreds, they're a little frightening. There was a restaurant, tables on a porch, and hummingbird feeders hung on the porch, and the quick small long-beaked birds darted around near our heads, and that took some getting used to. All that incredible movement . . . that was like the silence by the river, when there was not more light but just slightly less darkness, and the bats left their nests and darted, flashes of shadow, between me and the reflection of the moon below. And my little thoughts didn't seem like mine; they seemed to be darting here and there, hummingbirds and bats, leaving their nests and feeding . . . my thoughts seemed to have little to do with me, until I thought of something my brother Aldo said:

"You and your life, intimate lovers but never friends."

He meant it as a general "you," but he said it to me, and it was more true than I wanted it to be, but maybe that was changing.

You come when a friend calls. I felt called and I was there, on this little perch of life. A little progress was being made. As though the reflection of the moon had dared me to catch the moment when it disappears. To teach me that you can't. Or I can't. I never took my eyes off it. Once dawn truly started I really never took my eyes off it. Delicate shade by delicate shade, the sky took light. The cliffs of the river became their raw sienna. The river became its slightly bloody brown— too brown to reflect sky or clouds, though now and then, in a temporary swirl or eddy, a cloud would appear and disappear like a white shadow. The moon's reflection had moved, of course, as the moon moved above, so the swath of river I concentrated on shifted slightly downstream, but I concentrated. And I thought I was still seeing it when I realized it was no longer there, and I hadn't seen it disappear, hadn't been aware of the moment. It was still in my eyes when it was no longer on the river.

I laughed. I never felt better. Some words came to me:

"You make the path by walking." So wrote the poet Antonio Machado.

Not two hours later, an hour's drive north, through the Valley of the Gods, a long indent in the land out of which jut rock formations like nothing anywhere else . . . and a little later, we were the first people that morning to drive into Natural Bridges National Monument. As we drove the narrow road to the viewing points we saw only one park ranger in a pickup. You go to a cliff edge and look into the gorge, and there a stream had somehow, millions

of years ago, cut through the rocks to form them into arches, astounding structures. One is called by the Hopi word "Sipapu," which means "the place of emergence"—the handout they give you at the gate tells you this means "an entryway by which the Hopi believe their ancestors came into this world."

North Americans have walked here for 9,000 years. Not in droves. Singly and in small bands. Now and again. Some painted their images of the divine on the rock. Europeans, living in what was then an immense forest, had to build their cathedrals; the tribes of the West had no need for that. Cathedral-like formations were everywhere they walked, everywhere they looked. How could anything built by human hands compete?

The rest of America that August was sweltering under a heat wave, but here in the morning it was cool, we wore jackets, we looked at the Natural Bridges in as perfect a silence as there is.

Hannah . . . she's so many people . . . I'm so many people . . . often when we speak, only two or five of those people show up . . . but all the others are beside them, present and demanding representation . . . it's only when we're silent . . . it's only when we become part of that connective tissue, silence, which connects everyone to all things . . . it's only then that all those people make one circle and those two creatures we each call "I" stand together in the center of that circle . . .

and so, silent, with all our faces facing each other . . . I heard music.

Not a symphony, not jazz, certainly not rock, or blues, or anything like that. The sweet tinkly music of a nineteenth-century music box. It's made of wood. It has a simple mechanism inside it. Mechanical, not digital. You open the box and it plays a simple, elegant song. A little corny. An "I'm just a raindrop in a storm" kind of song. I heard a song as played on an old music box. I heard it as clear as anything.

"Hear that?" I asked Hannah.

She didn't. She asked what I was hearing and I told her.

I know I would not have heard it if I had not sat watching the reflection of the moon in the early hours.

We drove to another place to stare, in that silence, at another stone bridge.

I heard the music again. Clear as speech spoken close to your ear.

Again Hannah didn't hear it. She looked at me with some slight concern, but then she got what was going on, smiled, said: "God's such a tease."

Dirt road and stop sign, north of Lubbock, Texas, 1985

THIRTY YEARS AGO Janette was living in Amarillo. The city had three, maybe four, single-screen movie theaters and four TV channels. Foreign cinema and "art films" were known to Janette only by excited rumors spread by friends who'd returned from the big coastal cities or Austin. But one fateful afternoon (fateful, as it turned out, for me as well) Janette chanced to hear that Federico Fellini's *Juliet of the Spirits* was to be screened at Texas Tech, in Lubbock, 120-ish miles to the south. In those days who knew when, if ever, the film would come that close to Amarillo again? So she and another woman got in her car, sped down U.S. 87, and found the auditorium at Texas Tech just in time. Janette had never seen a Fellini film. His festive, chaotic rhythms; his seamless weave of grit and whimsy; his paradoxical vision of reality as a harsh environment that could be transcended but could not be escaped; his vast respect for the vulnerability of human beings; his sense of a secular sacredness that treated God respectfully but playfully—Fellini created a romantic cinema that had no need for happy end-

ings yet felt uplifting; a heroic cinema that had no need of heroes. And no one had yet splashed color on a screen as audaciously as Fellini in *Juliet of the Spirits*, his first color film, where drastically contrasting colored forms created illusions of perspective that seemed almost 3-D. The aesthetic excitement of it all thrilled Janette and her companion so deeply that when they left the auditorium they couldn't bring themselves to head straight back to Amarillo. (This will not have to be explained to anyone who's spent any time in Amarillo.)

Janette's friend had met a man who lived near the Salt Fork of the Red River, about a two-hour drive from Lubbock. Something about the Fellini film made her want to visit that man.

Here was art fulfilling its deepest function: not inspiring a duplication or imitation of itself, and certainly not getting its significance from an analysis or critique, but giving these young women a sense that life itself had just upped the ante, that the stakes were suddenly higher, and that there was more possibility in the night and in their lives than they'd yet considered. The work of art itself gave them the energy to fulfill its expectations.

That is greatness in art, and it is the only greatness that counts. By comparison, most of what we call greatness is merely a form of cataloging. Art is a repository of intense energy—"for USE," as the poet Charles Olson said in capital letters. In this sense art is "conservative" in that word's root use: Art conserves and condenses the most delicate and the strongest of life's energies in a form where those energies become available to any passing stranger.

So instead of going home, Janette and her friend drove the two lanes northeast across the High Plains and off the Caprock to the rolling gullied country that spreads out around the Red River and its Salt Fork. The man they went to visit—his name was (and is) George. A wild, wise, strange, paradoxical, and quietly great man whom most people will never hear of, but who would make all the difference in Janette's life. Through Janette, I and others would meet him, and George would make all the difference in our lives too—especially mine. To this day I call him my Teacher, and I owe much that I've become to him. But that is another story.

This story—is merely to note that so much was changed in so many lives (George's life as well as ours) because two young women had the impulse to see a movie and, more important, because they had to meet that movie more than halfway. The movie couldn't come to them. Couldn't even come to their city, much less into their homes. However they heard about that screening in a city 120-ish miles away, they had to meet the desire that creates art with an intense desire of their own; and it was their enacted desire that opened them to the possibilities of that work of art—opened them to art as no course of instruction ever could. And while the same thing might happen if they'd rented a video or had found the film on one of a hundred cable channels (neither of which was possible for them), the very convenience of these new technologies lessens the need of intensity in the seeker.

Which is a considerable danger. I cherish my video collection, and I love coming upon something unexpected as I zap through a hundred channels, but it is rarely recognized that these luxuries, like all luxuries, place a greater demand upon the seeker. We forget that convenience is a kind of confinement. We forget that to bring it all into our homes (instead of going out to meet it) is often to trap ourselves and put ourselves out of the reach of change. It is so much harder to release ourselves from the confinement of our habits if we needn't move from the setting of that confinement. The convenience undermines the art: for art's purpose is precisely to break through our confinements.

Now I own virtually every film Charlie Chaplin and Buster Keaton ever made, and that collection is among the last things I'd hock. Yet I can't avoid the knowledge that something of the mystique and romance of those films has been drained by my easy ownership. For I remember the winter of 1971, in Boston, when Chaplin (still alive) released fresh prints of all his major works for the first time since their creation. At that time you could be, as I was, a film aficionado, hungry for the art; and you could have spent most of your life in New York City, as I had, where more great films were screened than anywhere else in the world—and you could still never have seen, as I had never seen, *City Lights* or *Modern Times* or *The Kid* or *The Gold Rush*—or if you had seen them, rarely was the print decent or even complete. So the re-release of fresh prints of Chaplin's complete work at a real theater, one per week for weeks and weeks—the news went like a shock wave through those to whom such things mattered.

They played at a small theater in Brookline at the edge of Boston. I waited at a trolley station in the freezing New England cold, took the chilly trolley, and faced the prospect that when the film was done I might or might not be in time to catch the last trolley home—might, and sometimes did, have to walk an hour and more in twenty- and ten-degree weather. I, like the others in that theater, didn't

care. And because there was no way to predict when or even whether Chaplin would release these movies again, and there was as yet not even the dream that one might own these films, some of us would return to see our favorites two and three nights running all that winter.

In that setting, having to devote the evenings of the better part of two months to go to the films, putting much else aside, and braving the cold—the flaws of Chaplin's work didn't much matter. His sentimentality, his descents into mawkishness, his worship of the creature, the Little Tramp, that he'd created and become—who cared? All that mattered was the enchantment of his grace and the stark, elemental nature of a comedy that always stepped over the edge of tragedy. For we had to leave our confinements and even our social lives, had to come to Chaplin more than halfway, through the cold, and had to open ourselves to absorb his art, for it might be the only chance we'd get. Critiques were beside the point—they might be valuable in other contexts, but not after you'd missed the last trolley and were walking home on freezing feet, feeling more than a little Chaplinesque yourself, the films having opened you to the precarious beauties of a wintry city at night.

Once a fresh coat of snow had fallen during the movie. I could have caught the trolley but opted to walk in the almost unmarked whiteness. I was wearing thick galoshes over my shoes, and at the steps of my apartment building, fumbling with cold-numbed fingers for my keys, I looked back and it seemed that my galoshes tracks might be those of Charlie's oversized boots and that invisibly the Tramp had walked me home.

Now with all this art at our fingertips we get lazy and forget what art is. We can purchase it, or zap it to us with a click. It gives us the illusion of possessing that which we can never truly possess without going a distance to meet it—an inner distance or an enacted distance, it doesn't matter; Amarillo to Lubbock to the Salt Fork of the Red River, or a trolley ride in Brookline—it doesn't matter; but a distance must be traversed. For the video or the book of poems on the shelf is really very far away. It exists only to beckon us on a journey. And it can accompany us only as far as we've gone to meet it.

Across the road from the Cotton Club,
Lubbock, Texas, 1985

A TRAILER BY THE RIVER

Part I

SOMEWHERE in the canyons of Texas is a river, and a trailer alongside it. This is wind country, sky country, where the land is dry and trees are few and far between. A country of sweet air and suddenly violent storms that sweep in as though intent upon *you* personally. A world of armadas of bright high clouds, brilliant sunsets, starry nights. And dawn, and just before dusk, the beige ground glows golden and rose as though lit from within. You hear coyotes in the dark. Days, you see roadrunners, wild turkeys, quail, hawks, owls, the occasional heron. Horses. Turtles. Tarantulas. White, almost translucent scorpions. Cattle. Deer. When there's a storm the river runs hard; mostly, it's shallow, swift and gentle by turns, and clear. Always, in the soft sands by its shore, the animals leave tracks. You could mistake it for a peaceful place. It's not. Tornados and lightning always threaten. And there are voices on the wind.

People don't often find the trailer unless taken there by one who knows the way. No stranger who *tries* to find it ever does, though occasionally someone stumbles upon it by chance, as I did long ago. The man who lives in the trailer doesn't believe in "chance," so those who come by that means are always welcome. (Merlin told Arthur, "Do not dishonor your feast by ignoring what comes to it.")

I'll call that man George. He's twenty-odd years older than I, and twenty-odd years is how long I've known him, so when we met he was roughly my age as I write this—fifty. He laughs when he sees you, hugs you with what is still a fantastic strength, and looks into you with the most intense eyes I have ever seen. George doesn't tolerate small talk—not with anyone he respects. No matter how you came, no matter how you are, you start talking ideas. George radiates a sense that ideas are living things, wild animals to be trailed and chased; sometimes to be killed and eaten; often simply to be watched in their natural habitat, where, if we are still enough, they will come to investigate *us*, rather than the other way round. Every few months I drive to that place. Even when I don't call ahead, he seems to know I'm coming. "I see you've got your notebook," he says. "Ever get the quotes wrong?" "Never—almost." "You sure?" "Try me." I read a few old pages at random back to him and he gives me that small smile that says he's ever so slightly impressed. I say, "You'll see. I'll write a book about you one of these days." "You can't write about a man like me." (I can't be sure if he means that, or if it's a challenge, or both.)

George's definitions of some basic words can't be found in the dictionary—for instance, the distinction he makes between "thinking" and "thought." "Thinking is compromise. Thought is pure. Thinking is reaction—listing, figuring, cataloguing. Thought is a moment of consciousness. When an artist has lost himself in his art, and nothing exists outside of that circle of energy, then he or she is in *thought*. A poor artist wants to *finish* a thing, make it perfect; a great artist leaves some things in refrain."

"In refrain?"

"That moment of expecting the next verse, the next word. Things left in refrain are things left in motion, rebels on the move. In viewing a work of art, or a deed of the day, it is the bold stroke that gives hope. Communications in this heightened energy are housed in symbols: parables of silence . . . ointments for the afflicted . . . art with honesty, that comforts the loneliness of those held captive . . . symbols that cannot lie. A writer, in an exceptional work, will have painted his trail of destiny

between the lines, not in the linage. It's the difference between art on display and art as a way of life. A creative effort must never be wasted to put a smile on the face of the lazy."

We are far from the coffeehouses of the cities. When I was young, haunting those joints, I didn't imagine that some of the most useful talk about art that I would ever hear would occur in a Texas canyon, miles from even a small town, in a trailer by a river. I didn't imagine the variety of places in which truth could live and find a voice.

George says, "You're a messenger, I'm a messenger, but we too *need* messengers. We are all dependent upon messengers. If you miss the messenger, you're just putting in your time during this span. You call me a teacher. I work with, and I've always worked with, one type of person—a person who seeks the unexpected. People I admire are people who live by the code of the unexpected. I give credit to that nuclei of what you'd call 'normal people' as the backbone of the country, but I work with warriors who seek and appreciate the unexpected and pay the price—'cause they're the only ones who will ever be *reached* by the messengers. The messenger *appears*. It isn't, 'You go to the messenger.' The messenger shows up. But you qualify for the appearance by being strong enough to face the unexpected—and the appearance of the messenger is goddamned unexpected. How we are able to recognize a messenger depends on how well informed we are about how to handle fear, and how to handle time."

He pauses, then says, "Let's walk by the river."

My experience of such "sessions," as we call them, is that I leave with new nuances clinging to words like "fear," "messenger," "time." After talking with George, some words carry more freight the next time I use them.

The river is quiet. The sun is behind a thundercloud and the light of the land is subdued. I say, "Fear? Time?"

"Understanding time is understanding fear."

We had often spoken of how crucial it is to take charge of one's own time—and that this was especially true for what George calls "students" or "seekers." (Seekers after what? Oh . . . you know.) But I had never heard this equation of fear with time.

"You can learn about time in dreams," George says. "There is a time acceleration in the dream. You wake up and understand, 'Gee, time is not necessarily the same in two places in the same environment.' So when I go into the dream state in daytime, I can go at a great pace without fear. In a deliberately quiet time, you're able to comprehend at an amazing pace."

"I know that, George, but I don't know why it is."

"When you have a moment with yourself you have a moment with all of mankind. And with all of time. Michael, anything which is creative is a joint venture: it's between you and the rhythm of time. When you try to force time, you'll never know how good the work *could* have been. It's not a question of the abundance of time, it's the quality of time. The idea is not to look for days, or hours, or to wait for a vacation, but to go for moments. That's all you need, because in a deliberately quiet time you're able to comprehend at an amazing pace without fear. Time is consciousness. Consciousness does not recognize light or dark, nor fall nor spring. Just the way the dream does not recognize boundaries."

"But time and fear?" I ask.

"We live in a world of distraction. People are sick of distractions, but they're afraid to leave them. *Distractions are not time.* Distraction is just repetition."

"When I was still a poet," I tell him, "I wrote a line: Don't mistake repetition for time."

"You were having a good day," George says. "When you leave repetition and step into the quiet, you step into time. When you step into quiet you step into *yourself*—it's a harrowing experience. That's where the fear is. *The most disruptive thing you can do in the world today is to create a quiet moment.* To move into consciousness there has to be the disruption of the external, and the greatest disruption is quiet.

"Any act of consciousness, any entry into consciousness, is the result of something stopped. A pause. *If* you stop purposefully for a flicker of time, you are in consciousness. Then you're no longer in the world you were moving in. You're in the moment, and time moves at a different rate when you're in the moment—differently than it moves in the mechanical, in clock time. You learn to measure time not by the clock but by the amount of intake. So that your experience in seconds can equal an experience in days in mechanical time.

"And you only need a reasonable amount of experiences of that extraordinary energy, no matter what the subject is or what the experience is, for you to realize: 'During that moment I had no need to respond to any stimulation or provocation in the mechanical state.' Now you build on that moment. As you begin to sense the exaltation that you feel when you have purposefully stopped a mechanical action, you begin to see that there are two worlds, and that you can occupy them simultaneously. To escape once, is to know you can escape again—as long as the privilege of absence is not abused. There is no need to forsake responsibilities as a prerequisite to a time search—only to rise to required levels of management of

self. But you don't get a quiet moment free. The price you pay, the price of admission, is overwhelming the obstacle— working through the fear, working through distraction, leaving the expected."

An owl glided by looking for small creatures to eat. We watched it quietly.

Part II

A storm's come up. Wind gusts shake the trailer. When there's a lull, we hear the swift waters of the river. In these barren West Texas plains I always wonder where the birds and critters wait out such weather. The thunder rumbles for hours sometimes. People who don't know this country can't believe that, but it's true. Lightning flashes and flashes. Somewhere in this great expanse, funnel clouds swoop from the thunderheads and travel the ground. Most are never seen and cause no harm, but now and then one will flatten a town.

George and I drink hot tea—his herbal, mine caffeine. (George gets his caffeine from the Diet Pepsis that fill the fridge.) He has two TVs tuned to two ballgames. The sound is off. It takes a life-or-death emergency for George to miss his games—that, or lightning hitting the generator. But lightning usually leaves George alone. *[Note, 2009: Lightning left George alone until about four years ago, when, at his house in the Panhandle, it struck through the wall and hit close to his arm; the house caught fire and burned to the ground while he and the others under his roof barely escaped.]*

Some kinds of lightning, anyway. In his mid-sixties cancer visited George. The doctors said he had only months to live. Seven or eight years later, cancer's still a visitor with an honored if problematic place at the table. George talks of managing, rather than curing, his illness. He's employed every treatment—traditional and holistic, proved and unproved. But to this very unqualified observer, George has survived this long because of what he *thinks* about disease.

We often speak of it. The terminology, as always, is George's invention. He uses two terms that took me some time to grasp: "Old Memory" and "New Memory." "New Memory is a pause," he says. "Old Memory is a continuation." Old Memory is "body memory," genetic memory. It's what you're born with, and then it's conditioned, in turn, by the environment. New Memory is when you add an element that is beyond your programming—beyond what you were born with.

George believes that the body, like the planet itself, *is* memory: Both consist of cells and molecules *remembering themselves* from moment to moment as they re-create themselves. In short: Cells remembering themselves *in order* to re-create themselves. Memory, in his vision, is the glue that holds our physical existence in

place. So if you *really* go beyond your programming, even only for moments, you can influence basic structures on the material plane, including your body. You can change the rules of the game.

George has been badly damaged by his disease. There've been no miracles; the cancer's still there. But so is George. And if he says that his theories of Old and New Memory are how he's stayed alive, I believe him. I don't know how long he can do it, but nobody lives forever. *[Note, thirteen years later: He still has cancer, is very frail, but still alive.]*

As the rain pounds the trailer, he explains: "What I've discovered has been discovered by others in ancient times *and* our time. But there's an edge there that's still waiting to be discovered; it will bring a simplification, and take these practices out of the esoteric into very simple basic understanding. I'll try to explain again:

"When the mind usurps the genetic communication, time is stopped. You've shifted masters. You may still not be in control of your body, but you have a say. You're unable to alter the *inventory* of parts, but you're able to influence the *interaction* of the parts. The body does not respond to a lie, but it does respond to the truth. The individual's only course of study is within himself. There are no two identical styles, no two identical ways. No one can speak for any other person when it comes to entry into consciousness—and entry into consciousness is entry into New Memory."

A lot of tall men are running around both TVs, often jumping up and down, paying excessive attention to a large ball. George's eyes never leave the games as he speaks:

"The body does not belong to you. The body came into this identity as a result of millions of years of previous activity, previous thinking. Upon awakening in this life, you are faced with a body contaminated with millions of years of disease and negative thought. You're gonna have to compete with all that. You gotta be careful, 'cause the body's a good liar. It tells you, 'I'm okay,' while it has a disease it doesn't even know about because it picked it up millions of years ago. In order to challenge the memory in the body—which I call Body Memory or Old Memory, memory which gives you over to the lie—you set up New Memory, which works in coordination of the mind, over which you have some control.

"To compete with genetic intelligence [Old Memory] you were given, in the creation process, an opportunity to make your statement. You do this through developing a mind which could alleviate the lie in the body. This is not to disrespect the body. The body is trapped in its own memory, but the mind is not trapped. It also has the memory you feed into it [New Memory], which can be of a positive, exploratory, investigative nature.

This can alleviate the handicaps the body came into this world with. New Memory is for the purpose of complementing one's existence—of alleviating the discomfort *inherent* in the body that it didn't ask for and has no way of getting rid of without outside help."

The soundless jumping up and down on TV gets even more frenetic, and George gives this his whole attention. I'm grateful for the break. I'm a good note-taker, but I've been wondering if I'd be able to read my writing. I listen to the rain and the wind, and feel the constant thunder vibrate gently through every part of me that touches the sofa.

"The environment's not stable," George goes on. "That's what gets you in trouble, but that's also what can save you. I *believe* in traditional treatment—but why not give it all the help you can? There's no way of knowing just *what's* been helping in what proportions, but the doctors gave me up a long time ago, if you'll recall.

"I've learned a thing or two about the body: You don't have to directly affect it. You have to *entertain the idea* that there is a solution for this. You don't have to know the solution. Somewhere in the quiet moment it will be supplied. You just have to address it."

On the TV, several tall men are arguing with a short man in a striped shirt about the big ball.

"We mustn't ignore the possibility," George says, "that the DNA, on occasion, may bear false witness. The sanctioned theories claim that in evolution, DNA preceded the creation of the cell. That doesn't make sense. DNA *is* memory—coded memory, contained in molecular form. That's what it does; it passes on codes, which are memories."

"Wait up," I say. "You're saying that if DNA is just coded memory, then first it had to have something to remember? So the scientists have put DNA in the wrong place in evolution?"

"You *have* been listening," George laughs, "not just scribbling. The DNA blueprint, logically, could only have been based on existing information. DNA developed in the cell only after countless exposures to certain patterns of behavior, patterns that were sympathetic to survival in the face of adversity. At some point during all the repetitions of adversity, the cell finally noted the experience and logged it—logged what it remembered. Logging the memory of the experience represented the first genetic intelligence. That intelligence, once intact, elevated the cell to a higher stage.

"Think of the adversity! Think of what the cell, and then the DNA, had to go through to survive. That's why DNA, or body-memory, is so powerful—it had to come through difficult times, so it's justly defensive. It's in no mood to contemplate adjustment or change. That's why the human species resents change so much. A human being has to get up a full

head of steam to even consider change, and a *major* head of steam to cause change.

"The progress of disease runs from body-memory through the brain. The origin of negative emotion starts in the brain. When the two energies are mixed—disease in memory and negative emotion in the Now—then the chemistry can activate disease. Genes can have the earmark of disease, but disease can remain no more than earmarks if negative emotion doesn't spark a war of cells. But it's tough to pull this off with the memory deck stacked against you. And we have an environment that's 99 percent fear, so you can't blame anybody for negative emotions. So we need help. And dependable help can only come from one place: *thought*, directed at the cells, at the DNA. Replacing Old Memory with New Memory. Because the DNA's job is to log memory, I believe the DNA responds. Not 100 percent, but just enough to change the equation."

He's looking at me now, even though the tall men are still jumping up and down with the big ball. The trailer's rocking a little in the wind.

"We underrate the force of our consciousness, we undervalue it. We only sense the need when we get into a pickle, find out we're dying, and have to suddenly master all the forces we can."

"Well, George—either they'll have proved you right in fifty years . . . or not."

"Then we'll know that time is either our ally or our enemy."

Part III

In this raw West Texas country, there are nights when the wind sweeps down like something out of the Bible. The sky's clarity is almost painful, the starlight pierces you, and the land trembles beneath the gusts almost like a lover—as though only the most unrelenting wind could be a fit companion to these untamed expanses, these distances that seem to hide nothing until you get close and realize there are mysteries everywhere, on every dry riverbed, in every arroyo. Not far from George's trailer, for instance, someone found a conquistador's sword. We searched the books for records of an ancient expedition that had come this way. Couldn't find one. You feel something hidden yet present, secret yet insistent, calling incessantly through the wind.

I was searching through another kind of book this windy night. George had turned in. I'd intended to bed down on the couch. The trailer was sheltered from the wind's full force by a bluff, or it would have been crumpled like a beer can. But still the trailer shook, and the wind *did* howl. (I thought "howling wind" was a cliché 'til I got to West Texas, but there's no other word for that sound.) The wind howled, and screeched, and moaned, and I read.

The book is called *Light Years*, but you won't find it in any store. Every once in a while, George writes a book. He prints ninety-nine copies (that seems to be his favorite number), gives a few to selected friends, and lets the rest pile up here and there. Maybe strangers will find them one day, by chance or design, the way we all came across each other in the first place. He published a few paperbacks under other names long ago, but now he prefers to publish in this secretive, private way, as though to remind us what books are really meant for: that they're like messages in bottles, written by people struggling to survive—messages making their way over uncertain waters to who knows where.

Light Years is a story about an angel, a bear, an eagle, and a few people, interspersed with transcripts of conversations that George has had with some of us—Spider, Cathy, Semira, me. I'd read it many times. Being troubled by love yet again (for I am a very slow learner), I was searching out some particularly troubling passages. "Love is a living organism," George had written. I thought: If that is true, no wonder love has such power—being an organism and not (as we perhaps mistakenly perceive) a feeling, it exists on its own terms and not on ours. That would explain a lot. George went on: "It is the only organism tenured for the length of the universe, and it is always present before the perfect cell is woken to populate a chosen habitat." I thought: He makes love sound like a great, invisible, wild animal that appears in different guises everywhere—or is that just how I'm reading this? I read on: "But love—even in its most powerful state—is mankind's most fragile energy. It is the single most distinct example of oscillating polarities."

What in the hell does that mean? The wind seemed to underscore my question. He wrote of how "in a single second" love could oscillate between its widest and narrowest extremes, "which leaves one wrestling with a phenomenon endowed with chilling, contradictory dimensions." He said that this oscillation, beyond our control (for it's an organism, a creature that we encounter and become, not a feeling we have or own) can "drive the individual . . . to a state of madness that walks him/her along the edge of a cliff. It's a form of love/terror that penetrates deep into the psyche."

Penetrates *in*, rather than coming *out* from within. No wonder that to be in love can feel like such an invasion. The ancient Greeks spoke of this when they envisioned love not as a feeling but as an archer piercing you with arrows.

"The deeper the love," George goes on, "the deeper the converging danger. Conversely, the deeper the daring into the danger, the greater the potential enrichment."

Well, *that* much I understood.

"Is there ever enrichment without danger?" George continued. "Not in this dimension; danger is essential to complete the full cycle. But often, that's not as bad as the obscurities of a compromise that would keep one on the edge [of discovery]. When you tumble [off the edge, into love], you're tumbling into no less than a fresh choice-of-identity."

A fresh choice of identity? I'm having a tough enough time with the identity I'm used to. But love opens up the possibility of an unexpected, unpredictable identity—not only the stranger without, but the stranger within . . .

Now I was reading a passage about lovers whom fate has separated—how sometimes they seek a resolution, a meeting, trying to defy their fate. "Contemplating a resolution to the separation could create a time/slip in the cosmic . . ."

A *what*?

"A distraction that could thrust the existing alignment of the silent tenure of the loves out of sync. Out of sync is out of peace, and [then] love is often better left alone. Because it exists only when you give identity to it yourself. And if you're not careful, and let it lead you, you can end up a *whole* different person. Bye-bye to whoever you were before."

I nodded off for a few minutes. Some dream, or something in the wind, woke me suddenly. I got my notebooks out of my duffel and hunted for what he'd told me once about love and artists.

An artist is a person driven to the edge over and over and over. Every stroke of the brush may be one stroke too many. Every word may be one word too many. No artist can be saved from that. There's no refuge from that. But sometimes artists will look for refuge in love, and thus draw people to them who have been seduced into trying to give the impossible. The price of impossibility is the loss of one's identity. Bad luck all around.

At the instances when we are involved in the wrong use of time, the time-pirates are at work. Part of the wrong use of time is to pursue a path in which you are seeking to fathom out and bring to understanding a complexity which defends itself against understanding. That's often an excuse for a relationship.

The bad luck goes both ways. Within the bailiwick of the individuality of the artist, are drawn people who have complex problems. It's a horrible thing to say, but the animal of the artist has some kind of antenna that attracts people who are passing through intense psychic/spiritual difficulty. These people are convinced that their psyche's experience is a springboard to the domicile of the artist. They're wrong, but their inner state demands a great deal of notice.

Their inner state tries to compete with the inner life of the artist. But a so-called normal person cannot create sufficient distraction to compete with the life, the thought, of the artist, so they have to cre-ate a complexity that puts them in competition with the artist—and this often puts them in a bizarre condition. They present a Scarlett O'Hara countenance that simply is omnipresent. But there's no victim. The artist feeds on the complexity—and the 'guest,' as I call it, feeds on the artist. But it's make-believe. You can't give validity to make-believe, but you can play with it—recognizing it for what it is. But if you try to bring it to conclusion, like 'saving the relationship,' you go into madness. As I said, part of the wrong use of time is to try to bring a paradox, which defends itself against conclusion, to conclusion. That is self-indulgent.

People in relationships with artists often pick up the gestures intended for the art along with those intended for the lover, and can't distinguish between the two— and usually neither can the artist, until it's too late. These are all traits that make relationships with artists difficult. Because these two people come from different countries of the heart—neither better or worse than the other, but different. So, when together, neither party is ever really themselves except by coincidence. And it's in the moments of coincidence that some things feel decided. But the momentum takes you past that, and you move back into doubt.

I'd asked, "What about *two* artists?" He'd said, "That's like asking what about two storms, two earthquakes, two wars, two anarchists? Two artists? Can each artist give the other the freedom they demand and require for themselves?"

I hadn't tried to answer that.

Then, with a sudden intensity, he'd said: "Truth is a state of pursuit rather than arrival. When you get to a point of arrival, you run the risk of contamination at that point. You really need to stay on the move."

I put my notebooks aside. I guess I nodded off again.

George got up around dawn. The wind had died down. I hadn't even noticed. He smiled at me, said, "Don't you ever sleep?" "I nap occasionally. The dark is too inviting for sleep." "Well, you're only fifty—still a kid." "Someday," I said, "maybe you'll write a book with some rules to live by 'stead of things that just make us ask more questions."

I'll never forget the laughter in his eyes when he said:

"You know the rules: No rules!"

Signs and reflections, Molly's, somewhere in
America, 1986

HOMAGE TO A SORCERER

A SORCERER DIED not long ago. Liver cancer, they said, but the details are vague. Also vague is why it took so long for word to get out. There are strange rumors. No matter. All this is as it should be for a sorcerer. Strangest of all, in a way, were the obituaries of the media heavies, a blurry photo in the *New York Times*, tributes that were respectful in a distant and baffled sort of way. It's doubtful the *New York Times* ever before felt compelled to pay homage to a sorcerer. But that was Carlos Castaneda's mojo. Many who professed not to take him seriously nevertheless read him, remembered, and were haunted. Let them wonder whether he was born in 1931, as he said, or in 1925, as some immigration records said. Let them wonder whether he was Peruvian or Mexican. Wonder, even in such minor matters, will be good for them.

Carlos Castaneda has died. There aren't many to bear witness to or for him, because he didn't allow many witnesses. One met him by invitation, usually, and even that was more fluke than not. Those invited were of all sorts. I happened to be

one, for reasons that weren't clear (to me) and probably aren't important. Perhaps I was called to be a witness?

About twelve years ago a friend who worked in a bookstore in Santa Monica called: Carlos Castaneda was giving a talk in the cellar of the store (it *would* be in the cellar!), by invitation only, would I like to come? Who knew it was really him, I said? My caller, whom I had reason to trust, said, "It's Carlos, all right."

He was a small man. Impossible to tell his age. Didn't look much over forty, but his eyes were older, smiling eyes but deepened by a vague sense of grief. He laughed readily, didn't insist that we take him seriously, stood before us in an attitude of welcome. He wanted us to ask him questions. He said there was something he'd forgotten, and that sometimes he came out of his seclusion and talked to strangers hoping that a question would spark the memory of this forgotten thing. He didn't say this sadly. He was frank and matter-of-fact. That night nobody asked the question he was seeking, but every question brought forth a story of Don Juan, and every story had laughter in it.

As in his books, when Castaneda spoke of Don Juan the old Yaqui wizard was near and dangerous, inviting us to adventure. It was Castaneda's laughter, more than his skills as a storyteller, that convinced me of his sincerity and authenticity. He talked for free, had nothing to gain from us, spoke without artifice. People rarely laugh when they lie. At least, in my experience, they don't laugh sweetly. And there was an irresistible sweetness to this man. He described the most fantastic experiences as though they were *almost* jokes, but the joke was on him. I had the impression of a desperate man, but a man who knew how to live with desperation in ways that made it something else. He'd transformed his desperation, as a sorcerer must, into a search. (Was I seeing in him the man I would like to be, who, though fated to desperation, could be desperate in a wise and engaging and gentle way? Perhaps.) He was, at the same time, vulnerable and invulnerable: vulnerable in that he seemed a little lost; invulnerable in that he was on his path, a path of heart. If he was lost it was because that path had led him to unknown and unexpected territory. It would have been easier for him to face physical danger than to face that there was something important about Don Juan he'd forgotten. But he was facing it, and in public. More than magic tricks and the Sorcerer's Way, Don Juan had taught him to be brave. When

he finished speaking, and the twenty or so people in that cellar milled around, he greeted a couple of old friends. I didn't want to intrude, didn't introduce myself, wouldn't have known what to say anyway. So, in effect, I met him but he didn't meet me.

Then, about three years ago, another friend called. Would I like to go to lunch with Carlos Castaneda? Why I received this invitation I was never told. It turned out that there were four of us and Carlos. We met at the Pacific Dining Car, one of the best steakhouses on the West Coast. (Carlos picked up the check.) He had changed, and so had I. We had both lived a lot further into our very different desperations, and carried them with more assurance. He was much thinner, older—obviously ill. Whereas in the bookstore's cellar he had dressed casually, this day he was decked out in an elegant suit. But for all his fragility he seemed much livelier, happier, and even funnier. The food was very fine, but really we lunched on laughter. Even his saddest stories of Don Juan were, again, like jokes; but this time the joke wasn't on Carlos, wasn't on us—the joke was between the wizard and God, and a splendid joke it was.

I won't repeat those stories. I wasn't there to record them. They were his to tell or not. Best that anything he chose not to write should die with him.

But two moments caused not laughter

but silence. A woman at the table said she loved her job, her husband, and her child, but still she felt a lack—it was that she had no spiritual life. How could she achieve a spiritual life?

Answering this woman, Carlos didn't change the lightness or generosity of his manner; yet a steely thing came into his voice, a tone that made his words pierce all of us. He said that when she got home at night she should sit in her chair and remember that her child, her husband, everyone she loved, and she herself, were going to die—and they would die in no particular order, unpredictably. "Remember this every night, and you'll soon have a spiritual life."

Notice that he didn't tell her what sort of spiritual life to have, much less whether it should agree with his. He didn't suggest she read his books more carefully, or attend the movement classes he'd begun to teach. He gave her a practical instruction, something she could accomplish within the parameters of her life, and then assured her that this would set her on her own spiritual path, whatever that might turn out to be. This is the mark of a true Teacher.

Later in the conversation this woman asked how she could discipline herself to follow his advice, deeply follow it, so that it wouldn't be just an exercise. Carlos said:

"You give yourself a *command*."

On the page there's no duplicating how he said it. He spoke quietly, but it was as though he'd suddenly jammed a knife into the tabletop.

"What's that mean?" one of us asked.

"It means you give yourself a *command*." And that was that.

A command is not a promise. A command is not "trying." A command is something that must be obeyed. His tone invoked something deeper than the idea of mere will. His was a call to action. He wasn't talking about mulling or meditating or analyzing or wishing. To step on the path you *step on the path*. There is no substitute for that. After a nine-months–pregnant pause, the conversation took flight again. He told of a party at which a very tall and handsome Native American was saying, with great solemnity, that *he* was Carlos Castaneda, and revealing all sorts of Don Juan's "secrets." Did Carlos disabuse him of that fantasy?

"No!" he laughed. "He looked the way people expect Carlos Castaneda to look! Not some little round-faced brown man. And he was having such a good time! Why ruin it? Let *him* be Carlos for an evening!"

About a year later the woman who'd asked those questions at our lunch sent me a pamphlet that Carlos had printed privately. He'd requested she send it on to me. One passage goes:

Sorcerers understand discipline as the capacity to face with serenity odds that are not included in our expectations. For them, discipline is a volitional act that enables them to intake anything that comes their way without regrets or expectations. For sorcerers, discipline is an art: the art of facing infinity without flinching, not because they are filled with toughness, but because they are filled with awe. . . . Discipline is the art of feeling awe.

Any manifestation of the universe, any way in which it behaves toward us, isn't merely about *us*, isn't merely psychological, but is a movement of the universe, and as such what happens to us, no matter what it is, connects us to everything, and in that connection what can be felt but awe? "A live world," he wrote, "is in constant flux. It moves; it changes; it reverses itself." We try to defend ourselves against that, but we cannot. The only freeing response is awe.

When I saw him years ago in that cellar, an unhappier man than the dying man at lunch, I wrote: His presence was an admission that every truth is fragile, that every knowledge must be learned over and over again, every night, that we grow not in a straight line but in ascending and descending and tilting circles, and that what gives us power one year robs us of power the next, for nothing is settled, ever, for anyone.

Now I would add: What makes this bearable is awe.

Go well, Don Carlos.

Stranded shoes, downtown Austin, Texas, 1986

Tree and rear view, near Hunt, Texas, 1986

Near the Troubadour in West Hollywood—a stone's easy throw (if you could find a stone) from a sign announcing the boundary of Beverly Hills—Butch Hancock peered into a vending machine to take a closer look at a headline in the *San Fernando Valley Daily News*. Something about more suffering in Afghanistan. Then he noticed, above the newspaper's logo, a little photo of Joe Ely, Jimmie Dale Gilmore, and Butch himself. "Hey," he called to the other two, "that's us!"

What juxtaposition could be more apt? In this catastrophic time, where disasters ricochet off each other from country to country, there are the Flatlanders floating above the frantic headlines, singing irrepressibly joyful and generous songs that convince precisely because they incorporate an almost cosmic vision of pain: "The more you fear the kiss of death the more she licks her lips . . ." "Yesterday was judgment day—how'd you do? . . . Did you lay down in heaven, did you wake up in hell? I bet you never guessed it would be so hard to tell."

The Flatlanders are showing up everywhere all of a sudden. On Letterman. On the Don Imus show. On Larry King— where Imus issued his challenge to top-market radio stations to play their album. On the cover of *No Depression*, and even the cover of an entertainment supplement in the *San Fernando Valley Daily News*. Some would say this hoopla is long overdue, but I can guess what the Flatlanders would say: "You can tell me this is dreamin' or it's all in my head / You can tell me that I'm dyin' or I'm already dead / But it feels so good I might be right where I belong."

I remember listening to the first Flatlanders recording on a reel-to-reel in the living room of that house we all shared on 14th Street in Lubbock. That was January of '73. Fresh out of New York City, I'd never heard such music: earthy yet ethereal, sweet but savvy, fatalistic yet hopeful . . . and without a prayer in the world of being played on any radio station in our Broken Promise Land. After we listened to the tape, Butch took out his guitar and played his newest song . . .

he said he didn't write it, not exactly . . .
he'd heard it in a dream . . . and, in
Butch's dream, Jimmie was singing it:
"If you were a bluebird . . . if I was a highway . . ." I learned something crucial that
evening on 14th Street: Culture has no
center. Not New York, not Los Angeles,
not anywhere. The shifting center of a
culture, on any day or night, is where its
art is most alive—whether the audience is
a few friends in a living room or thousands of strangers in a stadium, a movie
that millions see or a poem written on a
napkin in a diner. That night in '73, there
wasn't any better place in America to hear
music than that house on a low-rent
street in Lubbock, Texas.

We were as silly as any wild bunch in
their mid-twenties, but credit us with this:
Our tribe of friends had no doubt of the
worth of what we experienced when we
heard it expressed in the music of these
songsters. I don't know if any of us has
ever thanked them, so I'll do that now:
Butch, Jimmie, Joe—and Jo Carol Pierce,
Terry Allen, David Halley—you've made
music of the lives we lived together, our
loves and adventures and disasters, and
we discovered many of our meanings and
purposes in your songs. Others have experienced the same since, listening to your
music, and that's wonderful . . . but it's a
more personal wonder for your friends.
What we lived is what you made music
of. That you could create such music out

of our shared lives made our lives themselves musical. "Thank you" ain't enough,
it never is, but: Thank you.

Now we're all just high or low of sixty,
but what you Flatlanders sing is something most of "the 14th Street tribe"
could say still: "My wildest dreams grow
wilder every day." From this perch on the
far side of middle age, that seems to me
our best and most difficult achievement.
"Remember when we used to be here
now / Livin' in the moment," the Flatlanders sing. ("Be here now" was a Zen
phrase we overused on 14th Street until
it became a joke—but a sincere joke.)
"The wind knows how we used to be
here now / It circles to remind us all . . .
Now it's now again."

It always is. And, come to think of it,
that's been the message at the heart of
every Flatlander song.

Well . . . as Butch, Jimmie, and Joe told
me their recent adventures in the band
bus parked across from the Troubadour
on Santa Monica Boulevard, all sorts of
associations awoke in the night. Did they
realize that this stretch of Santa Monica
Boulevard is also the final length of old
Route 66? Yep, Santa Monica Boulevard in
L.A. is Route 66! And 1,200 miles east,
just off old 66, thirty-ish years ago, we
were in Clarendon, Texas, working for
George, building a theater and two bars,
and we put on a play about Jesus, of all
people. (I wrote, codirected, and played

the part of Pilate. Butch shot the backdrop slides. Joe ran the lights.) And just across the street from the band bus, at the Beverly Hills Motel on the corner of Santa Monica and Doheny, I interviewed Carolyn Cassady, wife of Neal Cassady and sometime lover of Jack Kerouac. *On the Road*—that book influenced our 14th Street tribe mightily. Carolyn said, "Do you know what their letters to me were full of? Dreams of finding a nice little house and a nice little job and settling down. That's not their legend, but I've got the letters to prove it." So *that's* what those adventurers were looking for on their famous journeys. I wasn't surprised. To borrow a baseball phrase: Haven't most of our relentless long-distance drives been our way of trying to steal home? And if home eventually becomes a place you must leave yet again, only to search for another . . . well, that's part of what "the road" is all about. And it's about a kind of endlessness that frightens and excites by turns. As the Flatlanders sing it: "Did you hear the riddle of a road without a middle or an end?"

Put on the old and the new Flatlanders albums and hit "Random." Listen to the time, and the timelessness, that spans the thirty years between them. The younger sound is astonishingly pure and a little distant; the older, gruff and companionable. The younger songs are a music of discovery. The older songs are about the price

of discovery, and about how discovery isn't enough—you've got to *do* something with what you discover, and that's an entirely different order of difficulty.

The music of the Flatlanders' youth is a music of longing. Their older (though newer) songs are a music of experience. Experience is the one thing in this world that you can't fake.

Not for long, at any rate.

Perhaps the Flatlanders are finally finding wider public acceptance because a youth-obsessed pop culture is hungry for voices of experience. Voices not jaded, not discouraged. Voices battered but enriched by all they've seen and done. Generous artists sharing their vitality at a time of life when vitality can be hard to come by. Troubadours who know the score and are still willing to dare the odds.

Such a dare can be a valuable and catchy thing. America is a circus of false flamboyance where many are desperate for a daring that counts. A daring not backed up by money, military, or law; a daring that stands on its own. The Flatlanders make a music of the dare.

And speaking of the dare . . . that magazine defiantly titled *No Depression* . . . I opened it to a piece about Lisa Mednick. Lately I'd been listening again to her 1994 *Artifacts of Love*, wondering what's become of that profound, fierce, haunted artist, and if she'd ever record again. So here she is in this magazine with a new album, *Semaphore*. As different as it can be from the Flatlanders' *Now Again*, but just as valuable. In this time of catastrophe I've found nothing more encouraging than the Flatlanders and Lisa making themselves heard again. We need them. Lisa sings "I'll be your storm today." That's the kind of storm that clears the air.

It's an evil, hard time. "Hope" is a word I use with caution if not trepidation. I don't look for hope but sometimes hope finds me. And it finds me deepest in people who've faced the odds and are still willing to sing the dare.

A RAP WITH CAROLYN CASSADY

NEAL CASSADY was the very pulse of what became known as "the Beat Generation," and from him, more than anyone, emanated the twentieth century's literary romance with America's highways—for Cassady was Jack Kerouac's Dean Moriarty, the restless, reckless soul and hero of *On the Road*. In fact, Cassady's way of living ignited the travels and mayhems of dozens of writers, both famous and forgotten. His stream-of-consciousness, hours-long cascades of conversation influenced the prose of Kerouac and the poetry of Allen Ginsberg. Cassady continued as a character in several of Kerouac's later novels; was featured in stories by Ken Kesey; and was portrayed in Tom Wolfe's *The Electric Kool-Aid Acid Test*. In fact, I doubt any other person shows up in as many books and poems of the twentieth century as Neal Cassady.

But the public image of Neal Cassady differs, to say the least, with how he was seen through the eyes of his wife, Carolyn. Lewis MacAdams, codirector of the documentary *What Happened to Kerouac?,*

introduced me to Carolyn Cassady. The taped conversation that follows was the result.

MICHAEL: Jack Kerouac, Neal Cassady, you—when you met, in the 1940s, before you knew you were "the Beat Generation," what were your concerns?

CAROLYN: These guys were all concerned about the same thing: getting a home, settling down, finances—all the trivia of living.

MICHAEL: Nobody thinks of you guys as being concerned with getting a home and settling down!

CAROLYN: I know! But I've got letters to prove it. Picket fences, station wagons—it was really their dream! Of course, they sort of invented the commune. That was their idea—we'd all live cozily together. Jack was always, as he said, looking for home. I have letters full of these *houses*! When he first saw John Chellon Holmes' house he wrote me this great big letter saying, "Oh, you'd love it," describing every inch of it. So that's really what the drive was, to get in a position to be *normal*. Settle down in a home and *then* do what you wanted to do.

They felt they could, or wanted to, have a fairly conventional home and still be free to be creative. *They* didn't think of themselves as beatniks. And hippies were such a horror to them— you know, Neal was *immaculate*. Gosh! You couldn't muss a hair on his head! "Kiss me goodbye—but don't mess the hair!" No hippie casualness about that sort of thing. Neal would take a bath for a couple of hours, until the water was just all gone and he was covered with scum and stuff, and then he would go take a shower to get that off. And he washed his feet and changed his socks three times a day. And it was terribly important to him to work. He worked all the time. One of his proudest things was he could always get a job. It didn't cramp his style at all.

That's where he got his self-respect. That, and his family life. And Jack admired this, and of course envied the fact that Neal could do this, could be a home provider and also do what he wanted. The big, *real* ideal was to be able to do both.

MICHAEL: What was "what he wanted"?

CAROLYN: Neal? Oh, to chase women. Or help some poor sad soul. Teach them the meaning of life. Jack, of course, wanted to write.

MICHAEL: What did you want to do?

CAROLYN: Be a wife. Support the man, or men. I wasn't crazy about being a mother—that was put upon me, as it were, although it seemed natural, something you had to do. But Jack and Neal also didn't cramp my style any. If I wanted to paint or do theater stuff, there it was.

MICHAEL: This is fascinating to me. Nobody talks about the settling down part. It's left out of the legend.

CAROLYN: Well, Jack didn't write about it.

MICHAEL: Given the way you felt and thought—about art, about sex, about the spiritual, the political—did you all feel you'd have anything to say to the house next door?

CAROLYN: What I see in writers I know now is a new kind of selfishness— they're concerned with what *they* want. Whereas Jack and Neal were very much concerned about being a *part* of humanity, among others, and helping others, even if they didn't agree with them. They'd laugh at the square neighbors and all, but they had compassion for them. Jack certainly wrote about most all people as wonderful *beings*, whoever they were. They both had that. They didn't feel cut off until they were criticized or attacked, which happened a lot later.

Neal's great, great frustration was in having no outlets for that *mind* he had—a lot of energy and ideas he would have liked to express. It was wonderful watching him write *The First Third* [Neal Casssady's only surviving prose]; he was *totally* concentrated. He'd struggle and work with words. And he loved *playing* with words. Most of the letters he wrote me from San Quentin [prison] were games at playing with words—he'd write three or four pages, every word starting with the same letter, but each one *meant* what he meant to say, too. But, of course, drugs destroyed all that possibility.

He always did two or three things at once. I used to get irritated talking to him while he was watching television *and* reading the newspaper. I'd say, "Um, could I have your attention," and he'd say, "I heard everything you said," and he'd repeat everything I'd said. I still didn't quite like that, but I had to admit it was quite a feat. What a mind! But what are you gonna *do* with it?

LEWIS: How come he and Kerouac fell away from each other?

CAROLYN: They never did! Never. It was just that Jack was an alcoholic and Neal was in jail. *[Set up by two narcs, Neal Casssady was sentenced to five years*

for possession of one reefer. He served two; then, as an ex-con, found it nearly impossible to get a decent job.] And then Neal became a drug addict. And they were, then, hell-bent for—death.

MICHAEL: You mean during the Merry Prankster period Tom Wolfe and Ken Kesey wrote of?

CAROLYN: Yes. Occasionally Neal would come home during that time, crying and ill, and I'd say, "Why don't you *stop* living like that?" He'd say, "Well, I can't. Because they all look at me and expect me to perform, and I don't know what else to do." Then he'd go back to exhibiting all the things he hated about himself the most. All that blabbering, bubbling and performing like a trained bear. He'd just totally given up any kind of attempt to be what he wanted to be. And he was so destroyed by drugs he couldn't sit down in one place and write, anyway.

MICHAEL: Kesey and Wolfe write about him strictly as a kind of performance artist, before there was such a thing.

CAROLYN: They never knew him before he got out of jail. They never knew anything else. And they tried to take care of him, Kesey did, give him approval and so on. And they didn't realize what he was feeling or what the change was or anything like that. They just thought he was wonderful. I'm sure Kesey admired his mind some, too, but it just so happened that in caring for him there was condescension, which Neal *had* to have been aware of. It's just sad to me that most of the publicity about him is during those five years—though I don't know, maybe it has value.

MICHAEL: It's remarkable, a very strange achievement. A person who only wrote one thing, that we have—and most people have never read that—yet became a literary myth, influencing umpteen writers, filmmakers.

CAROLYN: Now Kesey's got this new myth going, that Neal died counting the railroad ties. *[Cassady collapsed while walking a train track in Mexico in 1969.]* I can't tell you how many young people love that myth. So—okay. But he wasn't counting railroad ties, he was going to get his baggage. He had left his baggage in the next little village and he was gonna go get it. The nearest witness said he was about three yards out of San Miguel when he collapsed. And we'll never know whether he drank the alcohol on purpose or whether it was "What the hell" or what—because he'd know what happens when you mix it with seconal. He didn't care. Or didn't think.

LEWIS: Do you think he was completely trapped in his mythology by then?

CAROLYN: I think he was completely beyond all that. All he thought about was metaphysics. He came home one time, and he was hallucinating, and I couldn't handle this, and when it was getting kind of rough he went into the bathroom and turned the shower on, so I wouldn't have to hear, and he had this big yelling conversation with the Devil. And I remember one time he said to me, "Now, I know you don't believe in him, but I know him, and we talk." Oh-kayyyyyy.

Now, I wish I knew then what I know now, and I could have talked to him about this. But at that point I thought you create your own devils. But he was very serious about this. So this was all he was doing in his head all the time. He was in another dimension. In the end, he never thought at all about things like *On the Road* or his myth or anything.

MICHAEL: When you say metaphysics . . .

CAROLYN: Christian metaphysics, at first. Then when he read Edgar Cayce it turned him around, and we went on reading everything related. He did believe in reincarnation and karma, and the past-life readings of his are . . . hairy. He was really working out these complicated metaphysical theories that just went over everyone's head. And I think his struggle was he couldn't be what his idea was, but he *knew* all about it, so it was even tougher because his emotional desire-body was the ruler, and he couldn't overcome it.

This particular life-reader we'd go to—and remember, this was in the '60s, long before it became a kind of fad—would give readings a year apart. The first year was supposed to be the physical-emotional lifetimes, and the second year you got the spiritual ones. Well, my second-year ones were kind of like the first ones; they did say something about where I got my talents, that kind of thing, but they were still these kind of dull, mundane lives of frustration. But his, his second ones, the spiritual ones, were just like one great long prayer. This, whoever this thing was that was talking through the medium, would go off on these rapturous things, and in fact instructed the medium to listen to the tape back, and she listened and said she'd never heard anything like that, ever. Of course, Neal was a sobbing wreck on the floor. So the mystical was another big struggle—this horrible battle of being a sex maniac on the one hand, and so spiritual on the other, wanting such perfection and creativity. I think that his appeal was that people felt this. This was the magnetism he had for so many, even in the Kesey years, when he was doing just a stumblebum kind of thing.

LEWIS: Were people drawn to Kerouac the way they were drawn to Cassady, like in a room full of people?

CAROLYN: No, because Jack was so self-conscious, and he'd say rude things when he'd get drunk, get belligerent, fight in bars. Whereas Neal wouldn't fight, he'd run. He didn't feel it was cowardice; it was good sense. He couldn't possibly hit anybody, ever.

Something else that may be a surprise—both men were very modest. They'd go to Big Sur, where everybody takes off their clothes and jumps in the hot tub, and the only two that wouldn't were Jack and Neal. These wild men would not remove their clothes. Oh, Neal may have, finally. But Jack *wouldn't*.

MICHAEL: It's very refreshing to hear this stuff.

CAROLYN: Nobody'll listen, don't worry. They'll go back to the same old myth. [*She laughs.*] They'll just say I'm making it all up.

MICHAEL: They went pretty crazy. You seem to me pretty sane. How do you think that happened?

CAROLYN: Well, I never did think I was one of them. All these people come to talk to me and I think, "Oh, they think I'm one of this group," and I fought it tooth and nail the whole time. I can't stand Bill Burroughs' lifestyle, or one word he writes. And a lot of Allen

[Ginsberg]'s stuff is just revolting! His little-boy-behind-the-barn sex attitude, things like that. But especially the drugs. Because, from what I've seen, it doesn't pay.

What was beautiful about Jack and Neal was their magnetism, their compassion, and—jolly good fun. Anyway, I had to keep doing what I had to do: Get them kids raised.

Lubbock for all reasons in the snow,
Farwell, Texas, 1986

Gassing up Baby, California, 1988

ACROSS THE GREAT DIVIDE

Old age ain't for sissies.
BETTE DAVIS

I'VE LEARNED the hard way that there's a crucial difference between problems and trouble: you can think your way through a problem, but you have to do something about trouble. Sure, sometimes, you can consult a friend or a therapist and *understand* your way through to the other side, but if, say, you're addicted to drugs, nothing will work until you *do* something—change your circumstances, clean up your act. Running out of money is trouble. If you're going to land on your feet you *must* act—your circumstances must change.

So let me state it plain: the money ran out—not all the way out, but I could no longer afford to live as I'd been living. When you're pushing sixty and your money runs out, as mine had, that's more than a problem. That's trouble.

For twenty years, I'd lived in Los Angeles and had long ago learned the difference between being what I call "Hollywood-broke" and "broke-broke." Hollywood-broke: you've got just enough to make expenses and live more or less as you like—no European vacations, no splurging on the latest high-tech, but things are manageable. Broke-broke: it's a week until rent day and you're sweating. For years, I'd been Hollywood-broke, but pretty soon I was going to be broke-broke.

It was clear that I had to leave a city I'd loved for many years—and leave people I loved and things I loved to do. It was clear that I had to move someplace where my newly reduced earnings would keep me afloat.

I'm fifty-nine years old as I write this. A friend of mine said recently, "At our age, people set up their lives so that they never have to leave their comfort zones." My comfort zone had turned into the red zone, where if you leave your car unattended it will be towed. This isn't what any of us expect at this age. Yet, in my more reflective moments, I pondered that my situation was a 3-D metaphor for being my age. Call it the age of "pushing sixty." The age when, like it or not, admit it or not, we're about to be old. Our fundamental comfort zone—a body and mind in more or less working order—will become an increasingly red zone as time goes on, and that time is short. Even if we have money and try to do everything right, our bodies (and perhaps our minds) will soon change beyond our ability to will them otherwise. Trouble is on the way, and much of it will be trouble we can do little about.

So the practical question of "Where do I go from here?" became also an existential question, a question that most of us who are pushing sixty try to avoid. My checkbook was doing me a kind of favor: to think about moving to another place forced me to think about moving into another, unavoidable passage of life.

A friend to whom I related these musings said, tongue-in-cheek, "Hey, Oprah said fifty is the new thirty, and now they're saying sixty is the new thirty!" Well, that may be what Oprah thinks, but there's nothing "middle-aged" about being in your fifties. Fifties ain't the middle. Average life expectancy these days is holding at about seventy-six. For most people, fifty ain't half, or near half. Fifty is about two-thirds of the way to the end. When you're pushing sixty . . . you're getting old. I was getting old and going broke, and the one seemed not unlike the other.

I needed to think. Well, there are many ways to do that. Meditation is one—I've meditated every day for many years. Another is just sitting down and trying to be logical—I'd done that and it

had taken me to a certain point, but that point wasn't as far as I had to go. Another is to wait for the solution to present itself, but I didn't have time for that. And there's yet another way that sometimes works for me: just say "The hell with it!" and do something that under the circumstances some might say was, to borrow one friend's favorite word, "wacko." So I called up Dave—who's about six months older than I, and who's been my trusted friend since we were ten—and I suggested he fly down from Oakland while I drive up from L.A., and we'd meet in Vegas and tie one on. Dave's a normally sober individual who does taxes for a living, but he's been having his own problems lately, and he readily agreed.

The odd thing is . . . it turned out that an impulsive trip to Vegas was, after all, the mature thing to do—probably because I'd left my familiar surroundings, my familiar strictures, my familiar lies, and gone out into an open-ended situation in which something new could enter my awareness.

AS I DROVE into the desert at night, a thought came to me—as they sometimes do, suddenly and without warning, at a turn on the road. At around 1:00 a.m., I rounded that curve on I-15 where suddenly Vegas is laid out before you in all her gaudy glow, looking like an aging whore with a heart of steel and neon eyes who lives by the proverb, "Scared money never wins." And this is the thought that hit me:

It takes fierceness to grow old well.

When I arrived at our room at the Stardust, I couldn't turn on the light because Dave, who'd arrived earlier, had fallen asleep hours ago. (Taxmen go to bed earlier than writers.) I threw my gear on the empty bed, took a yellow pad from my satchel, sat by the window twenty-odd stories up, and wrote by the reflected glare of Las Vegas' frantic night, trying to run the thought down. I wrote:

It takes fierceness to grow old well. It takes a fierce devotion to the word goodbye—learning how to say it in many ways—fiercely, yes, but also gently, with laughter, with tears, but, no matter how, to say it every time so that there's no doubt you mean it. When you're pushing sixty, the rest of your life is about saying goodbye. Your greatest work may yet be demanded of you (though odds are against that). You may find more true love, meet new good friends, and there's always beauty (if you have an eye for it)—still, no matter what, slowly, you must say goodbye, a little bit every day, to everything.

Goodbye, for instance, to your face. Sometime in your early twenties, you developed the face that's yours, give or take some wrinkles, until your late forties or even your early fifties. But, gradually, that face becomes a different face—and you'll never see the other, younger face again, not in a mirror. Even in photographs, the face you had for so long will begin to look like a stranger's. And you're saying goodbye to the faces of your friends—the faces they had when they became your friends. If you haven't seen them in a while, it can be a bit of a shock, these new faces of theirs, and their sagging wrinkled skin and grayed or dyed hair. Something hasn't been so much taken away as added to their visages: the approach of Death. Call it whatever you like, but that's what it is, that's what we politely call "aging." Seeing Death slowly mark the faces of your friends, you reluctantly recognize its mark upon your own.

Goodbye, face that was mine. Hello, Death—near? Or still a ways off?

By your late forties, you're losing your looks; by your late fifties, you're losing your capacities.

You're saying goodbye to your body every day now—or it's saying goodbye to you. You can choose to live with the face or hair you now have or you can play tricks with it, force it to look younger, but you can't do much about your hands. Or your feet. The skin changes. The toenails change. The belly. The ass. The slackness. Hello to that, and goodbye to the body you'd assumed was yours—you never realized how much you'd assumed that you'd always be smooth and quick and strong. A silly assumption, but you didn't know that. Smooth, quick, strong, svelte—goodbye to that.

And you're saying goodbye to things like . . . how you used to drive a car. I stop a lot more to pee, and I learned the hard way (skidding off a Nevada two-lane) that my night reflexes aren't what they were. And the gas-pedal knee throbs after a couple of hours. Once you could run with no pain. Walk with no pain! Now there's that twinge in the knee that sometimes turns into real hurt. Hello, pain. Something always hurts now, a little or a lot. You hardly notice it anymore. When you see people in their seventies walking so slowly and carefully, you realize now, in your flesh, that they walk that way because it HURTS. You'll walk that way, too, one day.

And then you begin to learn to say goodbye even to your memory. It's no longer so dependable, no longer at your beck and call. It's weird and scary: you know exactly what it is you don't remember, but, somehow, you can't actually remember it—you just feel a blank space where the memory should be. Then the name, or whatever, comes to the surface, hours or days later—but one day maybe it won't. Alzheimer's? "A senior moment"? You get used to it and hope for the best. Ain't nobody can do a thing about it anyway. Goodbye.

I'd come to Las Vegas and something about "fierceness" and "goodbye" had been given to me. Now what? For I was still in trouble and there was still something to do. Clarity begets clarity, contemplation begets action—if, that is, one's contemplation is rooted in the real. Move from L.A. I must—not in dejection or defeat, but fiercely. Where? Three decades ago, I'd wandered into Lubbock, Texas. I'd found good friends there, and they were good friends still. I made inquiries and, yes, rents in Lubbock are half of what they are in L.A. In fact, everything's cheaper in Lubbock. Restaurants, movies, gas, groceries, and even a scarce commodity in that part of the country: water. Why, a manual laborer—a mechanic, a plumber, a trucker, even a teacher— might still afford to buy a house in Lubbock! Lubbock, then. As Lubbock's most famous son, Buddy Holly, once sang: "Rave on!" Hello, I said to fate. Hello . . . Lubbock.

WITHIN WEEKS, my stuff was packed, my arrangements were made, my goodbyes were said. The movers had carted off my belongings, to be delivered in Lubbock after I arrived. All that was left was the choice of a road. I wasn't looking for the most direct path. Rather, I was thinking of a line from an Edward Albee play that "sometimes a person has to go a very long distance out of his way to come back a short distance correctly." So I chose

Route 50. They call it "The Loneliest Road in America," and they know what they're talking about. It winds through the center of the country, from the Pacific coast up the Sierras on the old Pony Express Trail, through Tahoe, down into the Nevada Desert at Carson City, and then across Nevada, up and down the barren basin-and-range country, where it's often a hundred miles and more between towns, through spectacular Utah (still a hundred miles between towns), climbing the southern Rockies in Colorado, across the Great Divide, down onto the High Plains—then, at Lamar, Colorado, you hang a right and head due south to Lubbock.

In the California mountains, climbing toward Tahoe, you're in a thickly wooded world with occasional startling vistas, a world of life all around—trees, lakes, rivers, animals, people—the world as most of us wish it to be, grand but human, a live exchange between our nature and Nature, wild enough to be invigorating, but settled enough to be secure, fairly safe, with fun to be had and help never far off. And isn't that how most of us imagine the ideal life? But life never remains that way for long. Nor does Route 50. Past Tahoe, the road winds down into the Nevada desert, where nothing is safe, where the sun can kill, where often there's no one in sight for miles and miles and miles—yes, a hundred miles between towns, and the towns

so small. And each has saloons, joints with names like Old Fogey's Saloon, Break-a-Heart Saloon, and the prize, a saloon named with a jaunty sense of heartbreak, Kathy's Somewhere Else.

She sure is. I thought of all the "desert rats," as they call themselves, who drive miles and miles to saloons like Break-a-Heart and Kathy's Somewhere Else for comfort, company, and whiskey. These are joints for old fogeys indeed—the jukeboxes play old songs, hair is mostly gray, and most of the patrons are over forty. Way over. Bars for people pushing sixty. It's an old American adage that "nobody takes anything small into a bar." What the desert rats took into these bars was the old dreams of love that keened from the jukebox.

At our age, we're a bit amazed that romantic love is still a problem—a problem that, for many of us, stubbornly refuses to pass. I thought of my late father—past eighty and recovering from a major operation when he drove his pickup in the wee hours through torrential Florida rains, mad with jealousy that his girlfriend hadn't come home yet. Kind of funny, a little pathetic, but proof for me, if proof was needed, that the demons of romantic love are no respecters of age.

It takes a special fierceness to face love at this age, when so many of us have seen too many of our relationships and marriages become, to put it mildly, untenable. Most who've stayed married have a fierce resignation and acceptance of all that marriage isn't. It isn't, for instance, a solution to loneliness. They've said goodbye to dream after dream after dream . . . They've met their spouses over and over again as the years passed, as each changed, as they've had to accept and/or reject, love and/or avoid, each new version of themselves and each other. They've had to accept (or reject) their children as the strangers that children really are—hello to that, goodbye to the hopes and dreams of those shining little people on whom we could project anything. Most marriages that last are equal monuments to surrender and fierceness.

And those of us who are alone now, yet still looking for love . . . I like to remember something my brother said: "A young guy loves a woman with his dick; at our age, you love a woman with your life." I take that to mean: you never lose what you've done—the good and the bad of it, the large and the small of it. To be this age is to have done a great deal—not in accomplishment, necessarily, but simply in the days and nights of one's life; and to love at this age, really to love, is to love with the momentum and gravity (as in "force of gravity") of all you've done. (To not have done accompanies you, too.) Whatever the joy of love at any age, there's also a kind of solemnity to it now. It's like the joyful, solemn wonder of watching a sunset. It's glorious, but it's most definitely not a sunrise, though the

colors may be similar. But these colors will be followed, soon, by darkness—and you're facing in a different direction. Goodbye to the coming day. You won't live to see it. There's something to be said for a love with little future—that may be a love with more room for the truth than any other. But truth takes fierceness, at any age.

Route 50, Nevada. There's nowhere for the eye to rest, your vision just goes on and on and sees—nothing. Desert, desolation. The day is terribly bright, the night is just as terribly dark. At night on Route 50 in Nevada, you can't see past your headlights, there's nothing but you in the vastness. No help anywhere. You feel your psyche attempting to expand to meet the expanses, you feel your psyche strive to assert itself here, something in you tries to say "I!" but it comes out as squeak. You're small. You're a little, tiny being, surrounded by Universe. What could it possibly matter if *you* grow old and die?

Then, driving in the harsh daylight of Nevada's Route 50, you notice that beside the road, in the middle of nowhere, truly Nowhere, for miles and miles there are— names! Names written in carefully placed stones and pieces of broken glass. It must be high-school kids, the lonely kids from the tiny towns, leaving their mark. I've worked as a high school teacher, and I can imagine the kids filling their cars with booze, driving out into the vastness, partying, playing their car radios loud, making out, choosing the stones and broken pieces of glass, adding their names to the miles-long line of names. Their "I" isn't a squeak, it's a mark.

And so it is: we meet the Universe with the fragility of our identity and insist on leaving our names, somewhere, even here. What were those kids trusting? The stars. They were placing their names to face the highway and the stars. Hadn't I done the same on every article and book I'd spent my life writing? And all the writers of all the tomes ever written, hadn't they done the same, all the way back to Plato and the Upanishads? This is what the Universe calls out of us—a response. That's all that's required: a response. To the vastness.

But every one of our responses is, finally, tentative, temporary. That may be the hardest lesson that we who are pushing sixty must learn. We must say goodbye, too, to the usefulness of our response, our knowledge—not our wisdom, but our terribly temporary knowledge. Things move so quickly now that a skill once essential often becomes replaced by something beyond your ken—yet instantly mastered by a teenager. If you're lucky, there are some young folk who value your wisdom, maybe even a little of your out-of-date knowledge. They ask you for help. You give them what my teacher George once called "bread-crumbs."

Goodbye to the dream of who you thought you might one day be. You *are* who you'll be. Hello to that.

Goodbye to so many dreams. Most of them just got in the way of who you really are. Not that they weren't helpful. After all, your dreams are important not because they come true, but because they take you places you'd never have otherwise gone, and teach you what you never guessed was there to learn.

And wasn't that what this journey to Lubbock was really about? A test of faith? Faith that my reversal of fortune would take me where I never would have chosen to go, and teach me what I didn't know was there to learn?

And then, on a nameless stretch of Route 50 in Nevada, I came upon The Tree of Shoes.

There must have been an underground spring somewhere about, for in the middle of the wasteland was an enormous tree, and from that tree hung strings of shoes—shoes tied together by their shoelaces, strands of five and ten and twenty shoes, hanging from every limb. You've got to love high-school kids. They remind you of what it is to be alive. Their names weren't enough to offer the Universe. They—and who was the first to think of it?!—came out here, took off their shoes, tied them together, climbed the only tree in this part of Nevada, precariously, and hung their shoes. Whitman said in his "Song of the Open Road,"

"Here a great personal deed has room." "Great" doesn't have to mean that everybody knows your name or is affected by your actions. A great personal deed.

Personal, private. The response called forth by the Universe doesn't have to be something the world takes note of. It can be as humble as a shoe—and yet be grand.

I'm an old man on a long drive into what is, in all humility, the Unknown, and I can think of each word that I write, each word that I say, each feeling I have, as a shoe hanging from a tree in the middle of nowhere, but marvelous for all of that by, as Kierkegaard would say, "virtue of the absurd." It's as absurd to expect a life to have meaning, in contrast to the vastness of the Universe, as it is absurd to take off your shoe and hang it from a tree, but both are wonderful in their way—for I assure you, if you could see that tree, you'd think it wonderful, you'd approve, you'd think that in a wacko way something had been done, something worth doing. And I wondered how long those shoes would hang from that tree.

For that's the deepest of all our goodbyes: goodbyes to all the friends and family who die. Getting old changes more than our bodies and more than our relationship to ourselves; getting old changes our relationships to everyone, everything, the living and the dead. Whose shoes were those, really? Mine? My parents'?

My parents are dead; nevertheless, my relationship to them changes as I get older. My parents were in their early twenties when they married and began to commit the mistakes that became the foundation of my life. But now, when I see people in their early twenties I think, affectionately, "Babies!" Not babies as infants, but as innocents. Just as I was in my early twenties, my parents were committed to ignorant certainties and hopelessly unrealistic hopes—and bitterness leaves me as I realize that those babies— my parents—can't be condemned or blamed for their inevitable innocence. I forgave them long ago, but what I feel now is more than forgiveness; now I join them, as the twenty-year-old I was—I join them, stand beside them, am one with them in my impossible twenty-year-old assumptions, and there's no longer a question of forgiveness or blame. It was just life, as they lived it and as, later, I lived it.

My mother was thirty-five when psychosis first struck—a relatively young woman in my eyes now, in poverty, with four small children and a failing marriage, who succumbed to pressures she couldn't bear. My eight-year-old feelings of abandonment, nursed for most of my life, are finally gone. How do I see her from the vantage of my present age, this thirty-five-year-old woman young enough to be my daughter—and who, somehow, by the alchemy of age, becomes daughter-like in my heart? I feel a tenderness and sympathy I didn't think possible: Oh mother, daughter, I only wish you'd had the help and friends to withstand your trial, and I hope to God that now you've found your peace, or at least an oblivion where there's no suffering. And when I think this, the bewildered and terrified eight-year-old I've carried so long within me fades away and is freed.

My father was forty when he abandoned us—I was ten. I can't help but wish he'd been a stronger and a better man, but I'm now far too experienced to expect anyone to be anything other than they are. And now I know what it is to be forty and to feel an utter sense of failure and futility and an unquenchable desire to run. I've failed enough people myself that I can look back on my forty-year-old father and, again, join him, in his guilt and shame and inability. So, yes, I'm much older now than my parents were when they made their worst mistakes, and if I've made less of a mess, perhaps it's only that I didn't take on as much. So I'm happy, at last, to say goodbye to them as "parents," and goodbye to the younger man I was who could see them as nothing else. And within that goodbye is a hello. As a friend put it, "What the 'hello' is, is that at this point in life, you can really be a fucking grownup, maybe for the first time in your life, and that's no small thing." With my parents' deaths, I'm the eldest in my direct family. With my father's death and the death of my

mother's brother, I'm the oldest male in the entire extended clan—the oldest of the Venturas and the Scandurras. Who's left to answer my questions about them? The gaps in my knowledge are now permanent. Parts of my history are now irretrievable. When, as an elder, I'm asked certain questions, I don't know the answers, and I don't know because I didn't take the responsibility of asking enough questions. So: goodbye to those stories I neglected to learn. They're gone forever now.

When Aunt Mary, Uncle Jack, and Aunt Laura die, there'll be no one left who remembers me as a small child. I was too young to remember and my siblings are too much younger than I to have a clear memory of me before I was ten. So, in a strange way, I must say goodbye to my early childhood. Except for some dreamlike fragments and some photographs, that little boy is almost gone from the world. For when there's no one left to remember, what's left? The effects of that history live on, but they live nakedly, orphaned, stripped of story, stripped of memory.

So much dies with each of us when we die. A great gift of getting older, of becoming old, is to realize that I, too, am a precious vessel—quite apart from any idea of self-worth I might have, quite apart from anything I may have accomplished, I'm a precious vessel because of all that I've seen, all the stories I know, all the images and memories that will die with me. In this way, we're all precious vessels. And it isn't that we must get frantic about preserving all we've seen and all we know. Preserving all the stories isn't a human possibility, for all will be forgotten one day. But to know that I'm such a vessel, and that you are, makes me more attentive, makes me more available to anyone who asks for what I know, makes me speak more carefully, with less of the judgmental and more attention to nuance—makes me try to speak more slowly and reflectively, and to be like . . . an older man, the kind of older man I once admired: tolerant, receptive, at ease in his age, not trying to be anything he isn't, not trying to be younger.

MILES AND MILES LATER, in Utah, I stopped by the side of the road in an area called the San Rafael Swell. There's no describing it, not adequately. You're a bit higher than 7,000 feet. The geological formations all around you, as far as the eye can see, are so massive that it's as if the grandest cloud formation you've ever seen had turned to stone and the rounded shapes of the clouds were carved sharply by some unsentimental sculptor into shapes that have nothing to do with human aesthetics, human values. A helpful plaque teaches that 180 million years ago this was the shore of a great sea—a sea level that rose nearly a mile and a half into the sky! What unstoppable forces

could accomplish that? And what's a human being beside that? Those forces are still at work! It's all still going on. The swamps of Florida could be the top of the world one day. The rock at the top of Mount Everest is limestone formed 5,000 feet beneath the surface of the sea; somehow, that limestone rose 35,000 feet into the air! And they've recently discovered that underneath the Arctic's ice are the remains of a tropical forest. Yes, that process continues as we speak. And what does that mean to an aging man? That I'm part of something so much larger than myself; and I'm part of how that "something" happens.

Surely, that's enough, whether I can pay the rent or not.

The next day, I drove up and up and up. There seemed no end to the steep incline, until I rounded the top and the sign said: "Monarch Crest—11,312 feet." Another sign said: "The Great Divide." All rain that falls east of the Great Divide flows ultimately into the Atlantic Ocean; all rain that falls west of the Divide flows into the Pacific. There I was, at the top of the world, crossing the Divide. Again, geology became psychology; before this stage of my life, all the "rain"—all my experience—had fallen in the direction of my birth, my youth. Henceforth, all the rain would fall in the direction of my death. The late songwriter Townes Van Zandt sang, "You cannot count the miles until you feel them" . . . adding, in that same tune, "I'm thankful that old Road's a friend of mine." It sounds corny, but even so, the statement is simple; the reality it describes is highly charged: if you can accept death—the death of anything and of everything, for there's nothing that won't die—then all the parts fall into place, even failure.

And so I arrived in Lubbock. Older. Old. And new. "Goodbye" and "hello" met in a harmony that was no less harmonious for being dissonant.

And I remembered that night at the Stardust writing beside my sleeping friend . . . I could see the two or three miles to the Rio, its crimson and purple neon, where Dave and I sat on the nineteenth floor the year we turned fifty. That night, I saw that room from the same time in the morning, four-ish, and he'd said: "We're fifty and we're better than I

ever thought we would ever be. I didn't expect that." I replied: "Indian summer, baby."

Nine years later, Dave slept as I wrote by neon glow. Indian summer is over. Say goodbye to what was, so you can welcome what is. Death approaches with something like a smile. Smile back. That's the only way Death will respect you. It's no small thing to be respected by Death.

Goodbye and goodbye and goodbye. Hello and hello and hello. It takes fierceness to grow old well. In Lubbock, I remembered that Vegas dawn when I was tired and a little drunk, when, appropriately for Vegas, lines from forgotten stars in forgotten films came unbidden to my vigil—this, from a noir relic, *Walk Softly, Stranger*: "They say you haven't lost anything important until you've lost your nerve."

Street reflecting tree snow, Ft. Sumner,
New Mexico, 1986

I N 1950 JAMES BALDWIN wrote one of the most daring and prophetic sentences ever penned: "The world is white no longer, and it will never be white again." That truth took its time showing up in the American West. When I first drove the West in the 1970s, I drove through a white world. You saw some Hispanics and some blacks, but (save in New Mexico) not many—they kept to their own neighborhoods except to work, and the world they lived and worked in was white. But throughout the West and Midwest today there's no denying Baldwin—these lands are white no longer, and they won't be white again, in the sense that "white" calls all the shots. Which is what the furor over Hispanic immigration is really all about.

Two facts tower above all others regarding Hispanic immigration. The first foretells how this issue will eventually be resolved. The second measures the injustice that these immigrants suffer. Yet in all that I've read and seen since the nationwide demonstrations of May 1, 2006, nei-

ther of these facts has been given much serious attention.

The first fact is: "The latest census reports . . . [that] nationwide nearly half the children under 5 . . . are Latino or other minorities" [CNN, "Wolf Blitzer's Situation Room," May 10, 2006]. This "half" is mostly Latino. Already California, New Mexico, and Texas have non-Anglo (mostly Latino) majorities; New York and Arizona are 40 percent non-Anglo (mostly Latino), as are Maryland, Mississippi, and Georgia [*The Week*, August 26, 2005, p. 16]. Florida, New Jersey, and Illinois (among other weighty states) will likely sooner than later have non-Anglo majorities. The trend will continue. The outcome is obvious. No matter what happens now, eventually Hispanic Americans will be this country's decisive voting bloc and immigration law will be whatever they want it to be. The political party that helps them now will be the political party of the future. The party that obstructs them will be doomed to insignificance for decades as this young generation grows up, remembers, and votes.

The second fact was noted by Anna Quindlen in *Newsweek* [May 15, 2006, p.78]:

> Although the conventional wisdom is that immigrants are civic freeloaders, the woman with a sign that said I PAY TAXES was reflecting the truth. Millions of undocumented immigrants pay income taxes using a special identification number the IRS provides. They pay into the Social Security system, too, even though they're not eligible to collect benefits. In fact, they may be helping to keep the system afloat.

Read that twice. In *practice*, the IRS—that is, the federal government—recognizes the legality of undocumented workers. Our government knows where millions of them work. Our government, and everyone who cashes a Social Security check, spends their money. It's well known that many U.S. corporations pay no taxes, and President Bush cut taxes for the rich, but these "illegals" pay. Their labor and the fruit of their labor is *in practice* legal, with legal arrangements for tax collection—but the workers themselves are illegal. The hypocrisy of ranting about "illegals" while pocketing their coin—*that* should be illegal.

Since the federal government benefits from undocumented workers, something

is owed those workers in return: Justice. The just resolution is simple. All immigrants who pay taxes should, immediately, be issued green cards. *Then* they can get at "the back of the line" for citizenship, with the not so unreasonable stipulation of learning English (immigrants do that anyway, eventually).

It is extraordinary that these two facts—the first demographic, the second financial and governmental—are virtually absent from both print and broadcast journalism.

Nor was I any less ignorant than my colleagues until I was shocked out of my ignorance and complacency by the demonstration in Lubbock on May 1, 2006.

Lifelong residents of Lubbock tell me that this city, "the Hub of the Texas Panhandle," never before witnessed a demonstration 3,000 strong. That was the figure quoted next day in the *Lubbock Avalanche-Journal*. The number seemed, to me, low. Extrapolating from a count of those within about a hundred feet of where I walked, and standing on a height to view the entire march, I estimated 4,000-ish, maybe more. *At least* 3,000, then. A first in Texas Panhandle history.

We gathered at St. Joseph's Catholic church, in the northeast area of the city. We walked behind a marvelous hand-painted banner of the Virgin of Guadalupe—bright colors on a white background, brilliant in the sun. On either side of the Virgin, folks carried signs: VOTE – IT COUNTS. As was typical of the May 1st marches everywhere in America that day, there were lots of kids, tiny ones and midsized ones, running about or in strollers or on the shoulders of fathers or big brothers—kids who will never forget this day, and who are being taught by example to stand up. Also typical, most Lubbock marchers were adults under, say, thirty-two—which means this movement may ebb and flow but it isn't going away. Everyone was excited. Many were smiling. There was no sense of discomfort, no scent of fear. The atmosphere, happy! (I've walked many demonstrations, and only at Woodstock—a concert, but also a kind of demonstration—have I seen a mass of people *happy*.) There were many U.S. flags, some Latin American flags, many handmade signs. An Anglo's read WE ALL COME FROM SOMEPLACE ELSE. A Latino's, JUSTICA PARA TODOS. Justice for all. And there were chants, and when one chant died down you never knew who'd start the next—it might be an old woman, it might be a young man, it might be three high-school girls walking hand in hand. SI, SE PUEDE! Yes, it can be done! EL PUEBLO UNIDO! JAMAS SERA VENCIDO! A people united will never be vanquished!

My father was six before he spoke his first English word. My mother was eleven or twelve. She would become the first woman of her lineage to graduate college. They didn't often speak their native Italian and Sicilian tongues around their kids because they didn't want us to face the crap they'd faced before they overcame their accents. If they were alive, they would have marched that May 1st. In New York City when I was young, Sicilians weren't quite white and weren't quite not. It depended on the neighborhood. I guess I thought I was white—because in 1973, to the shock of my naiveté, I discovered that in Lubbock, presto, I wasn't white anymore (if, indeed, I ever had been). An aged Anglo barber left a line of blood across the back of my neck to ensure that his establishment would not again be sullied by this particular spic. In memory of him and those like him—and for my parents, myself, and, yes, the honor of humanity—I'd've marched that May 1st, if need be, in a wheelchair. And, in fact, in Lubbock some did march in motorized chairs and in wheelchairs pushed by relatives and friends. (Note to the future: Such folk don't scare easy.)

When we gathered at the Federal Building, most speeches were pretty fine. A priest began with a prayer that God "keep in our hearts [Jesus' words], 'As you did it to the least of these, you did it to me.'" Lubbock County Sheriff David Gutierrez sang the daylights out of "God Bless America" (with marchers joining in). And a graying Anglo judge named Rusty Ladd said this:

Every founding father of this country broke the law; every escaped slave and anyone who helped that slave broke the law; every Texian (of any color) who fought for the independence of our state broke the law; all those civil rights marchers and protestors of the 1950s and 1960s broke the law and our nation is the better for their having done so. . . . If our legislatures . . . pass any law . . . that tells me I cannot offer food or drink or medical attention or shelter to any neighbor of mine, or passes a law that restricts my ability to treat my fellow man with dignity and respect, then save me a cell in the local jail—for on that day I shall become a lawbreaker as well.

That is the spirit that has eventually, with struggle, righted the great wrongs of society. These people were standing up, nonviolently but insistently, to prove that spirit is alive and well in the Texas Panhandle.

The spirit of that day will ebb and flow over time. The movement will have good years and bad. It takes more than a day of marches to teach the importance of voting and to induce America as a whole to recognize the justice of a cause. But time and demographics are inexorable. The day will come when this will be another long struggle won.

TO LOSE SOME NERVE

T HREE YEARS AGO October, in eastern Arkansas—driving west through flat, moist country—I saw the strangest cloud. Until then I thought that I'd seen every possible cloud in North America. Given the least excuse I brag that I've driven my '69 Chevy from Key West to Bellingham, Washington; from Tijuana to Waterville, Maine; and from El Paso to the Montana–Canadian border—driven every state, in fact, but Michigan, in all weathers and all seasons. So I had a right (as such rights go) to believe I'd seen every sort of cloud. But never had I seen a cloud like this.

It was about ten in the morning, a bright day, warm but not hot, blue sky overhead. Not an hour before, in a motel room in Brinkley, Arkansas, the Weather Channel reported thunderstorms to the west. The Doppler configurations on TV didn't look unusual. I figured I'd be driving west on I-40 at seventy-ish miles per hour, the storms were moving eastward pretty fast, I'd be through them in no time and it would be fun. Until that morning I'd enjoyed driving through storms. Friends have sometimes ques-

tioned my sanity when I've gone out of my way to drive into a thunderstorm, or when I've headed straight for a blizzard though I had plenty of time to take the long way around and avoid the danger. I tried often to explain that storms gave me something, something hard to come by. I tried to communicate that in my first novel, *Night Time, Losing Time*, when Jesse, a rock 'n' blues piano player, is driving late with his young son Jes:

Jes and I were driving back from Shreve-port in the rain. We were a little east of Houston. Jes was pissed that I wasn't let-ting him work the gas pedal, like I often did, but I wouldn't do it in weather. The rain started coming down so hard, the windshield wipers just sort of smudged it around, the glass never really cleared. It was a two-lane and the on-coming cars were just big double blobs of smeared light. If you turned hard, you'd skid. If you hit the brake, you'd skid. You couldn't tell where the white line was, or the shoul-der. I bent to the wheel. . . . We hit a turn too fast, the old car held the road, but it was so fucking scary both of us were shaken. I said, "I'm sorry, Jes." . . . And the rain beat down. And the spray sound of our tires on the road. And every car that passed the other way raised a wash of water on us.

And suddenly I felt a weird elation. We were completely cut off from the world. We were Out There. Together. Hurtling through something that was and wasn't a storm. I mean, of course it was a storm, but it was also an intoxication, something meant, I mean meant, to induce a state of mind, or out-of-mind . . . I felt the storm vibrating through the steering wheel, loved the pounding drops on the hood, the watery hiss of the wheels, and felt approval in the storm, knew it pleased the storm to be driven through like this, and must have had some crazy grin on my face because when I looked over at Jes again he was surprised and said, "What?!" "Isn't this a great STORM!" . . . And I prayed he'd remember this . . . And that maybe he'd psyche someday, sooner than I had, that the storm is there for our elation as much as for the crops.

Elation is complicated. It can be joy, but it can also be terror—and it can be both, and more.

Elation lifts you up and cleans you out, and bestows, in its wake, a fresh sensation of balance and an eagerness for whatever's coming next.

Anyway . . . with blue sky overhead, I drove west on I-40 across the Arkansas flats, and there was this cloud, if you can call it a cloud. Even from miles away, it loomed. As far as I could see to the north, and going on for almost as far as I could see to the south, it loomed, a massive wall rising straight up from the ground, I-don't-know-how-many thousands of feet high. White at the top, gray for most of its height—but its bottom hundred feet or so, where it met the earth, was a different, spooky white. And I said aloud, "What in Heaven's name is that?!" It looked like one of those giant tidal waves in an end-of-the-world movie.

Traffic was light. The highway was straight. There was nothing but an eighteen-wheeler maybe half a mile ahead. The vehicles in my rearview were many car-lengths behind. I had to bend over my steering wheel to look up and see the top of this cloud. And I felt a deep happiness to see something so magnificent, a phenomenon I'd never even heard of.

Then the eighteen-wheeler ahead entered the spooky whiteness at the bottom of that cloud—and disappeared. And I noticed that, on the eastbound side of the highway, vehicles kind of popped out of the cloud, with their headlights on and their windshield wipers furiously flapping. And just as it struck me that I couldn't see two feet into that cloud, I entered the cloud.

And couldn't see the hood of my car.

There were no raindrops; there was water. Pouring. I lifted my foot off the gas pedal, held the wheel straight, hoped the road would stay straight, turned on my wipers and headlights, slowing now to about thirty-five, hoping no one would ram me from behind, and I still couldn't see anything. After some moments, I could see two slashes of the white line as they disappeared under my left wheel. I steered to those two slashes, holding my car straight and steady, slowing even more. And then there was wind. Sudden and vicious. And stuff in the wind—couldn't see what, but could hear stuff hit the car from my right, little stuff and slightly larger stuff, by the sounds. It became all I could do to keep Baby (my car) going straight.

A '69 Chevy Malibu is heavy, made of metal, not fiberglass. It's wide and low to the ground—a grownup can't crawl under it. Low center of gravity. Even skidding on ice, Baby doesn't swerve much, just kind of shimmies. A good car for a storm. But it was all I could do to keep Baby level with those two slashes of white line that were my only guide. And then time slowed down, the way it does sometimes when things are really bad. In a kind of out-of-body way I noticed, with great surprise, that my arms and legs were shaking—no, "shaking" doesn't describe it. My limbs were like wild rubber bands. I started to laugh, because how could my

hands on the wheel and my foot on the pedal remain steady while my limbs were crazily trembling? Yet it was so.

Also, someone was screaming. "FUUUUUUUCCCCCKKKK!" It had to be me. Still out-of-body, I checked my throat and mouth. Yes, they were screaming. But it felt kind of distant. Over and over, "FUUUUUUUUCCCCCKKKK!" There's a Springsteen verse I've long loved, about a guy driving into a hurricane and getting splattered all over the road: *I wonder what he was thinking when he hit that storm.* Well, now I knew. He was thinking "FUUUUUCCCCCKKK!"

Then my luminous out-of-body-ness ended abruptly, because of a sound.

How can wind sound like metal? The cliché is that a tornado sounds like a freight train. Not really. Tornadoes sound like enormous metal plates clanging together. Way louder than a freight train. If you hear that sound once, you never forget it. I'd heard it once. But not like this. That sound around me was (forgive the capital letters) TOTAL. I couldn't see it, because I could barely see anything. But steering got even tougher, and the sound was everywhere.

I don't know how I wasn't swept away, but after a timeless time the sound passed. Rain and wind subsided into only the worst storm I'd ever seen before this one. And then suddenly it was all blue sky and daylight! I'd driven through the wall. I was gripping the wheel so hard that it took me some miles to free my fingers. (It was two days before my hands stopped hurting.) I was still shaking, but not as wildly. The next day the papers reported that a swath of "killer tornadoes" had wreaked damage, injury, and death across eastern Arkansas. Nevertheless, though you Google your heart out, you won't find an explanation of that cloud. I've tried. (If any of you are luckier at it, please let me know.)

I'm not sorry it happened. It's a privilege to experience such immense, elemental, impersonal power—to experience that and yet live. But I've suffered—what can I call it?—a loss of nerve. Elation has been granted me by many storms, and most of all by that incredible cloud. My many faults do not include ingratitude. But on my drives now a puny drizzle makes me anxious. I'll hunt for no more storms. I'm proud of my feet and hands— they didn't panic. But the rest of me did. I've lost and gained. Lost what I never thought I'd lose. Gained what I didn't dream to gain. Stared into the face of a "something" I couldn't name. Beyond elation is something greater. It makes you smaller and larger. (In a whisper I say, "Let's leave it at that.")

Caddy, I-10 W, Arizona, 1986

THE MOM, THE BOOK, THE KID, AND THE NUN

PSYCHOLOGY and sociology pretty much explain my life until about age ten. After that, something else, for which I have no name, took over.

My mother must have pondered what to do with her ten-year-old when New York City's public school system informed her the kid's reading score was that of a high school senior. Or junior. It was an "nior" sound. I can't swear which. What with caring for five-year-old twins and a three-year-old, Mama hadn't much to spare for her eldest anymore. (Pa, he went thataway months before.) But she made time to discover the Landmark Book Club, which sent out volumes designed for curious children.

I'd been reading encyclopedias hungrily since the end of third grade, but a Landmark volume, *The Wright Brothers*, was the first hardcover that was all my own, read again and again until the next arrived, *The First Men in the World*—a book that changed our lives. On its colorful jacket a mastodon upset two blond men clad in furs. They held spears. Cro-Magnon men they were, successors to Neanderthals. Difficult, now, to express or decipher my love for that book—read it so many times it was almost memorized, until the word "evolution" seemed, magically, the key to all mystery.

Wednesdays, Catholic kids left public school early to attend catechism classes at a Catholic school. We were instructed in our religion by a stern nun whose name I've forgotten. Came her lesson on Adam and Eve, I eagerly raised my hand and explained that Adam and Eve must have been Cro-Magnons, or perhaps Neanderthals. The word "evolution" passed my lips. Sister bade me step forth and put my hand on her desk, palm down. She rapped my knuckles with six swift strokes of a wooden ruler.

I didn't resent the punishment as such. If you messed up, you got hit. That's how things were. But I'd never been good at anything, and here it was recognized by no less an entity than New York City that I was good at something, even if it was only reading—not much street cred for reading, but better than nothing. That nun's ruler drove me to tearful fury. I declared I was standing up for truths I'd discovered, but really my response had more to do with pride. To be punished for the one thing I was good at was more than my ten-year-old pride could tolerate.

"I'm never going back there," I announced to my mother when I got home. "I'm not a Catholic anymore."

I meant it, and my mother took me at my word. I was that kind of kid and she was that kind of mother.

We searched for a different church. Tried Quaker services twice, our tribe of five dressed in our best and even the twins awed into stillness. But Mama probably figured that, being Sicilian, we'd make lousy Quakers.

Next came a church with a name that didn't sound religious: Unitarian. Mama attended the service while my siblings and I were put into Sunday school classes by age. What was discussed in my first Sunday school session? Evolution! I was overjoyed. What a church! I needn't believe in God, I needn't believe in anything, and the people were so nice. As far as I ever learned, a commitment to reason and kindness was the ideal of Unitarian belief. For them, the word "God" seemed to mean the principle of reason in a reasonable universe. (Not until I grew up did that seem as naïve a notion as any in Christendom.)

Now my tale becomes intricate and long, but its telling must be brief.

At that Unitarian Sunday school, I met Dave. Remember that name. Poverty and insanity plagued my family, and when I was thirteen it fell apart. I was on my own. After a circuitous, solitary, and serendipitous journey, a Unitarian minister's family took me in, saving my life, while All Souls Unitarian Church of Manhattan supplied funds for my support. I attended a small, extraordinary high school, Coburn Classical Institute, in Waterville, Maine, where Mr. Carlo, Mr. Judson, and Mrs. Willard taught English and history remarkably well. Without them I could not have become a writer. (I would spend two fragmentary years at colleges where education wasn't nearly as rigorous. Those Coburn teachers constituted all my formal education.) Throughout high school Dave and I kept in touch.

And here it gets weird. Stripped of nuance, it goes like this.

I'm twenty-ish. My siblings, my mother, and I live in a two-bedroom apartment in the Bronx. Mama works as a file clerk, I'm a typist, and we make ends meet. While I'm doing that, enter Irene and Anne—women my age, of whose existence I am unaware. They meet by chance at a hostel in Europe. Their meeting is the most pivotal event of my adult life, and I wasn't even there. Had no idea.

Not much time passes. Anne meets Dave. They marry. More time passes. Irene is now in New Mexico, where she meets Janette. Janette goes back to her native Texas to be with her boyfriend, Butch, in Lubbock. Irene drifts to Lubbock. Irene meets Crash. Crash has never seen the sea.

By this time, Anne and Dave live in Oakland. I'm drifting around the country, twenty-seven-ish by now. I stay a few weeks in Oakland with Anne and Dave, then head to Santa Cruz to live on the sofa of Sarah and Duke—Duke being a friend met at a Unitarian summer camp during high school. Irene and Crash visit Dave and Anne so that Crash can see the sea. I visit Dave and Anne while Irene and Crash are there. I'm about to hitchhike to Nashville for Mikey's wedding. Crash invites me to ride with him and Irene as far as Lubbock. I'd never heard of Lubbock. I go with them and stay at 14th Street and Avenue W during a snowstorm—among other residents of that house are Butch Hancock, Joe Ely, and Jimmie Dale Gilmore. I dig it there. I bus to Nashville for Mikey's wedding, hitch to New York to see my family, get a ride to Boston to see friends, and run into Watson, who was a camper in my cabin when I was a high school counselor at that Unitarian camp. Watson tells me he's about to drive to New Mexico. I say, "Drop me off in Lubbock." After two years in the Panhandle I drift down to Austin just as some wildcat journalists start *The Austin Sun*. They give me a job. The rest of my life happens next: thirty-odd years, so far, as a working writer.

(A strange aside: I'd decided not to visit Dave and Anne's for dinner with Irene and Crash. A voice out of nowhere—in my head? from capital-e Elsewhere?—said, "Go. It will change your life." Cross-my-heart-and-spit, that happened.)

If Mama hadn't subscribed to a book club . . . if I hadn't protested my punishment . . . if Mama hadn't found the Unitarians . . . if, through them, I hadn't met Dave, Duke, and Watson, and gone to camp and Coburn . . . if Irene hadn't met Anne, if Anne hadn't met Dave . . . if Mikey hadn't married Martha . . . if Irene hadn't met Janette and Crash . . . well, my life is unimaginable without all that, yet these crisscrossing meetings had little to do with me. What does one make of a pattern like this? What does one call it? How does one possibly untangle its elements?

That nun, whom I've maligned all my life—now I see that had she been tolerant and kind, she'd have ruined me! Nothing that guided my path after age ten would have happened. What does one do with a fact like that?

Every now and again I go to Mass. I sit in the back. I like the atmosphere of Catholicism. Next time I mean to light a candle for that nun, thanking her and the saints she believed in—the Blessed Mother who looks after children, Saint Christopher who guides wanderers, and Saint Anthony who finds what's lost. Her vehement faith and stern ways had as much to do with setting me on my path as anything else, and, until now, I've never thanked her.

How did G'Kar of *Babylon 5* put it? "A brilliant cascade of cause and effect. Isn't the universe an amazing place? I wouldn't live anywhere else!"

My nun would have expressed the same idea differently: "God works in mysterious ways."

Legs passing on by, California, 1988

'D JUST MOVED back to the Texas Panhandle when the documentary *Lubbock Lights* screened in a theater on Lubbock's Buddy Holly Avenue—a venue the Flatlanders played that night, or the next night. Jesse Taylor (may he rest in peace) played his last hometown gig the night after. Many of the bunch we call "14th Street" showed up for the screening, and it was weird, it was flat-out weird to see that old brick house on 14th and Avenue W up there on the big screen with its most famous residents—Joe Ely, Butch Hancock, Jimmie Dale Gilmore. We thought we were pretty outlandish in '71, '72, and '73, when many of us lived there and many others passed through, but we never dreamed anything as unlikely as that one day that house and everything it meant to us would be a documentary lauded at film festivals . . . or that Stubb's Bar-B-Q in Lubbock would be a landmark . . . or that Stubb would have a statue . . . or any of it.

It was a snowy winter morning when I first walked into "the house they call '14th Street'" (the phrase is dear Irene's, and may she, too, rest in peace). Yes, as the film relates, there was usually someone playing music and a party that ebbed and flowed but never quite ended and continuous night-and-day conversation . . . but there was something else, something not part of the legend (*if* it's a legend) that impressed me that first day: The house was full of books I'd never heard of.

I was a Brooklyn Yankee (a Brooklyn small-d dodger, too). With Yankee arrogance, I figured I was pretty well read in history, literature, science, psychology—but there were only six books in that house that I knew. Four of them were Lawrence Durrell's *Alexandria Quartet* (in my Top 10 of the twentieth century's fiction); the other two were by Carlos Castaneda. Like most Euro-Americans back then, I wasn't much aware of Islam and had never heard of Sufis, but here were Idries Shah's *The Way of the Sufi*, *Tales of the Dervishes*, and *The Pleasantries of the Incredible Mulla Nasrudin*. And somebody else I'd never heard of, Gurdjieff—many books by and about him. Plus esoteric books on Christianity. And *The Kybalion: Hermetic Philosophy*, "by Three Initiates," a work that Butch Hancock, Janette Norman, and I pondered endlessly (and ponderously). I have a copy in front of me, and I still wonder about its publisher, "The Yogi Publication Society—Masonic Temple—Chicago, Ill." Masonic Yogis! Yogi Masons! Yogi Berra! (Before I got to 14th Street, "Berra" was the only word I associated with "yogi.") And who was Krishnamurti anyway?

That material is more or less familiar to literate people now, what with New Age and all. But "New Age" is a phrase and a spectrum of notions that wouldn't become current for about a decade. From my perspective at the time, I'd landed in the middle of nowhere amongst fantastically talented people who were well schooled in wildness and who'd collected (and constantly discussed) a mysterious library of philosophies and mysticisms. It's not much of an exaggeration to say I felt I'd been admitted to an isolated, hedonistic, country-western–folk-music–Zen–rock-&-roll–honky-tonk/monastery.

I beg forgiveness for the pun (I forget who I'm stealing it from), but: That was Zen, and this is now. I invoke those 14th Street bookshelves to say it's no surprise that some of those people are publishing books nowadays. These friends of mine were always writing books—thick notebooks of drawings and words. Dream logs. Journals. Verbiage. Nothing taciturn about this crowd.

Terry Allen, for instance. Terry never lived "at 14th" (as we say), but he went to high school with most who did; he's part of "the tribe" (as we also say). Two years ago he published *Dugout* (UT Press). Terry claims not to be one of the mystics, but he also claims (rightly) that we're all liars. I'm opening at random (cross-my-heart-and-spit) . . . the narrator speaking in verse and capital letters of his baseball-player father and his honky-tonk mom:

SHE SAYS A PERSON HAS TO DIG INTO THE HEART OF/EVERYTHING . . . AND WHAT LITTLE GETS DUG OUT IS ALL / THERE IS . . . OR WILL EVER BE. / HE SAYS HE REMEMBERS EVERY GAME. / SHE SAYS SHE REMEMBERS EVERY SONG. / AND IT IS NO LONGER ABOUT JUST THE TWO OF THEM . . . / IT'S ALL OF IT. / MOST OF WHICH CAN NEVER BE SAID. / IT JUST LAYS IN SECRETS IN THE DARK . . . LIKE THE BLACK / GAP BETWEEN THE TWO BEDS THAT HOLDS THEIR HANDS. / IT HAS NOTHING TO DO WITH GROWING OLD.

Dugout is about baseball, music, love, and a boy being raised by wildness and by the thought of the end of the world. (We used to talk all the time about the end of the world. Vicki had dreams about it, of incredible vividness.) *Dugout* is full color, with drawings, photos, sketches, as vivid and nonlinear as anybody's dreams: "Odd-painted creatures on porcelain plates. / After the fire, they are all that is left." "Once he told a young Busher with a promising arm . . . 'Your life just turns into a bucket full of stories . . . with a little bitty hole in the bottom.'"

I knew this afternoon I wanted to write about Terry's book, but I couldn't find it—which was me paying the price for how I despise alphabetical order. Many bookshelves, no order. I called m'lady—she knows my apartment better than I—asked if she knew where it might be, she said, "Below the glowing Virgin." OK, that takes some explaining. A friend gave me a plastic statuette of the Virgin Mary that glows white in the dark. It's on a bookcase. M'lady was right and *Dugout* was below the glowing virgin. OK, alphabetical order has its uses, but if you're too orderly, nobody instructs you to look below the glowing Virgin. Which reminds me of Jo Carol Pierce—who also never lived at 14th but went to high school and cavorted with those who did, befriending this errant Yankee somewhere along the way—and her song cycle *Bad Girls Upset by the Truth*, with its vision of the Virgin's sudden appearance in a supermarket in Lubbock, resulting in the rebirth of Jesus as the prettiest baby girl. Jo Carol called me not long ago and read me a lyric she was working on. Its refrain: "We didn't come here to stay." So let's don't bitch about getting older. "We didn't come here to stay."

Anyway, I found Terry's book.

I wish I could find Butch's book, but

he hasn't published one. He will. All those thick notebooks he writes and draws in. Butch's book will be like what he wrote me from the Roman works at Bath, England:

> *The rocks are worn, corners rounded . . . colors changed who knows how many times? What? Maybe a couple of thousand generations know. Perhaps a few thousand or a few hundred or maybe only ten or twenty pairs of eyes each generation could remember the fading colors over that generation's span of years . . . the living wave of consciousness from generation to generation . . . No way to pass that memory on except in dreams and genes.*

And there's Joe Ely's book, *Bonfire of Roadmaps* (UT Press; it includes a CD). When I hit 14th, Joe wasn't there; he was exploring where I'd been—Brooklyn, the very blocks where I'd lived—Decatur Street and Myrtle Avenue. Joe walked those streets because Henry Miller (who also grew up on Decatur Street) wrote of them. Joe was checking Miller's veracity. You young musicians, read Joe's book. It's the life of a rocker on the road, written as it happened. As Nelson Algren used to say, "That's the way it is, gentlemen. That's the way it *really* is." When Joe got back to Lubbock, the circus was in town. He and I joined up. I carried stuff; Joe tended animals. When the circus left town, Joe left with it. I didn't because I was in love with Kathy. I left later, on the run, when I started half-believing in Kathy's pact with God, which is all she talked about. I'd lain "below the glowing Virgin," oh wonder . . . and I'd best shut up about that.

Opening *Bonfire of Roadmaps* at random: "In Phoenix the crowd stood back / And looked upon us with suspicion / That is, until I turned myself inside out / And served my still-beating heart on a Styrofoam platter / Afterwards I gravitated to the pool table / Where I showed off my skill and insincerity." "Do I attract Psychotics naturally / Or is it that music brings out the psycho in people / Lucinda feels it too, the Prowlers, the Sycophants / In a race with sanity, stalk our skinny white asses." "There are no answers for gypsies who Question / Just questions, mysteries, mazes and riddles / And no good reason for any destination, / Other than living in the present . . ." And: "We must live it as it comes, catch it as it passes / The road goes on forever but we'll never be the same again."

Read our stuff and you can tell we all know each other, each a student of the road, schooled alike to a mix of jukebox existentialism, two-lane mysticism, and truck-stop practicality.

"And," as Terry sings, "I'm holding what I am: the wheel."

It's not so bad, never to be the same again. Nor are we all that different. Just older.

"Be here now," we used to say, only half getting the joke. Be here now? Well—there's nowhere else to be.

For reasons that may not be reasonable, we'll dispense with names and call our trio of travelers by where they sat: Back Seat, Shotgun, and Wheel Man. Shotgun was a keen observer and she asked sharp questions. Wheel Man enjoyed the sound of his own voice, but making sense was not always part of his game. Back Seat, she could question or answer with the best, and her preference for that back seat was practical as well as wise. In that old car, the back seat was like a sofa and, so Back Seat claimed, afforded the best view.

The front seat was sofalike too. Better back support than in your newer cars. A heavy, wide, low-to-the-road cruiser, designed for comfort and long distances. (At which point Back Seat might tell Wheel Man, "Let's don't go on about the car, eh?" She's quick with aid and good advice.)

On U.S. 60 in New Mexico, west of Magdalena, this trio marveled at the Very Large Array—twenty-seven radio telescopes, painted bright white, each about six stories high, supporting a dish wide enough to contain a baseball diamond.

They range across the edges of space and time.

To borrow our mutual friend Fox Eyes' words about her child, there is nothing more thrilling than that time of life when you "discover discovery"—except, perhaps, the moment you discover that discovery can be shared, as happened to Wheel Man at age eleven when he wrote a "book" about astronomy, a brown pocket notepad illustrated with crude drawings into which he copied astronomical facts, writing (and misspelling) on the last page, "I hope anyone who reads this book benifets by it." It mattered little that no one would read, or "benifet" from, this work; his thrill was in the offering. To stand dwarfed by the Very Large Array brought that all back.

Shotgun and Back Seat, too, shined with wonder at being part of a species that reaches out for what is Other. There may be no good reason to chart this vast universe, yet we can't help feel there is something pure in discovery for its own sake. We are never more human than when we explore.

The Very Large Array recently discovered something no one expected: "a hole in the universe." Our galaxy is 100,000 light-years across and contains at least 100 billion stars. That "hole" is an area 10,000 times the size of our galaxy in which there is nothing. No stars, planets, gaseous masses, so-called dark matter—nothing. This "hole" makes hash of every theory of the birth and growth of the universe. What does one do with a fact like that but bow in humble wonder and drive on?

Later, in Arizona, Back Seat and Wheel Man decided the explanation given in the brochure did not account for the Petrified Forest. Wheel Man is a speculative sort, but Back Seat is firmly evidential and practical. Shotgun impressively mixes all these qualities and was convinced by their doubts. Strewn across a swath of the Painted Desert are thick tree trunks preserved, in minute detail, in stone. Once this desert was a forest. Something turned it to stone. Some explanation must be offered to tourists, most of whom won't spend an afternoon and a morning walking from tree trunk to tree trunk arguing with the brochure. Satisfied that the Petrified Forest was yet another mystery unsolved, our trio drove on.

Back Seat and Shotgun engaged in erudite discussion of the historical importance of Pullman porters, whilst Wheel Man struggled to tune out their voices and concentrate on vistas of mesas as they made their way to Canyon de Chelly. Toward sunset the sky was a marvel of

slate and white clouds streaked with orange, indigo, and rose.

First the Anasazi, then the Navajo, have lived in Canyon de Chelly hundreds of years. Beauty is no one's possession, and to be drawn to beauty is simply to be alive, but a traveler who doesn't feel like a trespasser here isn't feeling. Trespassing happily, Shotgun, Back Seat, and Wheel Man drank it all in, imbibing the beauty and enjoying one another's company too much to apologize for history.

Next afternoon, in the rain, they headed back to Albuquerque.

Somewhere around Window Rock, Shotgun told Back Seat about a conversation months before with friends whom we'll call the Sharers of the Mountain. Wheel Man's rap had gone more or less like this:

"The human psyche is not separate from Nature. It is a creation of Nature, a force of Nature. It is the nature of the human psyche to create culture—that is its *natural* function. So any cultural creation of humanity is as natural as anything else in Nature. The atom bomb, a can of Coca-Cola—like it or not, they are as natural as a rose. You needn't enjoy or approve of that fact to recognize it as fact."

Back Seat jumped all over that, as had the Sharers, particularly the biologist, a woman who pointed out that a Coke can hasn't the ability to evolve. Her argument stopped Wheel Man cold. "Before I go on with my theory I'll have to think that through," Wheel Man said, stumped.

"Have you?" queried Back Seat.

"Lots. What could be more natural than a rock? Big or small, a rock doesn't evolve any more than a can of Coke. Once rocks are formed, their elements slowly break down and become something else, but they don't evolve. The ability to evolve defines the biological, not the natural. This planet is mostly rock and water. Both change, but neither evolves. So my argument stands. Sort of."

Sentences ricocheted; digressions ensued. Back Seat said, "Conveying our intent for each other takes up a lot of our vocabulary." She contended that a sense of morality was our birthright. "We need to believe in a moral universe." "Perhaps," said Wheel Man, "but our need for that belief doesn't make the universe moral."

"So," said Back Seat, "in your 'Nature,' is there such a thing as perversion—since, according to you, everything that *can* happen is 'natural'?"

"Terrible behavior exists within an ecology of behavior. It is not to mitigate horror that one can see a horrible act as part of an ecology of behavior larger than any particular act. Which doesn't mean you don't punish or fight what you're calling perversion. It's perverted in relation to the larger ecology of society. Popular usage equates 'natural' with 'good'—but that's a belief, not a fact. Either humans aren't part of nature at all—which is ridiculous—or we are, and that means everything we do or create is 'natural,'

the result of the force of Nature that is humanity."

"Do you see right or wrong in anything? In your system is there no universal law? You would say that the wrong is part of nature?"

"The bad exists in dialectic with the good. There is *always* good and bad, right and wrong, moral and immoral—and because that's *always* so, the existence of both must be natural. Both are part of a human ecology that is larger than either good or bad, right or wrong. I don't mean that to do a terrible thing is OK. I just mean it's part of what naturally happens. Fighting what's terrible is also part of what naturally happens. That dialectic is what human society *is*. As I see it, this vision ennobles every choice for good. We are more moral than the universe tends to be."

They drove on. Wheel Man wondered what that hole in Space and the Petrified Forest says about "universal law." Given his druthers, he'd rather believe in Back Seat's moral constants than in his anything-goes Nature. He'd rather, but he couldn't.

Who was the wiser was revealed when Shotgun asked, "If your house is on fire and you could take only one book, what book would you take?" Wheel Man didn't hesitate: "*Out of Africa*. My favorite of all books." An answer easily beat by Back Seat: "I think I'd take the one I'm currently reading."

Trucks over truck over underpass,
Austin, Texas, 1986

To A STREET KID in Brooklyn in the 1950s, Texas was a movie—and Texas was the West. Films like John Ford's *The Searchers,* shot in Monument Valley on the Arizona–Utah line, claimed to be Texas. Randolph Scott's films, directed by Budd Boetticher and shot in California, were supposed to happen in Texas; either that, or Scott would claim to be a Texan. Half the horse operas filmed on sets in Hollywood, Culver City, and Burbank told stories of Texas. A movie about New York always showed the same New York, but movies about Texas could show whatever they wanted.

It was a stunning geography of the mind: John Ford's mesas, Anthony Mann's mountains, Budd Boetticher's deserts, incredible landscapes, places with no boundaries. And what if most of the town scenes were filmed on any of three or four identical sets in L.A. or that Western set near Tucson? Each town opened out to something called "Texas," something endless, wide open, thrilling. It gave a kid the sense that anything could happen in Texas.

Anything could happen, and in the most vivid of colors. It wasn't just that these were the days of black-and-white TV, and that there was nowhere to see such color but at the movies; it was that New York was a black-and-white town. Shoot New York in the gleams of black-and-white film and you capture how that city feels; shoot it in color and you get a palette of grays and browns that bleed into each other. To step from gray New York into the Technicolor brilliance of Hollywood's Texas was to step from a world where brutality expressed itself in sameness and mercilessness into a wider world where brutality could be confronted and transformed.

A wider world—there was that, too, the wildness of the place, the sense that you could go off at any time in any direction. In Brooklyn you walked street after street of tenement after tenement; each building the same color and the same size; each street pretty much the same length; everything laid out at right angles. A pattern too orderly to be a maze, but so huge (especially to a child) that it seemed inescapable. Yet sit in a movie theater and watch Hollywood's Texas, where every horizon was unobstructed: this was a vision of freedom that went beyond any political definition, beyond any childhood urge of rebellion, into a landscape that could not be measured in miles. It could only be measured by the depth of one's longing.

Walt Whitman, another Brooklyn person responding to the promise of the West, said it in his "Song of the Open Road": *Here a great personal deed has room.*

Yet these expansive feelings, these feelings that taught so many of us that a world of greater possibility might exist somewhere—where exactly were these feelings felt? In a strange, funny, and slightly violent place called the Starr Theater on the corner of Starr Street and Knickerbocker Avenue. "Brooklyn's Finest Showplace," the sign said. Even we children of seven or eleven, who had never seen another showplace, knew enough to laugh at that. Twenty-five cents admission, ten cents for popcorn, five cents for a Coke got you fifteen cartoons, a serial, a monster movie, maybe a war movie, and a Western. Every Saturday. The theater full of kids, noisy the whole time, with nothing between us and mayhem except a big matron in a white uniform with a long flashlight. She paced the aisles, flashed her beam, shouted, and now and again whacked someone over the head with that flashlight.

Back then no parent would have

dreamt of suing. In fact, our parents expected her to ride herd on us (an image from the Westerns). Tired of smacking us themselves, our parents were grateful to her. And I don't remember any of us kids thinking the matron was unfair or harsh. Actually, we thought it was kind of a game: who got away with what, who didn't, who got hit, who ducked, who fixed it so that their buddy or their enemy got hit. Between our contests with the matron, and our feuds with each other, the action in the theater reflected the action on the screen. Randolph Scott was living dangerously and so (we thought) were we.

We were living more dangerously than we knew. Children of a lying country, absorbing a lying history, and being taught to lie in turn. Poverty children of a country that called itself affluent (though in the 1950s at least 25 percent lived poor), being indoctrinated with a code of heroism in order that we might defend somebody else's affluence. Children of the McCarthy era and the Cold War, watching a freedom on that screen that we couldn't find on our streets. You can see how the word "Texas" became mythic for us.

In the 1950s there were still a few horse-and-wagons in Brooklyn, and at least one working stable. They were the last of the ragmen's carts: huge slow horses hitched to wagons piled with junk, atop which sat old, usually Jewish men—

men with exhausted eyes who talked funny and had come from far away. They were the last of their kind, and they drove the last working wagons in America. Once, leaving the Starr in the late afternoon, we chased one of these old men on his wagon. We shouted like Indians, trying to spook his horse. The horse didn't react; the man didn't either. Some of us became furious at their indifference, picked stuff up from the gutter, and threw it at the wagon and the horse. We probably called the old man a "kike." Ugly, as all children can be ugly. But he'd heard it all before. He just went on.

What we really wanted, I think, was to ride on his wagon. Ride it slowly out of Brooklyn. Ride into what "Texas," that mythic word, meant for us. Ride a lie into a dream.

What could be more American than that? That if you live your lie long enough, it will turn into your dream. (The Westerns were teaching us well, weren't they?)

But were those Westerns lying? The truth was there to see, if we wanted to. All those movies of wide skies were full of men who hung out in saloons and on ranches, in forts and in towns; hung out in packs, always agreeing with each other, always armed, always easily swayed, easily cowed, equally available for a lynching or a rigged election, as long as the drinks were on the house. These were by far the most numerous and most permanent

men in those movies. It was they who formed the contrast, the backdrop, for that other, rarer man, the man who rode alone.

That man who rode alone, be he John Wayne or Randolph Scott, Gary Cooper or Glenn Ford, Burt Lancaster or James Stewart, Alan Ladd or Audie Murphy—he was advertised as the true Texan, the true Westerner. But he was always coming or going. Passing through. He never stayed.

The real true Texans, the real Westerners, were the other guys, the guys who didn't come and go, the guys who lived in those towns, apparently spending a great deal of time in saloons away from their women, and always agreeing with each other, easily swayed, easily cowed. (There are, after all, many nuances to the word "cow-boy.") Individually, they were no match for the man who rode alone. They stepped out of his way, though they carried the same gun he did. His solitude, not his gun, marked him as a hero. And though the man who rode alone loved his West, his Texas, he didn't love those towns or those townspeople. He wasn't about to settle and become one of them.

At the end of almost every picture, they'd implore him to stay, but he'd just ride off. He didn't believe he'd fit in their Texas. Didn't believe they were sincere in asking him to remain. And he was right. He was trouble, and they didn't want trouble. He was free, and they didn't want freedom. They wanted a quiet, orderly life where they would not be bothered by the trouble of freedom. Or rather, the only freedom they cared about was the freedom to be quiet and orderly, and the man who rode alone wanted more.

It was as though he knew what was coming next. Knew that Abilene and Sweetwater would be taken over by the churches and go dry. Knew that Houston and Austin would be controlled by the bankers and lawyers. Knew that everybody would breathe easier once he left. The schoolteacher would marry her storekeeper. The rancher would acquiesce to an economics controlled not far from the Starr Theater in Brooklyn—just across the river, on Wall Street. The cowboys could play at freedom all they wanted, but the banks would control

their ranches sooner or later. The man who rode alone didn't want to stay around for that. He knew those Texans weren't going to fight the real fight, so he rode off into his own sunset, his own struggle with his own spirit, taking his liberties where he could find them while there was still some liberty left to find.

These people who waved him goodbye said they wanted peace, but what they really wanted was order. That's what they still want. They think that if they can control the way others live, they'll feel safer. They won't, but they'll have to find that out for themselves. Meanwhile, somewhere west, under that wide sky, something calls to us still, and it can still be measured only by our longing.

Concrete truck and rear views,
Austin, Texas, 1989

WILD BILL HICKOK had elegant penmanship. His was an era when "a good hand" was expected, but Hickok's was exceptionally graceful, and his lines on unlined paper are almost perfectly straight. It's a kind of calligraphy. How and why did an unruly Illinois farm boy, dismissed by his father early on as a "dreamer," who'd lead a violent life almost all his life—how and why did he learn to value painstaking, gorgeous aesthetics in his handwriting? The reason is lost to history. Everyone knows the cards he held when he was murdered in Deadwood in 1876 at the age of thirty-eight: aces and eights. Ever since they've called that a "dead man's hand." (Some gamblers, superstitious to the core, fold that hand even when it may win.) And is there anyone within a mile of a TV who hasn't heard of Wild Bill? Eyewitnesses testify he was an incredible marksman with a handgun. Long before he died his exploits were trumpeted (often invented) far and wide. But there's nothing in the legend of Wild Bill to tell why he took such care to make his letters lovely.

No hesitation in that hand—the letters swirl and swoop, full here, thin there, exact. An aesthetic sense! Almost effete, in a kind of manly way. We know his killings, weaknesses, excesses—but how this sensibility of beauty lived in him, we'll never know.

Calamity Jane, at least as wild as Bill, gives a clue in her diaries: "We both lived a life of lies."

Was the lie to be found in the difference between—or the nexus connecting?—what they did, what they were said to have done, and what they felt?

Feelings and the inner life weren't what these people wrote about. It was considered unseemly, in their time, to express private feelings verbally, much less in writing. But they did write: Hickok's letters, Jane's diaries, the autobiography of John Wesley Hardin, the many writings of Bat Masterson and Wyatt Earp, and Seth Bullock's record of founding Deadwood. The movies don't portray them as people who might write. Their intellects are not so much dismissed as never considered. But they wrote. These were complicated people.

It's morning in Deadwood at the Adams Museum. I'm reading Wild Bill's last letter in a glass case, thinking, "Just who the hell were you, Wild Bill? That kind of penmanship doesn't happen by accident." The letter was written to his wife (a former trapeze artist ten years his senior) on the day he died. He wrote it, then went to a card game at Saloon Number 10, a few blocks from here, and sat with his back to the door. I don't sit with my back to the door. People who've lived with danger rarely do. We like to see what's coming and we're aware of activity at every entrance and exit. Did Wild Bill decide to be killed? But if I explore that idea, am I in danger of being censured by Seth Bullock? Seth Bullock, who wrote to chastise legend makers, calling them "that *pertinacious* source of so much misinformation offensive to the real pioneer."

Seth Bullock, long overdue, has finally entered Western legend through HBO's superb series *Deadwood*. We owe Seth Bullock more than you might think. Born in Ontario in 1849, he left home early and was on his own in Montana by the age of eighteen. At age twenty-two he was serving in Montana's Territorial Senate; he was sheriff of Helena at twenty-three. When twenty-two, he introduced and guided the passage of a resolution in Montana's legislature to recommend to Congress the establishment of Yellowstone National Park. Congress approved.

Conservation wasn't a nineteenth-century ideal. It took a cultivated aesthetic, plus a sense of history and a knack for politics, for twenty-two-year-old Seth Bullock to envision and found Yellowstone National Park. How Bullock felt that aesthetic within himself we'll never know. The accounts then and the legendary portrayals now give no clue. We only know that without a deep aesthetic and historical feeling for the land, there could have been no result like Yellowstone.

In 1876 Bullock and his lifelong friend Sol Star (also portrayed in *Deadwood*) headed to Deadwood to start a hardware business. (Star would one day be the town's mayor.) Deadwood had been founded by gold miners on Sioux land. Until Congress legalized the theft, Deadwood was technically not on U.S. territory and not bound by U.S. law. Or any law at all. Of course it was a more complicated place than any film can portray. A plaque not far from where Hickok was killed: "In the autumn of 1876 the *Black Hills Pioneer* reported that Deadwood had 173 businesses, including an assayer, a bank, a bath house, 3 butchers, 2 brewers, 4 billiard halls, 11 clothing houses, 21 groceries, 2 dance houses, 14 gaming houses, 2 hardware stores, 8 laundries, 7 lawyers, and 27 saloons." Al Swearengen (another *Deadwood* character) owned the Gem, part theater, part brothel. (He made fantastic money for a while, but it is said that when he left town he was penniless.) Nor did Deadwood ever really go straight. Prostitution was legal, and brothels operated openly, until 1980! Gambling became legal again in 1979, and now a sign on I-90 boasts "1400 rooms—80 Casinos—See Historic Gunfights Daily!" (That use of the word "casinos" is a little loose. There may be 80 places to gamble, but there are only a few casinos, cozy by Vegas standards.) But old Deadwood's wildness can hardly be exaggerated. In 1878 one-third of its deaths were attributed to "violence caused by murder, suicide or accidents," though Seth Bullock wrote: "It was remarkable that with the number of outlaws of both sexes in the gulches, there were so few crimes of the graver character committed."

Bullock was twenty-eight when he became the first sheriff of Deadwood. He would be involved in its law enforcement, politics, and commerce until his death in 1919. In 1884 he was deputy U.S. marshal. Out riding one day he happened to meet Teddy Roosevelt, who had a ranch in the Badlands; Roosevelt, in the capacity of deputy sheriff, was escorting a horse thief he'd just apprehended. Seth and "TR" remained close friends all their lives. Roosevelt sent his sons to work on Bullock's ranch to toughen them up, and he would one day mention Bullock in a State of the Union address. It's likely that the president credited with establishing our national parks system got some of his inspiration from the founder of Yellowstone.

Morning in Deadwood. It's early June but chilly, jacket-and-scarf weather. The narrow town sits in a gulch. The surrounding Black Hills are steep—and from a distance they are black, because they've burned so often. I'm staying in one of its oldest surviving buildings, the Franklin Hotel, 1903. (The original wood structures burned or were destroyed by flood.) On every room door is a plaque with the name of a famous guest, names like Seth Bullock, Teddy Roosevelt, Buffalo Bill, Potato Creek Johnny, and, on my door, Lame Deer. (Modern names too, but they don't carry the same weight.) The fixtures are antique—push-button light switches, that kind of thing. On the shelf in my room: *The New Century Dictionary*, a century old. There is a manually operated elevator; the very elderly gent who takes you up and down informs you that there's only about a dozen such elevators left in the country. Early in the morning in the dining room, another very old gent plays piano—"Lara's Theme." Not exactly early-morning music, but incongruity somehow suits the place.

The legends show you where to go. Once you get there, you do your best to find out why you came. Maybe I came because, as a kid in New York, Western movies are what first taught me that the world is wide and that I might roam in it. When I can, I seek out the places that gave me my first legends. Like last evening, at twilight, climbing the *very* steep grade to the cemetery. No one about. Chilly. Too dark already to read names on the stones. But the graves of Wild Bill Hickok and Calamity Jane, buried near each other as she'd wished when she died in 1903, are hard to miss. Difficult to keep my footing, the slope's so steep, but I clamber around and find them. And remove my hat.

"I know little about you two. Nobody really does. Just legends and incongruous facts like your penmanship, Mr. Hickok. Your diary, Ms. Jane. The books and films give scant hint of your inner lives, though I know you couldn't have lived so restlessly—couldn't have become icons of our restlessness—without an even more restless inner life. I wonder about your demons and your angels but I don't try to fill in the blanks. You lived lives that captivate people who wouldn't want to live like you or even live next door to you—enjoying your darkness the better to be certain of their light, perhaps. Maybe you'll only be forgotten when people no longer need to leave home, in this country created by home leavers. Legends about people like you were my first clue to freedom. I guess that's why I'm here—a restless man, honoring you for doing your part to give restlessness it's good bad name. Well. Rest in peace, if there is any."

Tornado weather in the Panhandle, Texas, 1989

SOUTH OF RAPID CITY, up in South Dakota, driving the Black Hills, I pass a little turnoff marked "Gumbo Lily Lane" and slip into reverie. How'd that gal get that name? Maybe she hailed from Louisiana and made a mean gumbo. (In a mining camp? How'd she get the fixings?) But why had she come and what did she do, that a century later a "lane" repeated her name? Is she enough of a local legend to list on the Internet? Later, I search. There's her picture! She's not a woman, she's a flower, *Oenothera caespitosa*, native to the Dakotas. Pretty little thing. But for ten miles or so I'd had a fine time wondering about a wild gal. Of such stuff are Western legends made . . .

(Ok, she's a flower, a lily, but still: why "gumbo"?)

Back in Nebraska, between McCook and Ogallala, driving U.S. 6—6 once rode from Provincetown to Long Beach and is still our longest transcontinental highway, a notable distinction for a bumpy two-lane. Here 6 has no shoulders, grass bends over the asphalt. A two-lane's so different from an interstate—on the interstate you're *upon* the land, gliding over its topography, but a two-lane's *of* the land; it rises and falls, weaves and curves, and in the West (as in New England and the South) it's usually a tarred-over wagon road. Upkeep is erratic, especially this far north, where winters buckle the tarmac. This Western sky is wide, a view not like back East—there, roads feel like hallways through woodland; here, blue air and white cloud touch the ground on all horizons. The road ascends and descends gentle grades of small valleys, passing modest farms that still appear family-owned. One farmer's erected a rough billboard on his fence, hand-painted lettering over graying wood:

THIS IS A SIGN—God.

Nearer Ogallala is a valley with no farm, no poles and wires, no human vestige but the humble road itself. A creek runs through, cottonwoods shimmer along the waterline, and there's a stand of larger trees beside a pond. And suddenly I knew, I *knew*, they camped here, camped here often—it's perfect, there's water, good grazing for the animals, game for their cook fires and furs. The low hills that surround the valley protect from winter winds; on those hills, sentinels would see an enemy miles off. I felt it so strongly, they camped here often, before we came, Cheyenne and Dakota and Lakota peoples, in numbers large and small. No image arose—and where could I get such images but from movies and mostly staged old photos? No one living knows how their camps really looked. But they were here, and it was as though I could hear their memory spoken in the voice of the valley, wordless but definite, clear. . . .

I get crushes on towns the way I get crushes on women. I fell for Deadwood as soon as I got here. It's mostly only two streets wide, for it sits at the bottom of a gulch; the steep Black Hills rise, wooded, on either side. You walk Main Street's length leisurely in fifteen, twenty minutes. Its population of about 2,000 lives on hillside lanes so slanted you'd need a strong heart to go for a stroll. Deadwood thrives on small casinos, but woos me with history: many of its brick buildings (like the Bullock Hotel, built by Seth Bullock himself) date back a century and more. One wood structure escaped the early fires and is dated 1879. The Adams Museum is first-rate. I've spent hours there, where I learned that Sol Star, Bullock's friend and business partner, was the only non-Chinese person welcome at the Chinese Masonic Lodge. Star was also

Deadwood's mayor, 1884–1898, and a leader of a rare entity in the Old West: a thriving, respected Jewish community. An old photo shows an unnamed man in suit and Hasidic hat dancing Hebrew folk-steps—not your typical Western icon.

Wild Bill Hickok and Calamity Jane are buried up the hill. Stroll the family plots and you see small stones for many, many infants and young children from the 1870s, '80s, and '90s, more than I've seen in any other old graveyard. That Deadwood was a hard place to be.

I first came through last June. This June I'm here to meet with Dave. (We've known each other since age ten.) He was driving from Long Island back to Oakland on I-80, which passes some 220 miles south of Deadwood. I suggested I drive north from Texas and meet up with him here. We explore places, we share a love of history and have complementary ways of knowing: he can tell me (just by looking) how a building was built, and with what, and why; I can tell him who built here and what they were up to, and we compare theories about their thoughts and their hearts. Between us, we construct a place's history and share great satisfaction at standing, say, at the spot by the creek where gold was first found.

I've booked a suite (the only smoking room left) at the Franklin Hotel, built in 1903. Last June you could sit in the Franklin's dining room knowing that there dined Seth Bullock, Sol Star, their friend Teddy Roosevelt (Bullock was a captain in Teddy's Rough Riders), and maybe Calamity Jane, who died in '03 near here. Also, Willa Cather. But a casino's bought the Franklin; alas, the dining room is making way for slot machines.

I wasn't prepared for Room 421. It's immense. Two large bedrooms. A huge living room with an intricately carved bar (Dave explains its different woods and why no one builds like that anymore). And the sofa! Plush cushions covered with rich whorehouse-violet cloth, and its frame . . . imagine a kind of basketweaving, but of thick molded dark wood, and at the end of each arm, where your hand rests, the carved face of a beautiful woman. On the wall, a long, tall mirror framed in gilt. In the dining room, off the kitchen, a rectangular wood table, and six chairs . . . again, intricately carved wood. On their backrests, front and back, the profile of a devil, and devil's heads bulge from the legs and at the ends of the arms. A place for gambling men and wanton women. The suite pulsed with the psychic scent of sin.

Of hundreds of rented rooms I've known, from Manhattan's Waldorf-Astoria to Santa Rosa's Sun & Sand (the mattress deeply stained with blood), I've never seen the like. Deadwood doesn't disappoint. Though (alas again!) by year's end 421 will be "renovated," its uniqueness erased.

Dave is an early-to-bed–early-to-rise guy, I'm a stay-up-all-night guy, so for hours alone I read at that table, sipping whiskey, smoking, and forgetting my book for indeterminate moments, listening to the suite's ghostly whispers, too faint to make out, but still barely audible.

The day after next, a time filled with good conversation and fascinating history, Dave continued west, I headed due south . . . western Nebraska, where it's as though a great stormy sea, with sweeping rolling swells, suddenly stilled in place and grew prairie grass. Wind ripples the grass to the horizon, the land looks alive (and it is). My '69 Chevy startles some quail; they fly scattering in all directions before me; one bird is not quick enough and thuds sickeningly against my windshield—a chance death amidst the beauty. And there is a dancer-like, Shiva-like, many-armed lightning-struck tree, bare of bark, gray, dead . . . I say aloud, "The dead are beautiful."

You learn that when people you deeply love die. Their memory overwhelms you with difficult beauty.

Western Kansas, state road 27, another two-lane—wild turkeys and lovely pheasants cross the road now and again. (A trucker nearly swerved off the road trying to run a pheasant down. I'll never understand that.) Not so far from the Oklahoma border. Soon night will "fall," as they say—a strange usage, night doesn't fall, it emerges. Here the world's flat as an ironing board. No one born here, who had not been taught otherwise, could conceive of a round planet—but for that very slight curve at the far horizon. Between you and the horizon there is rarely a bush, rarely a tree. Some might not think a land so flat and featureless could be beautiful, here where the skyline sits several degrees *below* your gaze, and you must look slightly down to see horizon . . . yet sunlight plays upon such a topography as upon a canvas, you never know what subtle color will gleam next, and on a day like this, the sun sifting through clouds, your eyes are constantly

rewarded by tints no painter has imagined.

Sunset, huge and orange-crimson in the west. In the east, at the dark brim, the moon is impossibly large and silver, draped with the thinnest shifting clouds, an effect like lingerie. A being (almost) naked, playing at appearing (partly) clothed. The universe condenses into one word: *invitation.*

At seventy miles an hour, I grope for words of gratitude to say to this glory of a moon.

The words that arise are, "Thank you for the blessing of your beauty."

IT MAY HAVE BEEN the night I said to Mayer Vishner, "Every morning of my life I wake up angry and afraid."

"That," said Mayer, "is a terrific lead."

A "lead" is the first sentence, the sentence that leads the reader into an article. I probably wouldn't have remembered the line without a Mayer Vishner verdict of "terrific." Mayer is a precise editor who never idly employs a word. We were working for a paper in the place I call "a city by the sea," but Los Angeles is also a city by the desert, a city crisscrossed with fault lines where no one is more than five miles from an epicenter of a looming quake. The sea facing the desert with L.A. teeming in between, upon ground ever likely to shake—that expresses all the extremities of the city's character. In those days most people I knew were trying to be as extreme as the city. Certainly we'd have been extreme anywhere, but Los Angeles gave us a fantastic arena for fucking up.

On the night in question Mayer was insisting that L.A. is "unredeemed."

A bit of context: This was one of those nights when Mayer and I were hav-ing a noisy sit-down with our editor-in-chief, whom we'll call simply "J." We were in a Mexican joint on Sunset Boule-vard in Silver Lake (long before its gentri-fication), east of Hollywood. These sit-downs had a definite form. One of us (usually me) was very angry (usually at J); one of us (usually J) was upset and con-fused about the one who was angry; and one of us (usually Mayer) was trying to cool things down. But our roles rotated. This night, I think it was Mayer who was angry with J, while I tried to cool things down. In those days, you knew a situation was worse than bad when it fell to me to be the moderating influence.

Which leads to more context: Cut to the paper's first office, on a seedy stretch of Sunset Boulevard, on the second floor of what had been a residence. An edito-rial meeting. No one remembers precisely which meeting, *except* that it was the meeting I ended by throwing the chair. Actually, I threw the chair out the win-dow. The window was closed at the time. But that may not be the truth. We lied a lot in those days, then believed and repeated our lies. Several stories came out of that meeting—all agree as to the flying chair, none agree as to where it landed. There were lots of meetings at which that, or anything else, might have happened, and not with only me playing it crazy. To steal a usage from Jean Shepherd, our staff worked in "crazy" as sculptors work in clay. One of J's talents was finding such people and bringing out their worst as well as their best. (Not that he's to be blamed. We were quite happy to find an excuse to be at our worst.)

One final bit of context: Becoming a semifamous writer in Los Angeles stirred up all my terrors, and I did my best to mess myself up any way I could manage, except for the actual writing on the page. Doing stuff I should have been fired for. Or quitting—so I could be wooed back, a prime prima donna, drama queen to the max. The Death-Wish Kid, as I called myself, except I was no kid. I was also having a grand time. As I wrote for *L.A. Weekly*'s Thirtieth Anniversary issue (Dec. 4, 2008), "The good times, bad times and stupid times weaved together so tightly that even the best times were a little bad and a little stupid, and the worst were at least interesting." Alas, "interesting" is lame word choice; "flavorful" would have been better.

Cut back to the Mexican joint, circa 1985, three born-and-bred New Yorkers at odds in L.A.—Mayer so much a New Yorker he's never learned to drive. Our original intention was to have our sit-down, settle what had to be settled, then head to a Hollywood club where we'd get drunk while viewing a band formed by some of the young grunt-workers at the paper, thereby demonstrating that the paper's elite respected its proletarians. As Mayer has said, "We got a little ahead of ourselves." We were already drunk. Very drunk. And Mayer was saying that L.A. is "unredeemed."

J told Mayer he'd dig L.A. if he wasn't afraid to drive.

"I'm not afraid to drive. If you want, I'll drive us to the gig."

"Not in *my* car," said I.

Said J, "We'll take mine; it's a rental."

And, just like that, a suggestion that hadn't been at all serious became a plan. Drunk Mayer, who'd never driven in his life, would drive us to Hollywood. (As Mayer recently and passionately pointed out, a lot of wars have been started in just this way: People say a little of this and a little of that, and suddenly they're taking very seriously something not worthy of serious consideration—and acting upon it. Historians have never figured out why.)

J's rental was a tin can, two seats in front, cramped in back, *and* it was a stick shift. Mayer sat where he had never sat: in the driver's seat. I sat beside him. Mayer remembers J: "Sprawled out in the back as if he's on a couch—he puts his feet up on the back seat and he's lying back there." Also, come to think of it, a safer position in case we fuck up. (J was good at that.)

Mayer said to me, "I'll work the pedals and the wheel. If there's anything else that's gotta work, you gotta work it."

We were on a steeply sloped driveway. Mayer would have to navigate down the driveway, cross two lanes of eastbound Sunset Boulevard traffic, then turn left into the westbound lanes. I gripped the stick with my right hand, put my left on his thigh, just above his right knee, and kept it there, saying, "Do what I tell you when I tell you to do it."

We started down the slope. As Mayer remembered, "We roll down to Sunset and I can feel the *car* sober up." By now we knew this was nuts. Any of us could have said, "I'm not doing this," and stopped it. But, as Mayer now says, "We're good Americans! Once we commit to a stupid, harmful plan, we stick to it."

We made it across the eastbound lanes, into the westbound. I kept talking, telling Mayer things like, "The pedals are more responsive than you think; you don't have to press so hard." My grip on his thigh tightened or loosened in sync with my instruction to press the gas pedal, ease off, hit the brake *gently*, press the clutch, there, we're in first, there, we're in second, lots of traffic, keep in your lane, there's a red light, foot off the gas, ease on the brake, press the clutch, I'm shifting to neutral, "I don't understand," "You don't have to, just do what I say." A metaphor for L.A.: Three forty-something drunks in traffic on Sunset, and the guy who never drove is driving.

Mayer: "You were talking to me constantly, and I've told people it was like making love. You were very gentle and explicit."

J popped up from the back seat, "Michael, what are you worried about? What are they going to do, take his license away for drunk driving?"

At which Mayer and I exchanged a look. The look said it all. J (as often happened) didn't get it. We were endangering lives, strangers' and our own. What we were up to was great fun and drastically idiotic. If it went wrong, we'd go to jail. If it went greatly wrong, innocents would pay for our stupid excess. Mayer and I were conscious that we'd stepped over the precipice and were engaging in what was, in fact, an immoral and criminal act. *Yet we still didn't stop.* As for J, he seemed oblivious (which was not unusual). And he could always plead that he was in the back seat and not responsible. He was good at that. (And good at making stuff happen. He made my career happen. J was a package deal: opportunity, inspiration, and insanity.)

Mayer, his one time behind a wheel, drove, oh, two miles on Sunset, at night, in traffic, all the way to Vine. I guided him to curbside at a bus stop, then took over and parked. We got drunker. The band bored me to death. I don't remember how I got home.

"I'll write it funny," I told Mayer earlier tonight. Always precise, he edited: "If you stop at funny you miss the point. We really did a bad thing, and we were lucky to get away with it."

It's a dangerous world and you never know, not really, who the most cruelly dangerous people are. Some nights it may very well be you.

Running the crosswalk, Los Angeles,
California, 1989

A DAY'S RIDE, 2008

SOME MONTHS AGO I was startled by hard knocks at my door. I knew by the knock that I didn't like whoever was knocking. Opened the door to a nervy guy in expensive duds. "The apartment manager told me that's your car." He pointed to my '69 Chevy Malibu. I nodded yes and said, "Never." "What?" "You want to buy it. I'll never sell it." "I'll pay well." "Never." "Never say never. You may change your mind; take my card." "I don't need your card." He wasn't used to taking no for an answer from one he judged a social inferior. He held out his card. I just let him stand there like that. When he realized my no meant no, he walked off without another word. I thought: Never say never? That can't be right. "Never" is an important word. Each of us should have some things we'll say "never" to, and we'd best know well what they are.

(Told Danny the episode, with my concluding thought, and he said something I liked: "*Never* exists in this world.")

My Chevy draws all kinds. I was packing the car for a day's ride to Austin to see old friends and go to the *Austin Chronicle's*

Christmas bash. Three young men and one older, Latinos, gathered. "Hey," I greeted, smiling a little. The elder said, "We're just waiting till you start 'er. We wanna hear the engine. Still got the 307?" "No, when they switched to unleaded the additives fucked up the 307. This engine's a 350." We talked of this and that, then I started her up. They smiled wide when they heard that engine. There's nothing like a 350 in good shape. I headed for Austin.

Not long ago a petulant reader chastised me for my "most prideful possession," my "damn stupid car." I sympathize with his crankiness. We're all cranky about something or other. But everywhere I go—and I go everywhere—people who wouldn't otherwise speak to me are drawn to the car. We talk about the car and cars in general, then sometimes we talk of other stuff. Sometimes we go for coffee and exchange life stories. That's not why I'll never sell the car. You don't sell something you love. But the car is kind of my passport to America. People who might want nothing to do with me look at that car and know there's something about America we agree on—something embodied in a '69 Chevy Malibu—so we talk. In my profession, that's very helpful.

There's a yellow legal pad on the seat. I scribbled notes as I drove Route 84: 2008—its most remarkable event was that the American system failed so completely that right-wing Republicans quasi-nationalized housing, banking, insurance, and (as we speak) auto manufacturing. A centrist Democrat will try to quasi-nationalize health care and do a twenty-first-century New Deal to employ thousands. For a year, the stock market's gone up only when the government acts, which means this market isn't the market that was. What to call all this? It's certainly not capitalism, and it's not how dictionaries define socialism. But the rules of the American game have changed utterly, a fundamental reorganization has begun, and nobody really knows what the new rules are or if they'll work or if they're even rules.

I stopped at dark in Coleman, Texas. Gassed up at the Allsup's. Four young laborers climbed out of their beat-up pickup to talk about my Chevy. Two had smart eyes. Two had most of their teeth; one, just a few; another, none I could see. My street sense didn't trust one. The others I liked. The world I call "the world" is not the world they call "the world." With their manual skills, tattered clothes, rural accents, and laborer's manners, their

world is the only world that will have them. But they're vigorous. Laugh readily. And dig the sound of a 350. (A friend's family reunions are near here. He says most local youth do drugs. Lots.)

I checked into a motel and went to a steak house down the road. At the next table, two clean-cut, soft-spoken guys, roughly the age of the four I'd just met, spoke of their fraternity. The violence of hazing. The guy "who beat me up." The kid hadn't protested. Said no one does. Said the university knows of the bullying and allows it. The lesson these frat boys seem to be learning is how to take shit. The frat bullies are learning how to dish it. Both lessons are important in an education for the corporate world they spoke of joining. They're home for the holidays. Coleman no doubt considers them the best of Coleman. But in their faces was a brokenness—as though already they'd accepted that they would not be the men they'd hoped to be.

Those four laborers with missing teeth—they did not look beaten down and certainly didn't look like guys who'd accept bullying. Who knows but that they might do well, by their lights, in Obama's attempted New Deal? And who knows but that the frat boys won't? The old rules are gone, the new rules don't yet exist, and it's anybody's ballgame.

Back at the Allsup's, I bought a six-pack for the motel room. (The friendly cashier didn't have all his teeth either.) In

the parking lot, a guy in hunting garb, cigarette hanging from his lips, was at the
pay phone. You don't see people at pay
phones much anymore. Finishing his call,
snapping his butt stub onto the tarmac,
he went to his car, parked beside mine: a
small tin can, its entire right side stove in,
duct tape covering the cracks.

He said, "Looks bad, don't it?"
Smiled. Missing some teeth. I nodded
yeah, smiling. "Looks so bad, people
wave when they pass me now. They
didn't used to wave. Guess there's some
good in anything," he grinned, very
knowingly. We got in our cars. He
started his. It made a tinny sound, like,
"Do we hafta?" I started mine, and I
couldn't help that a V-8 350 just naturally
roars. The guy and I looked at each
other from behind our wheels, and he
cracked up, laughing so hard he couldn't
light his cigarette. There are traditions of
secret Hasids, secret Buddhas, secret
Sufis. I felt I'd met a man who might
qualify. His laughter was genuine. A man
well worth knowing.

My motel room stank of a strange
sweetness. On the desk (not, as is usual, in
a drawer) was a Gideons Bible. I opened it
to see if it was a King James, a New King
James, a Revised Standard—the transla-
tion makes all the difference. Opened it,
and that sickly sweet scent blasted from
its pages. A perfumed Bible! My first. I
raised my beer in a toast to whoever

thought of doing that. America—you can
ruin it, but you can't tame it.

Further on, next morning, I stopped
for an orange juice and an Egg McMuf-
fin (my one fast-food weakness). The
cashier was a thin, slight woman, about
thirty, blond, smart eyes. No Texas
accent. Long fingers—blunt, not tapered.
A wedding ring, simple, thin, gold. Two
interesting rings on her right hand. Not
from around here. What's her story in
2008? What will it be in 2009, 2010?
How did her smart eyes find their way
to a McDonald's on the early shift in the
middle of Texas? (I think she'd relate to
a song I heard in Austin by that remarkable twenty-year-old Sahara Smith:
"There's a quiet hunger I have curled
myself inside / And it's a thousand secrets
wide.")

I was in Austin five days, during
which three different kinds of people
offered to buy my car. "Never." The big
news was that some wag threw his shoes
at the president of the United States
while the world laughed. I didn't. It
pains me to see the country of the Bill
of Rights a laughingstock and pains me
more to know that, these days, mockery
is the least we deserve.

My last night in town I went to the
Armadillo Christmas Bazaar to hear Mar-
cia Ball's Pianorama. You've never heard
anything like it. And I've rarely seen so
many people grinning and unable to

keep still. Six piano players, each uniquely superb, played five pianos, all at the same time, extemporizing boogie woogie and blues, rhythms a century old and ever fresh, templates capable of infinite variation, irresistibly and incorruptibly funky.

I never heard a better embodiment of what we used to call "the American spirit." Can we, the people, again embody and enact that spirit? I won't say "no," I can't say "yes," so I'll just say "maybe" and head on down the road.

Publications and Dates

Essays and dates are listed under their publications in alphabetical order.

Austin Chronicle

8:15	August 3, 2007
A Day's Ride, 2008	December 31, 2008
A Life of Destinations	December 18, 1997
A Long Way to Llano	September 15, 1995
A Trailer by the River	March 29, April 12, and April 26, 1996
Below the Glowing Virgin	March 16, 2007
Between Window Rock and Albuquerque	June 19, 2009
Broke Down in Bossier City	February 3, 2006
Deadwood in the Morning	June 24, 2005
Death Wish in Traffic	December 19, 2008
Driving in Sin	July 17, 2005
El Pueblo Unido	May 28, 2006
Everybody Needs a River	June 27, 2003
Forever in Chimayó	June 25, 1999
Heartland	July 7, 2007
Homage to a Road	March 19, 1999
Homage to a Sorcerer	July 17, 1998
How Soft You Tread Above Me	March 16, 2001
Little Fleshlets on the Run	March 16, 2001
Love Is a Dog from Hell	March 13, 2008
Lubbockian Identity	December 7, 2007
McGuffey's Eclectic	April 27, 2001
Once Upon a Time in the Movies	March 18, 1994
Out of Hibbing	March 17, 2006
Panhandle Christs	September 2, 2005
Practice	September 2, 2005

Raindrops in a Storm [original title: Gateways–Pt. 2]	October 27, 2000
Red State Blues	March 30, 2007
Sorry We Missed Church	February 17, 2006
The Art of Being Beckoned	September 3, 1999
The Million Mile Commute	June 10, 2005
The Mom, the Book, the Kid, and the Nun	May 22, 2009
The Pace at Which She Walked	February 4, 1994
To Lose Some Nerve	September 14, 2007
Unidentified Frakkin' Objects	August 15, 2008
Volcano Days	June 24, 1994
Walk Across Texas	March 30, 2001
When We Were All Bluebirds	March 17, 1995

L.A. Weekly

A Rap with Carolyn Cassady	December 4, 1987
A Swastika in the Snow	January 10, 1986

Psychotherapy Networker

Across the Great Divide	January–February 2005

Michael in front of Lubbock or Leave It,
Austin, Texas, 1992

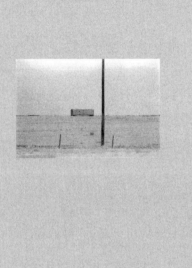